IMAGES
of America

GEORGIA'S LIGHTHOUSES

ON THE COVER: LIGHTHOUSE AND KEEPER'S QUARTERS, C. 1900. The keeper's dwelling is a Victorian design built of Savannah gray brick with 12-inch walls and heart pine floors. (Courtesy of Coastal Georgia Historical Society.)

IMAGES
of America

GEORGIA'S LIGHTHOUSES

Patricia Morris

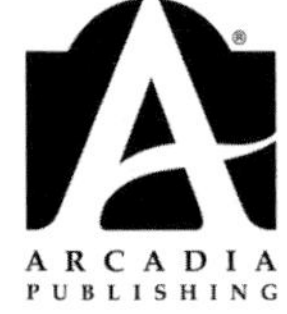

ISBN 978-0-7385-5305-4

Published by Arcadia Publishing
Charleston SC, Chicago IL, Portsmouth NH, San Francisco CA

Printed in the United States of America

Library of Congress Catalog Card Number: 2007930227

For all general information contact Arcadia Publishing at:
Telephone 843-853-2070
Fax 843-853-0044
E-mail sales@arcadiapublishing.com
For customer service and orders:
Toll-Free 1-888-313-2665

Visit us on the Internet at www.arcadiapublishing.com

The book is dedicated to
a lighthouse lover and great friend, Dr. Hal Fulmer.

Contents

ACKNOWLEDGMENTS

The photographs in this book were from the collections of Amelia Island Images, the Coastal Georgia Historical Society, the Tybee Island Historical Society, the Georgia Department of Natural Resources, the National Archives, the National Park Service, Fort Pulaski National Monument, and Cumberland National Seashore.

It is important to thank those people that made this volume possible: Cullen Chambers, Sarah Jones, Buddy Sullivan, Ed Mathews, Michael T. Ryan, John A. Mitchell, David Freedman, Charles Williams, and the staff of the Coastal Georgia Historical Society.

Introduction

Lighthouses are some of the most enduring of historical structures. Along Georgia's 100 miles of coastline, only five remain standing. Dating as far back as the earliest days of the colony, Georgia's lighthouse history is rich, and the beacons remaining today guided ships in the 18th and 19th centuries into port cities like Brunswick, Darien, and Savannah. This photographic history explores the history, mystery, and lore of these fascinating structures.

When Gen. James Oglethorpe landed with his company on the high bluff that he named Savannah, he immediately realized that the economic survival of the colony depended on the establishment of trade. In 1736, three years after the founding of the colony, Georgia's first lighthouse was built on Tybee Island at the entrance to the Savannah port.

Erected in 1736, the Tybee Island Light served as a day mark for the first few years. It stood only 90 feet high. Unfortunately, the lighthouse was built too close to shore and was toppled by a severe storm in 1741. Rebuilt in 1742, again too close to the sea, this second structure suffered the same fate. In 1773, at a site farther back from the ocean, a third tower was constructed of brick and stood 100 feet high.

By 1790, the Tybee Lighthouse joined the federally operated U.S. Lighthouse Establishment. It was at this time that the Tybee Island Light, using candles with large metal discs as an illuminate for the lantern room, changed its status from day mark to lighthouse.

A second, shorter lighthouse was built on Tybee Island adjacent to the first in 1822 and served as a range light. By sailing to a position where the two lighthouses were aligned, a sailor could accurately approach the Savannah River channel.

In 1857, a second-order Fresnel lens was installed in the main lighthouse. The Fresnel lens, invented in 1823 by Augustin-Jean Fresnel, produces a bright beam by concentrating and magnifying light.

Confederates stationed nearby at Fort Pulaski were sent to burn the lighthouse's wooden stairs and landings in 1861; however, Union soldiers repaired the damage and used the tower until the surrender of Fort Pulaski the following year.

After the Civil War, a new lighthouse was built using the lower 60 feet of the 1773 structure as a foundation. Activated in 1867, this 154-foot tower was reclassified as a major aid to navigation and required three keepers to staff the station. When the light was converted to electricity in 1933, there was no longer a need for three keepers. The Tybee Island Light Station remains one of America's most intact light stations. The station is now maintained by the Tybee Island Historical Society and is open to the public.

Two miles west of Tybee Island Lighthouse is Cockspur Island. Here the first Cockspur Lighthouse was built in 1849 and used to mark the entrance to the south channel of the Savannah River.

When this structure proved inadequate, the lighthouse was rebuilt with Savannah gray brick in 1857. The lighthouse was fitted with a fourth-order Fresnel lens and illuminated by a whale oil lamp. A twin channel beacon was constructed at the same time on the north channel of the Savannah River.

Unlike many lighthouses in the South, this small beacon received only minor damage during the Civil War. Soon after the war's end, on April 25, 1866, the beacon was relit and painted white for use as a day mark.

When ships with deep drafts were no longer able to use the south channel, the light was darkened in 1909. Today the little light has been restored and is owned and operated by the National Park Service.

A major shipping port during the early nineteenth century, the small seaport of Darien was a bustling operation. A small tract of land was sold to the U.S. Lighthouse Establishment for the sum of $1 in 1808 by plantation owner Thomas Spalding to build a lighthouse on Sapelo Island.

In 1820, Winslow Lewis of Boston was contracted to build a 90-foot brick tower topped by a 15-foot iron lantern. A fourth-order Fresnel lens was installed atop the tower in 1853. When Confederate troops retreated from the island in 1862, they removed the lens and destroyed the reflector system but left the rest of the facility intact. It was repaired and reactivated by the U.S. Lighthouse Service in 1868. In 1877, a cast-iron beacon, part of the range light system, was placed east of the main tower.

A severe hurricane in October 1898 seriously undermined the foundation of the Sapelo Lighthouse. Extensive repairs were needed but were never made. Instead, in September 1905, a new lighthouse—a 100-foot steel pyramidal tower with a kerosene-lit flashing light—was activated, and a new third-order Fresnel lens was installed. By 1934, shipping traffic into the port of Darien had become nonexistent, and the Sapelo Island Station was deactivated. Today the lighthouse is fully restored and open to the public. It is operated by the Georgia Department of Natural Resources.

The first St. Simons Island Lighthouse was built by James Gould in 1810 and stood 75 feet high. For economic reasons, most of the material used in the construction was tabby, a local mixture of oyster shell, lime, sand, and water. Gould became the first lighthouse keeper and held the position until his 1837 retirement.

In 1857, a third-order, double-convex Fresnel lens was installed that greatly improved the lighthouse's power and range. During the Civil War, the Macon Artillery troops and six field guns were stationed at Fort Brown at the base of the lighthouse to protect St. Simons Sound. However, when they were forced to evacuate the island, Confederate troops destroyed the lighthouse. Nothing of the first lighthouse remains today.

In 1867, the government ordered the construction of a second lighthouse. The 104-foot brick tower and adjacent keeper's house was designed by the Irish architect Charles B. Cluskey, who died of malaria in 1871, a year before the lighthouse was completed. The head light keeper, his assistant, and their families shared the dwelling.

In 1890, a fireproof, brick, oil house was constructed beside the lighthouse. This 9-foot-by-11-foot building could hold 450 five-gallon oilcans. The lighthouse was electrified in 1934 and completely automated in 1953. The station, maintained by the Coastal Georgia Historical Society, is open to the public.

The Little Cumberland Island Lighthouse is located on the northern tip of Little Cumberland Island in St. Andrew Sound. Built in 1838 by John Hastings of Boston, the tower measures 22 feet wide at the base, tapering to 11 feet wide at the top. Rarely used during the Civil War, the lighthouse on Little Cumberland escaped the war's devastation, and in 1867, it was reactivated after being fitted with a third-order Fresnel lens.

In 1874, to protect the lighthouse from the encroaching sea, a brick wall was built. Active until 1915, the keeper's house and all other light station buildings, except the tower, were demolished in 1968. Today a large dune protects the Little Cumberland Light from the ocean, but it can barely be seen from the water. It is now owned and preserved by a private foundation.

One

Tybee Island Light

Located at the mouth of the Savannah River, the Tybee Island Lighthouse was the first light along Georgia's coast. From the earliest days when Gen. James Oglethorpe first landed on its shore in 1733, the importance of this waterway to bring settlers and supplies was apparent. The need for a lighthouse to assure safe passage was paramount, and the Tybee Island Lighthouse has been guiding mariners safely for more than 270 years.

Tybee Island would play an important role throughout Georgia's history. The first lighthouse was completed in 1736 but was built too close to the shore. By 1741, it had washed away in a severe storm. A new tower was completed in 1742. The second, like the first, was built too close to the Atlantic Ocean, and in 1768, a third Tybee Light was authorized. Completed in 1773, it stood 100 feet tall. In 1857, a second-order Fresnel lens was installed in the lantern room.

The Fresnel lens, developed in France in 1827, used a molded glass prism in a brass frame to magnify the light source. Fresnel lenses, in general, are divided into seven classes. The first-order lens is the largest lens and was installed in coastal lights. Smaller lenses, such as the sixth-order lens, were installed in smaller lighthouses, such as harbor or breakwater lighthouses.

In 1861, Confederate troops burned the stairs and landings; however, Union troops repaired the damage and used the lighthouse to watch rebel forces at Fort Pulaski until its surrender in 1862. Finally, in 1866, a new brick and cast-iron lighthouse was authorized.

The Tybee Island Light Station is one of America's most intact stations, having all of its historic support buildings on its 5-acre site. Rebuilt several times, the current light station displays its 1916 day mark with 178 stairs to the top and a first-order Fresnel lens.

In all, four lighthouses were built on Tybee Island. The causes for the changes were due to a variety of reasons, including updating for modern conveniences to make the station more livable and easier to maintain.

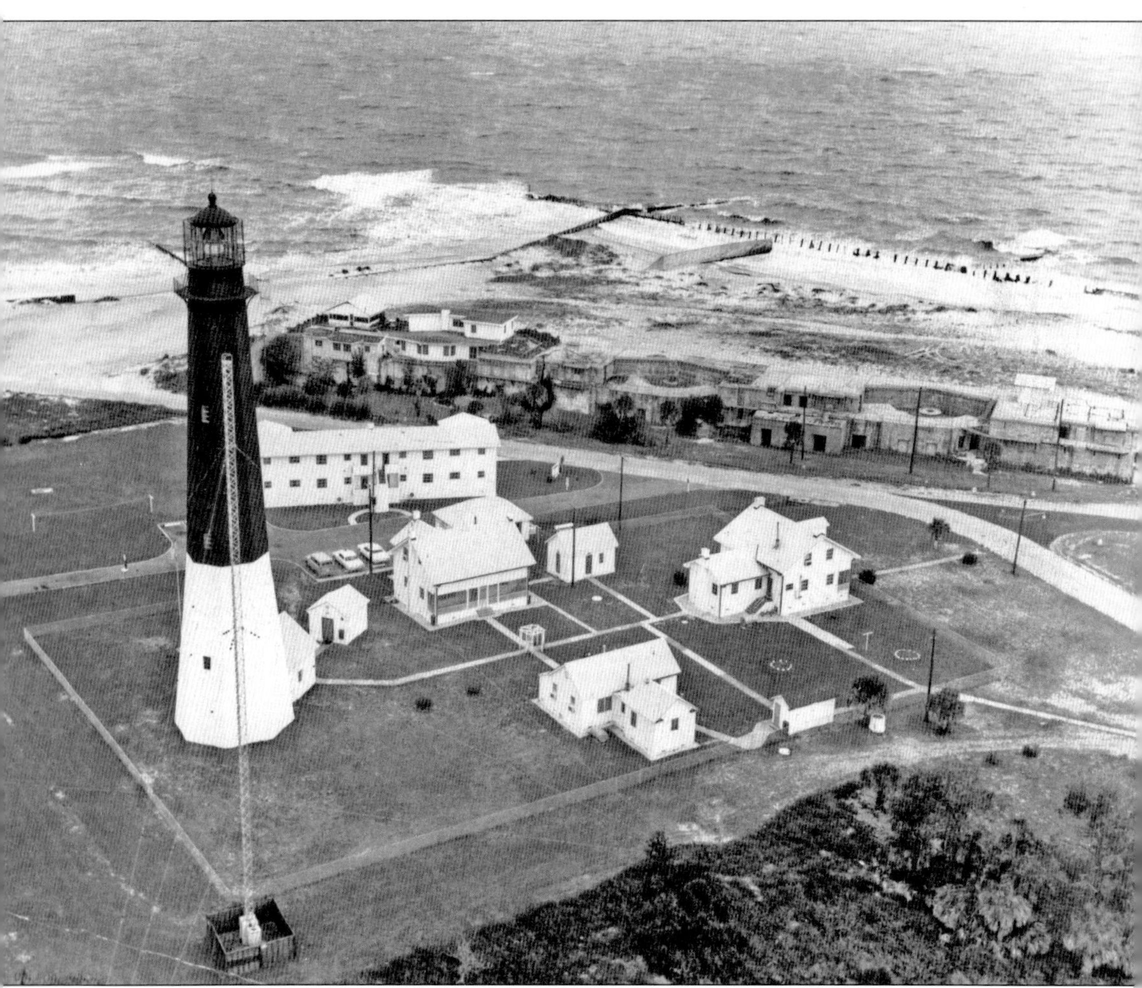

TYBEE LIGHT STATION, 1970–1986. During this time, the lighthouse was under the jurisdiction of the U.S. Coast Guard. Prior to 1789, each colonial government determined the need for a lighthouse in its colony, financed the construction, and oversaw the lighthouse's operation. In 1789, Pres. George Washington signed the ninth act of the U.S. Congress that had the states turn over their lighthouses, including those under construction and those proposed, to the federal government. With the creation of the U.S. Lighthouse Establishment, aids to navigation became the responsibility of the U.S. secretary of the treasury. (Courtesy of Tybee Island Historical Society.)

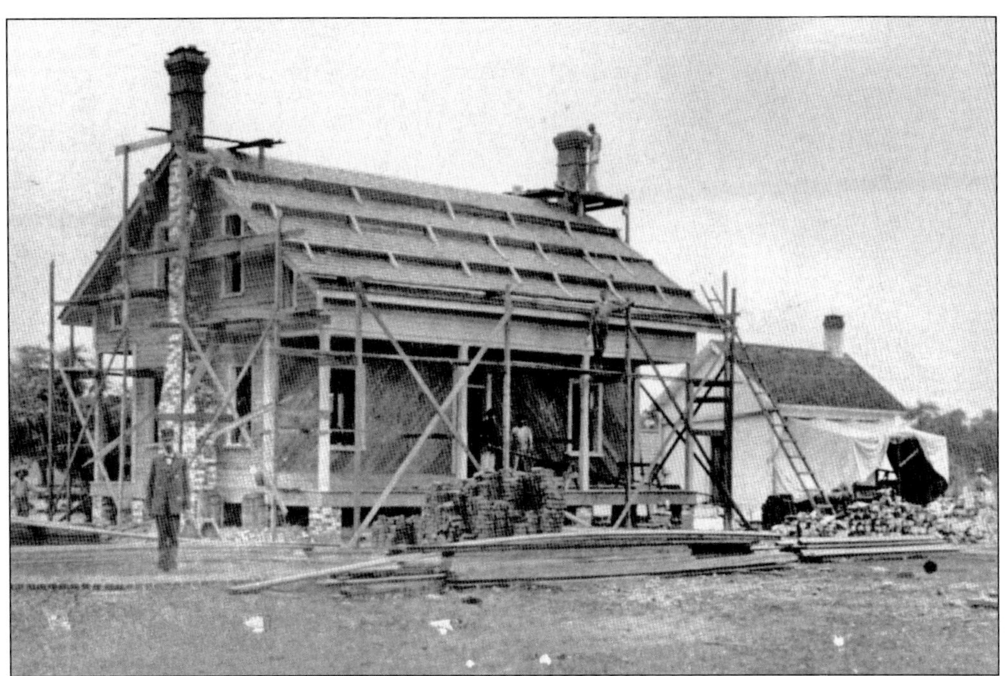

FIRST ASSISTANT KEEPER'S HOUSE, 1885. The house is under construction in late 1885 after it burned in early 1884. (Courtesy of Tybee Island Historical Society.)

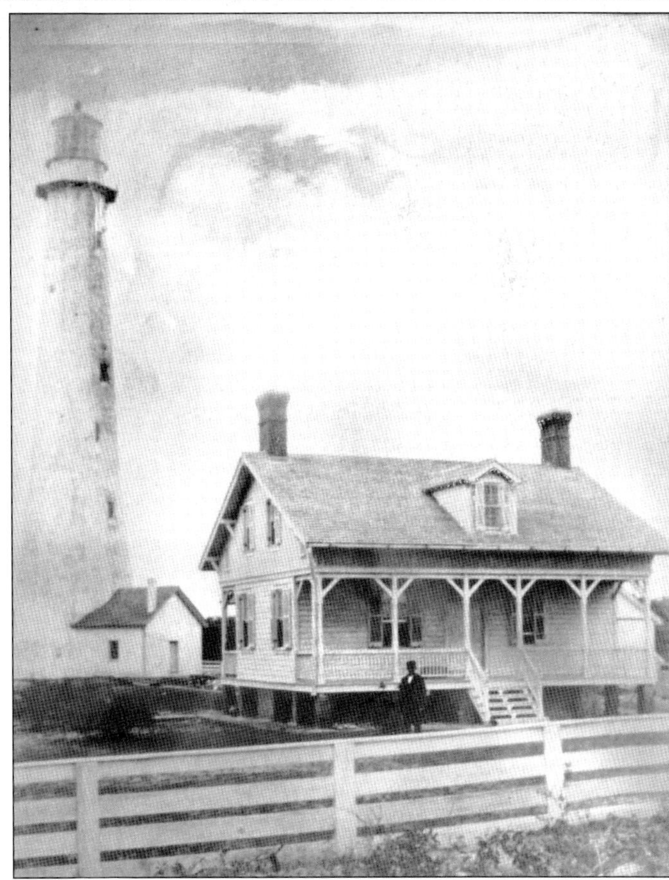

TYBEE LIGHTHOUSE AND HEAD KEEPER'S HOUSE, 1867–1887. This lighthouse was considered the first day mark even though only white paint was applied. (Courtesy of Tybee Island Historical Society.)

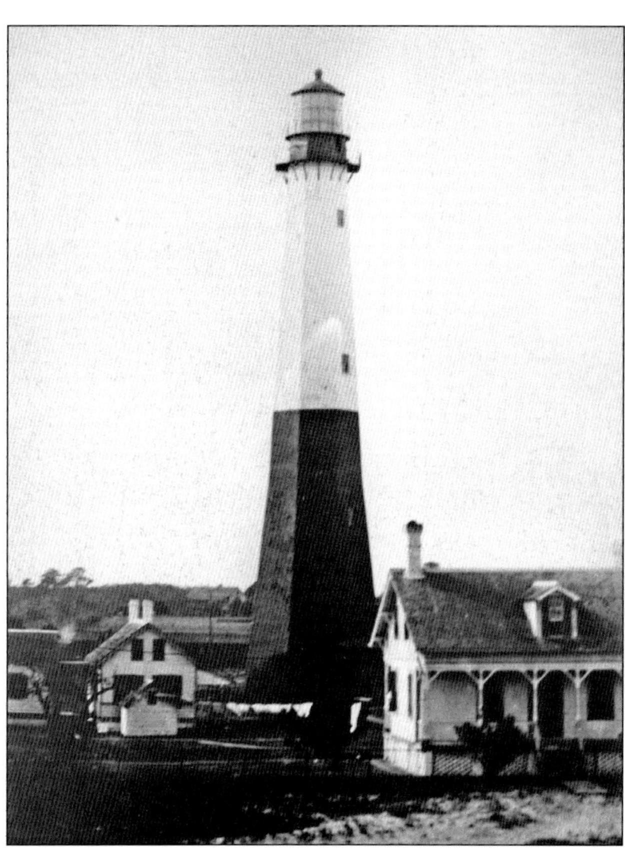

SECOND TYBEE LIGHT, 1887–1913. The second assistant keeper and head keeper's houses are shown in the foreground. (Courtesy of Tybee Island Historical Society.)

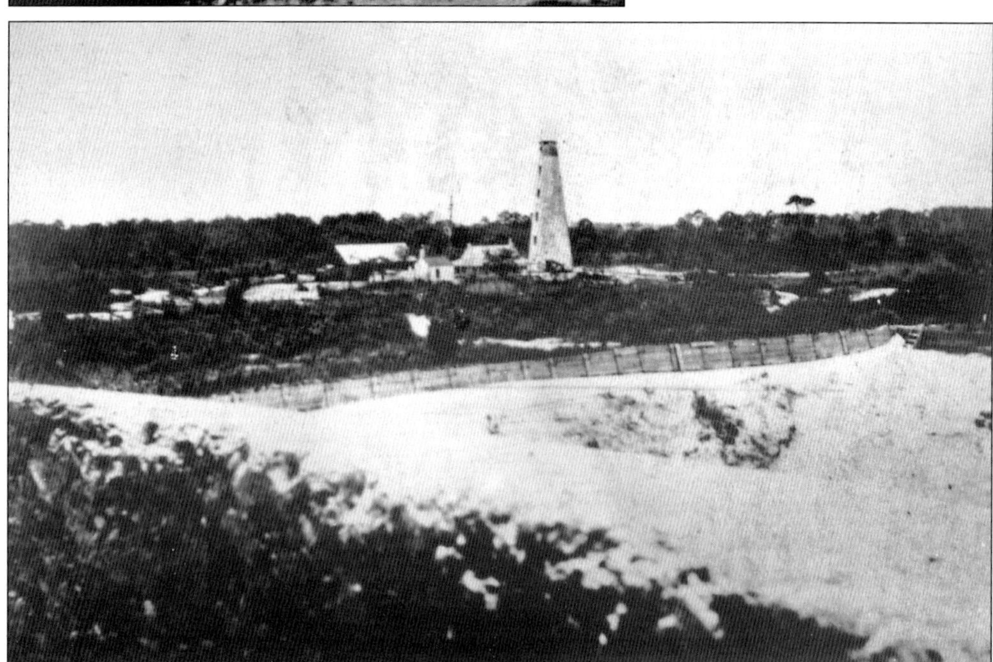

REBUILDING TYBEE LIGHT, 1866–1867. The building shown here is part of the original 1773 lighthouse that still remains today. (Courtesy of Tybee Island Historical Society.)

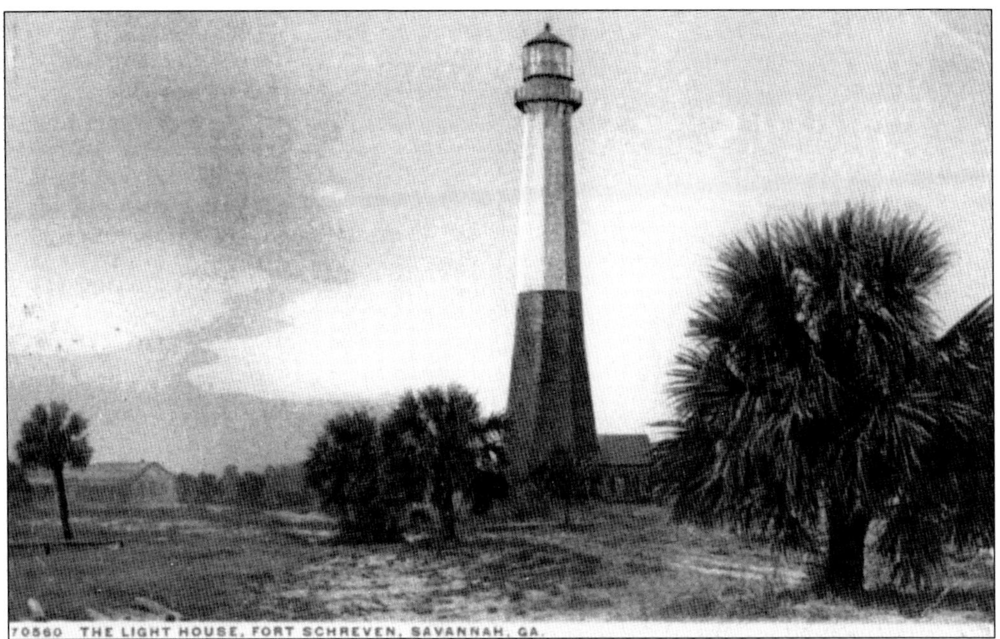

POSTCARD, 1887–1913. After the Civil War, Tybee Island began to grow as a resort area for local Savannah residents who wanted to escape the heat of downtown. (Courtesy of Tybee Island Historical Society.)

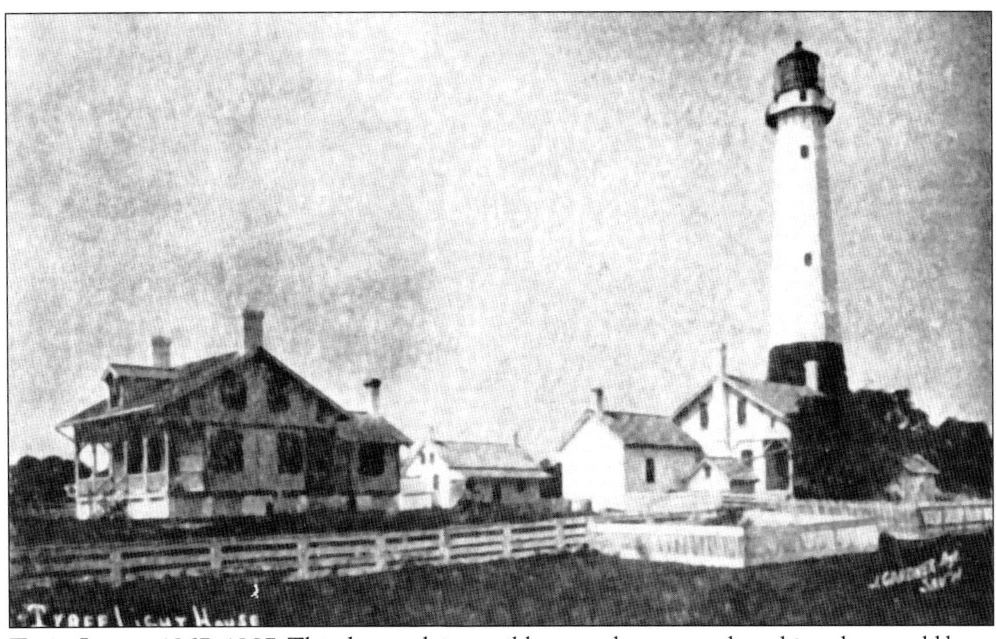

TYBEE LIGHT, 1867–1887. This day mark is possibly an undocumented marking that would have existed between the second and third lights. (Courtesy of Tybee Island Historical Society.)

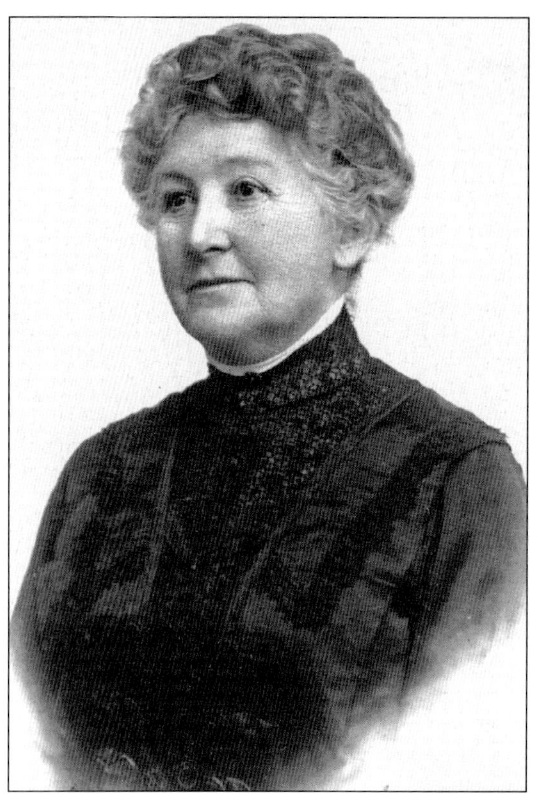

Alice F. Brodie Evans, 1900. Alice Evans was the wife of John Simmons Evans. She is believed to have acted as the interim lighthouse keeper after her husband's sudden death. (Courtesy of Tybee Island Historical Society.)

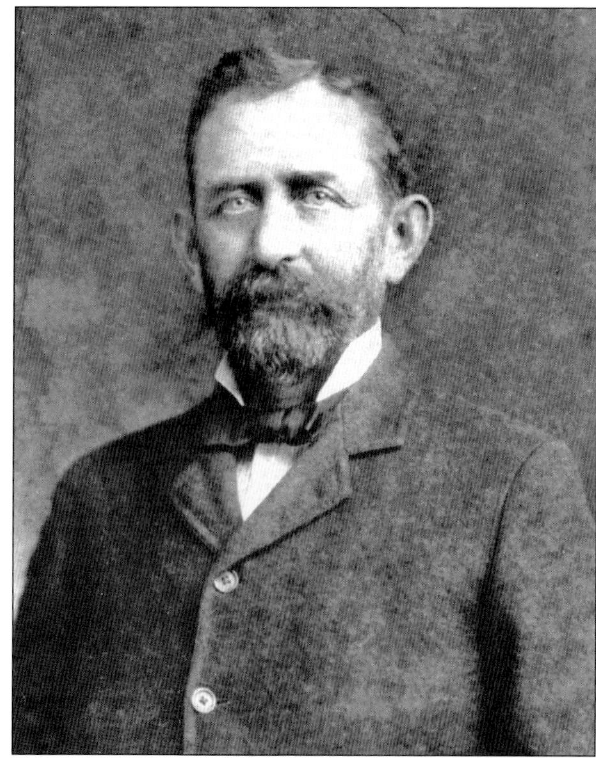

John Simmons Evans, 1900–1901. John Evans was the head keeper of Tybee Light between 1900 and 1901, and was the only keeper to die while in service. (Courtesy of Tybee Island Historical Society.)

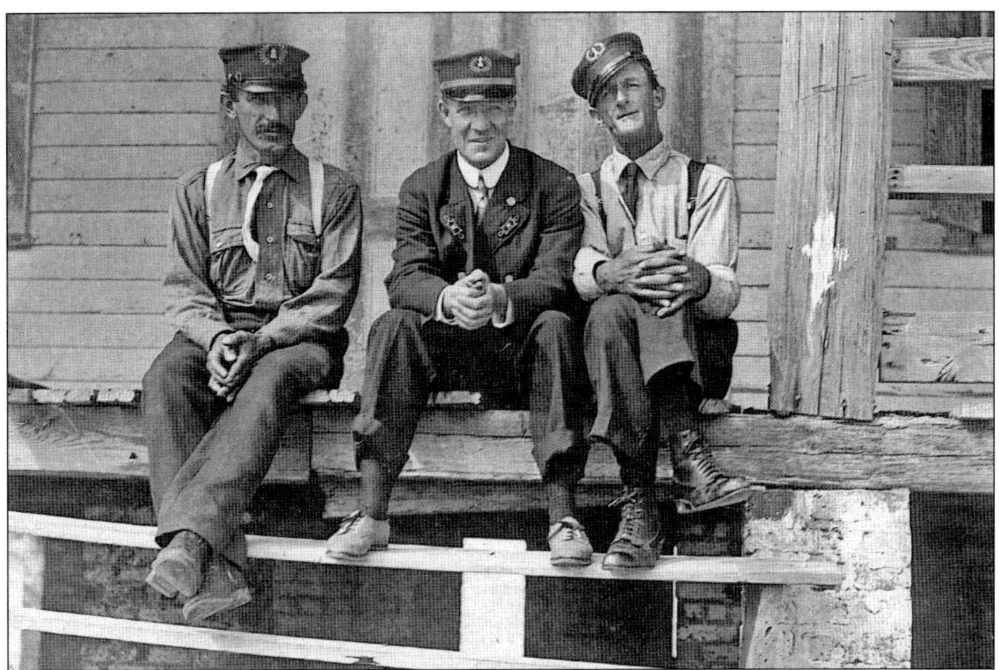

SITTING ON THE STOOP, 1905–1906. Pictured on the porch of the head keeper's house are, from left to right, J. H. Minges, the first assistant keeper; James E. Swan, the head keeper; and Charles Armour, second assistant keeper. (Courtesy of Tybee Island Historical Society.)

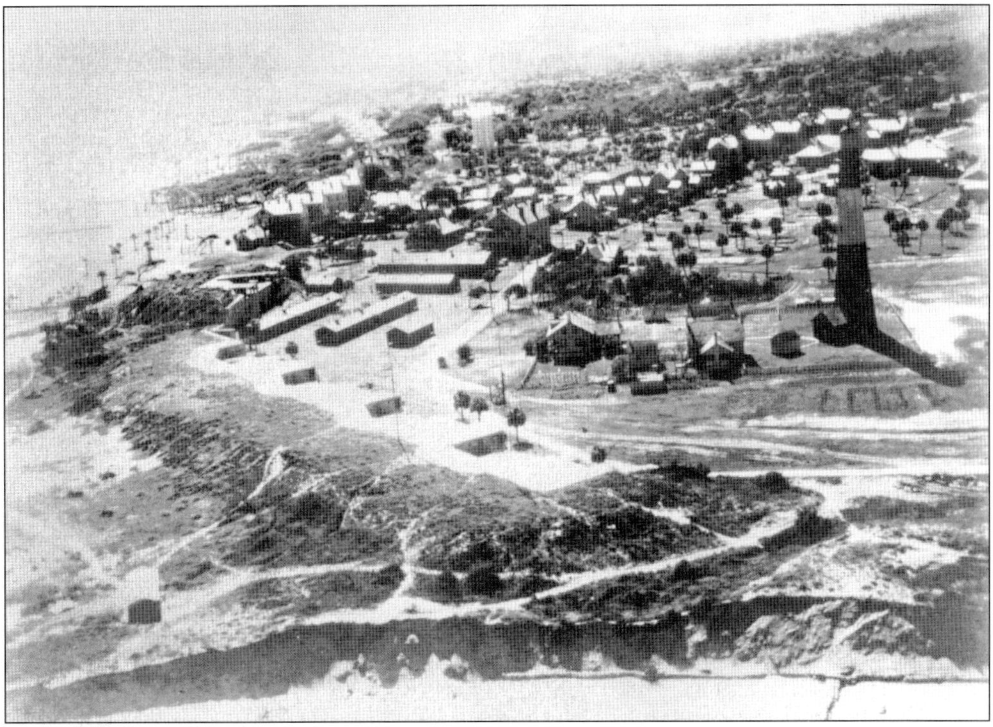

FOURTH DAY MARK, 1918–1930. This new lighthouse was to be a first-order station. It was built of masonry and metal, and was completely fireproof. (Courtesy of Tybee Island Historical Society.)

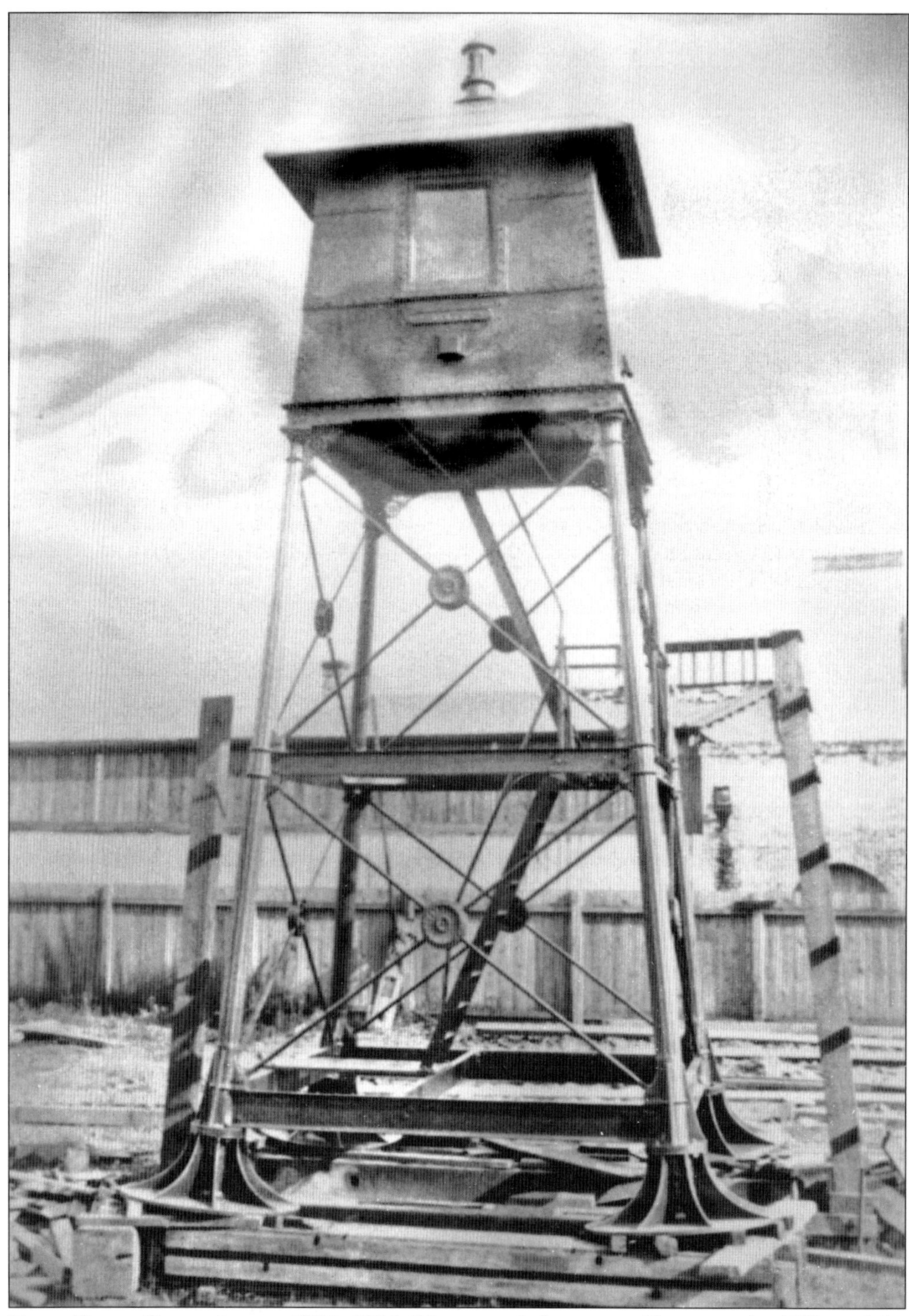

TYBEE FRONT RANGE LIGHT, 1870–1920. This range light operated between the 1870s and the 1920s. (Courtesy of Tybee Island Historical Society.)

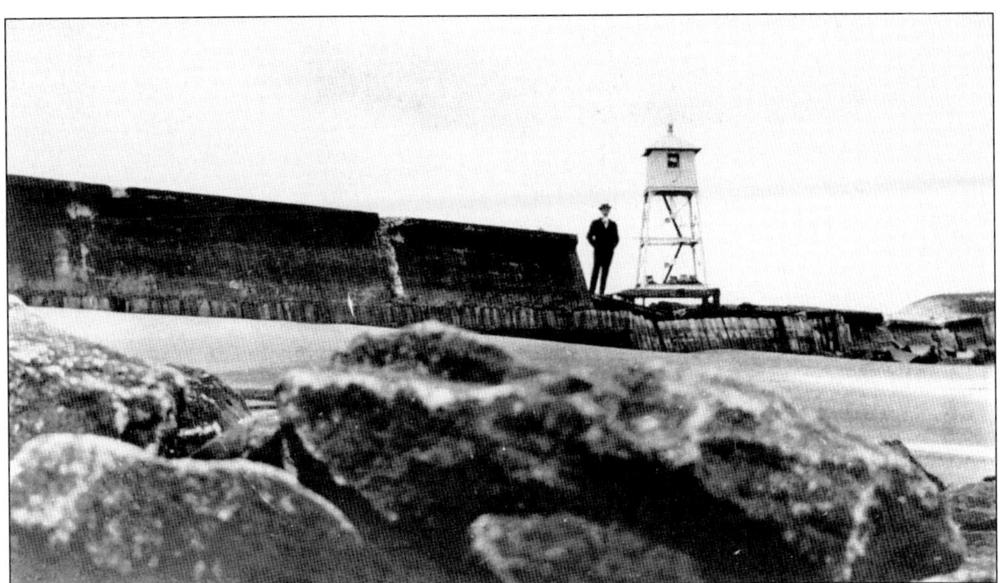

TYBEE FRONT RANGE LIGHT, 1870–1920. An unidentified man stands on a sea wall. (Courtesy of Tybee Island Historical Society.)

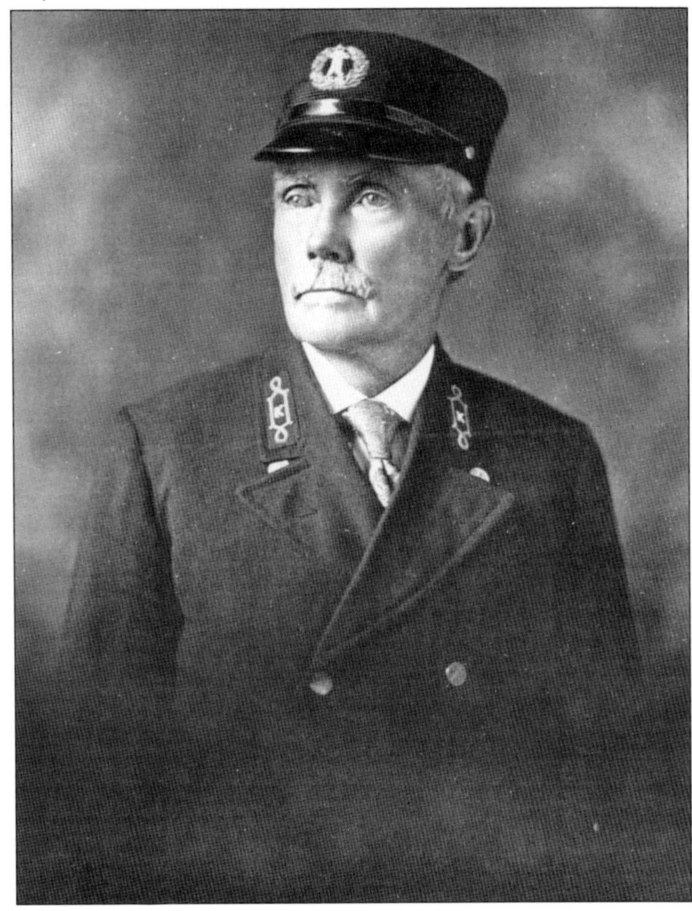

FREDERICK HENRY GATLIEB BRUGGEMAN, 1914–1931. Frederick Bruggeman was the head keeper between 1914 and 1931. (Courtesy of Tybee Island Historical Society.)

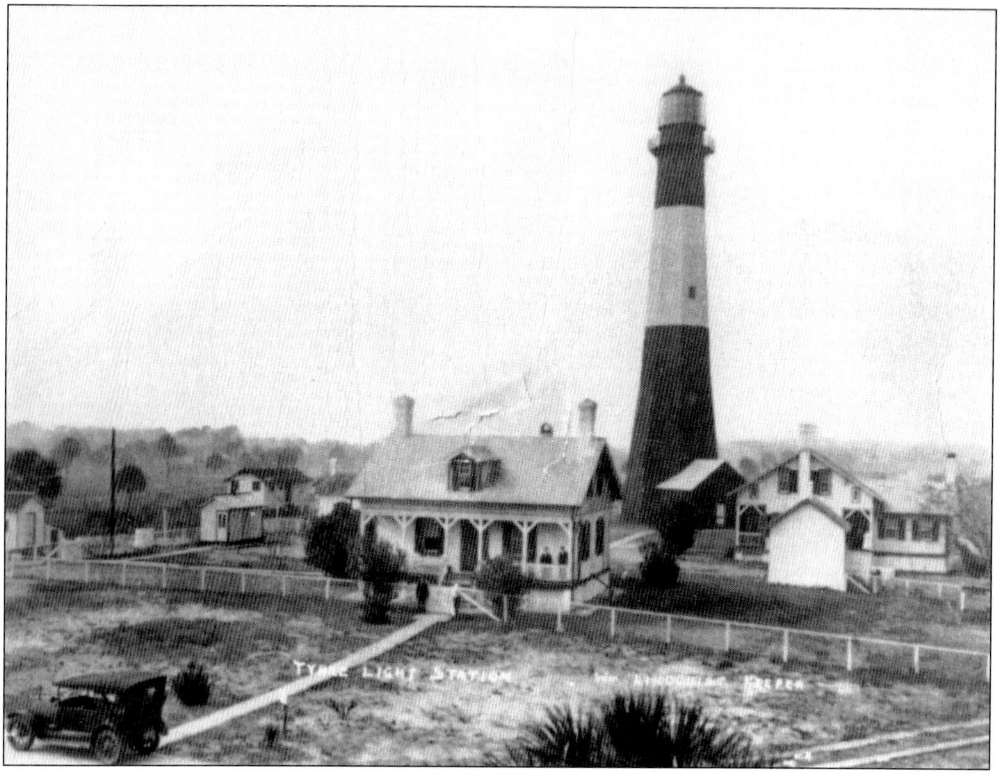

TYBEE LIGHT, 1930–1933. William Lundquest was head keeper during this time. By 1933, the light was converted to electricity. (Courtesy of Tybee Island Historical Society.)

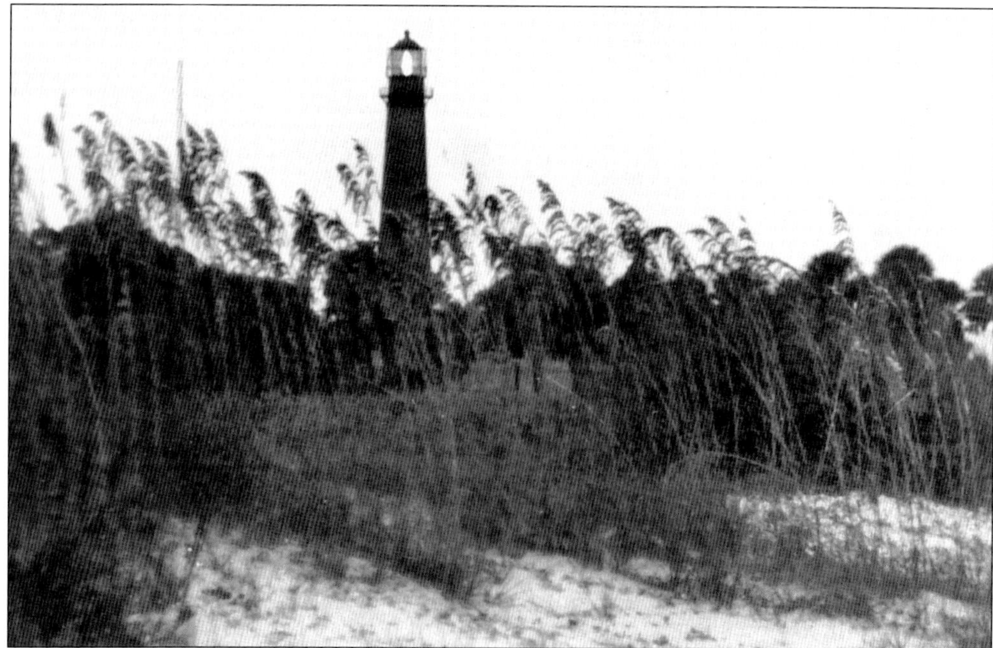

TYBEE LIGHTHOUSE. This image shows the Tybee Light with sea oats in the foreground. (Courtesy of Tybee Island Historical Society.)

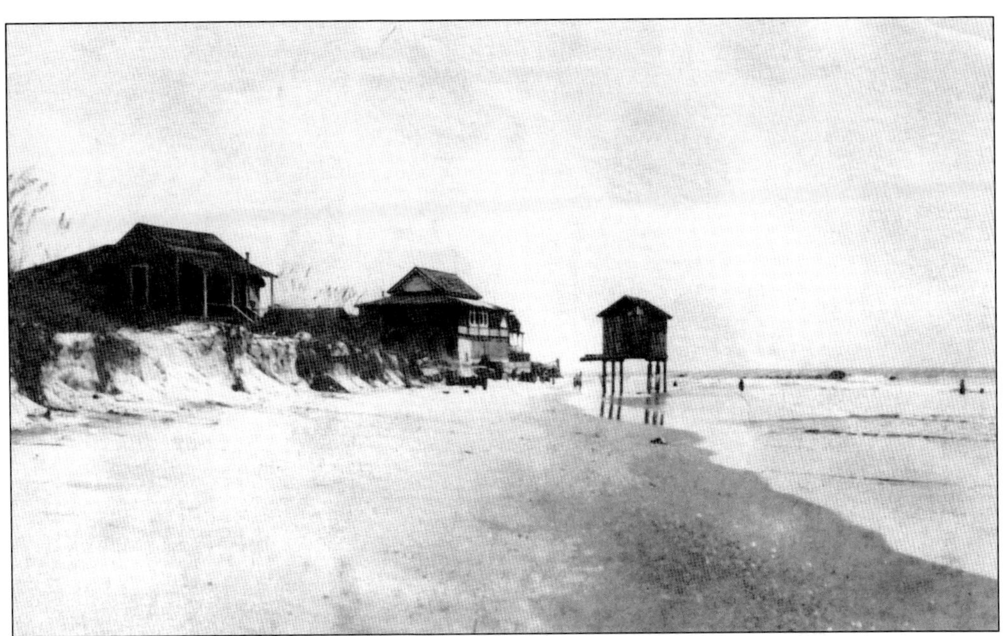

NORTH END OF TYBEE ISLAND, 1921. Beach erosion has always been a problem and is evident in this July 10, 1921, photograph. (Courtesy of Tybee Island Historical Society.)

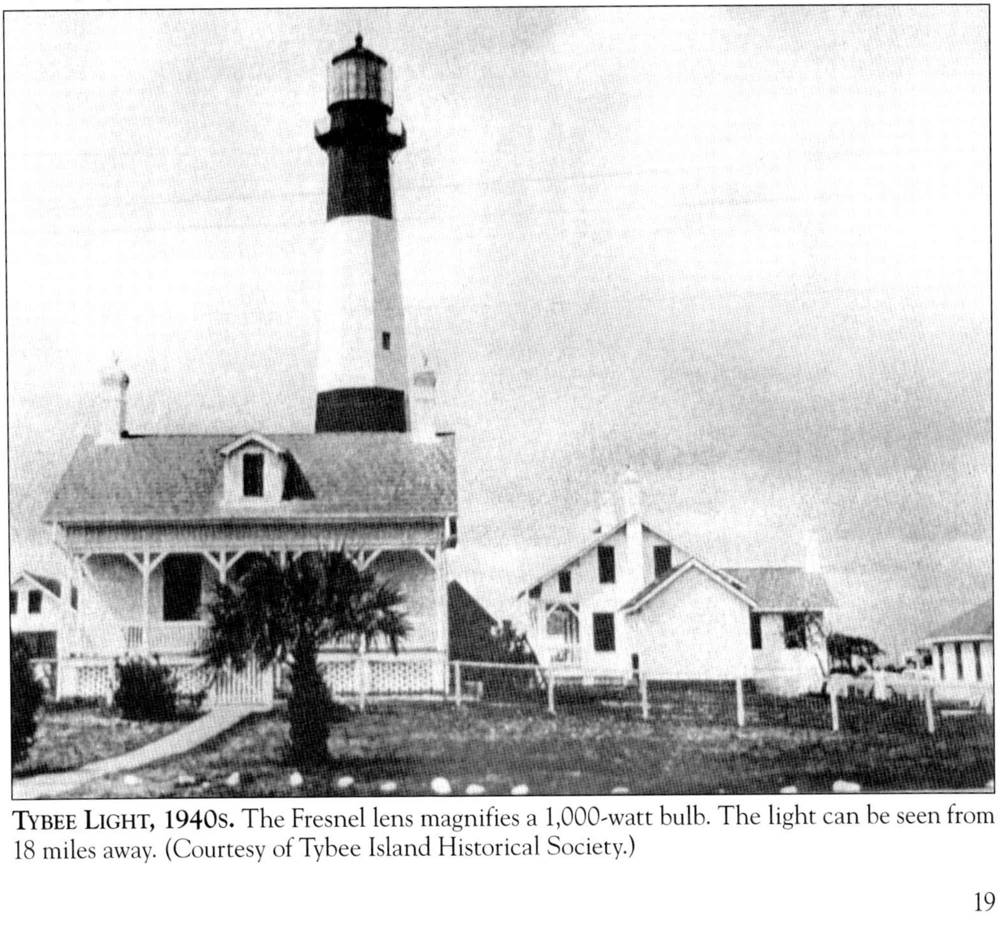

TYBEE LIGHT, 1940S. The Fresnel lens magnifies a 1,000-watt bulb. The light can be seen from 18 miles away. (Courtesy of Tybee Island Historical Society.)

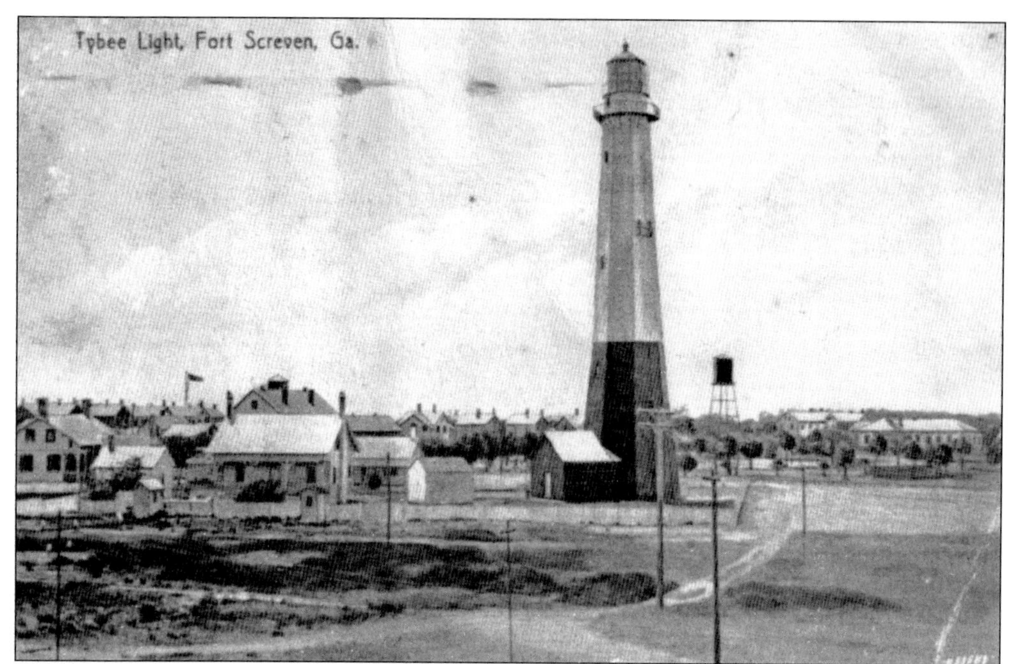

TYBEE LIGHT, 1890–1907. This postcard shows Fort Screven in the distance and an undocumented day mark. (Courtesy of Tybee Island Historical Society.)

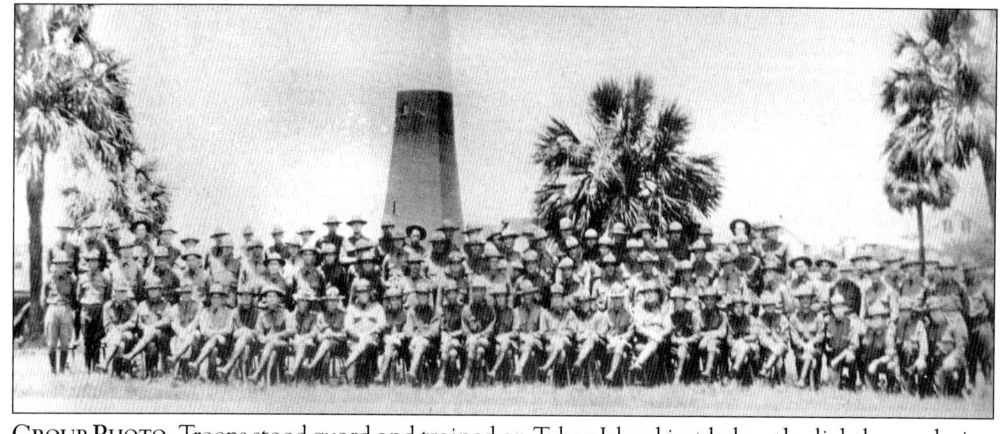

GROUP PHOTO. Troops stood guard and trained on Tybee Island just below the lighthouse during the Spanish-American War of 1898 and World War I and II. Fort Screven was sold to the town of Tybee in November 1945. (Courtesy of Tybee Island Historical Society.)

TENT CITY, 1930–1945. The exact date of this photograph is unknown, but a civilian military training camp operated in the area between 1930 and 1945. (Courtesy of Tybee Island Historical Society.)

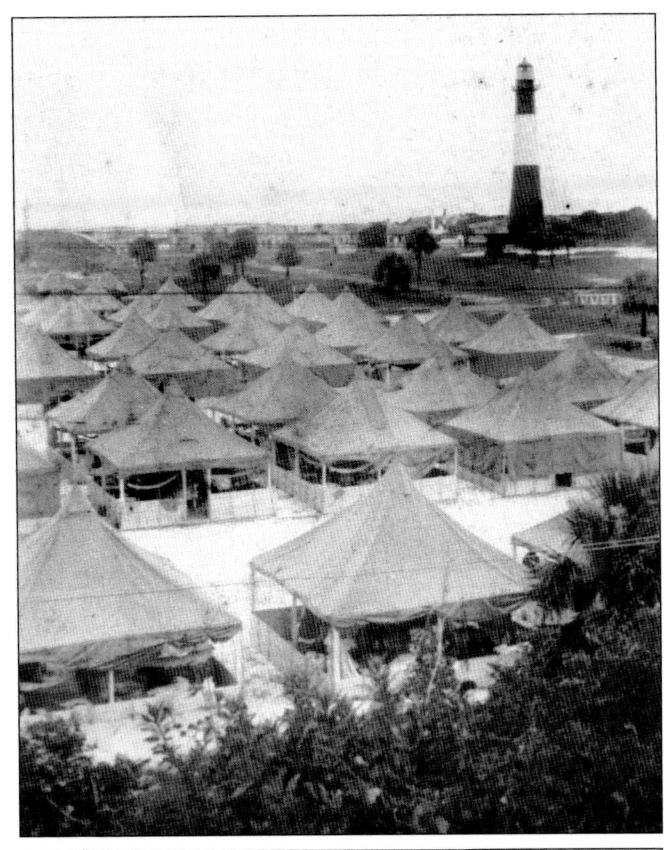

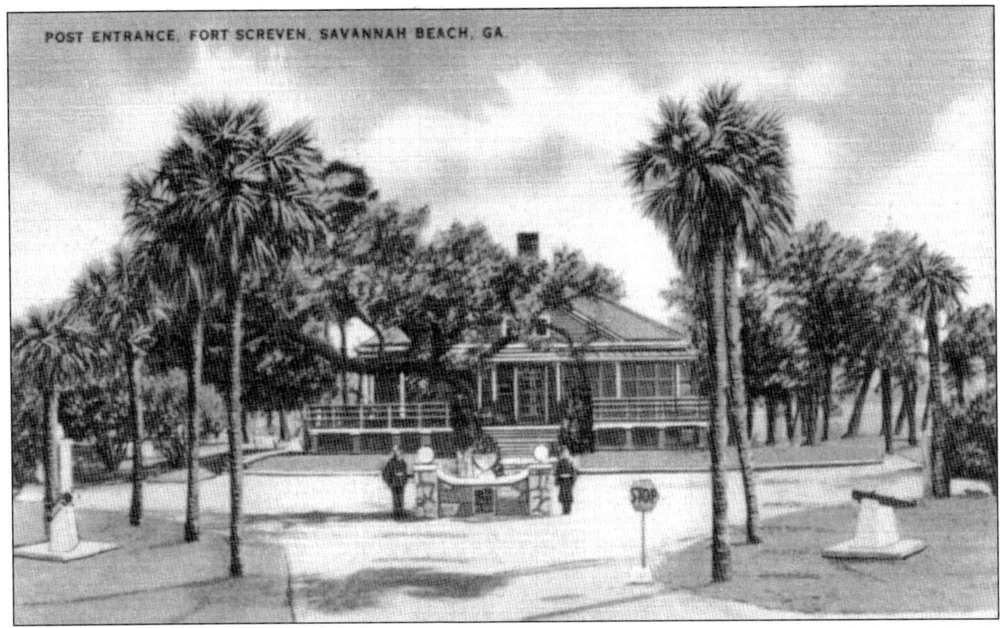

FORT SCREVEN GATE, 1897–1947. Fort Screven was built on the north end of Tybee Island. From 1897 to 1947, the fort was an integral part of a coastal defense system. (Courtesy of Tybee Island Historical Society.)

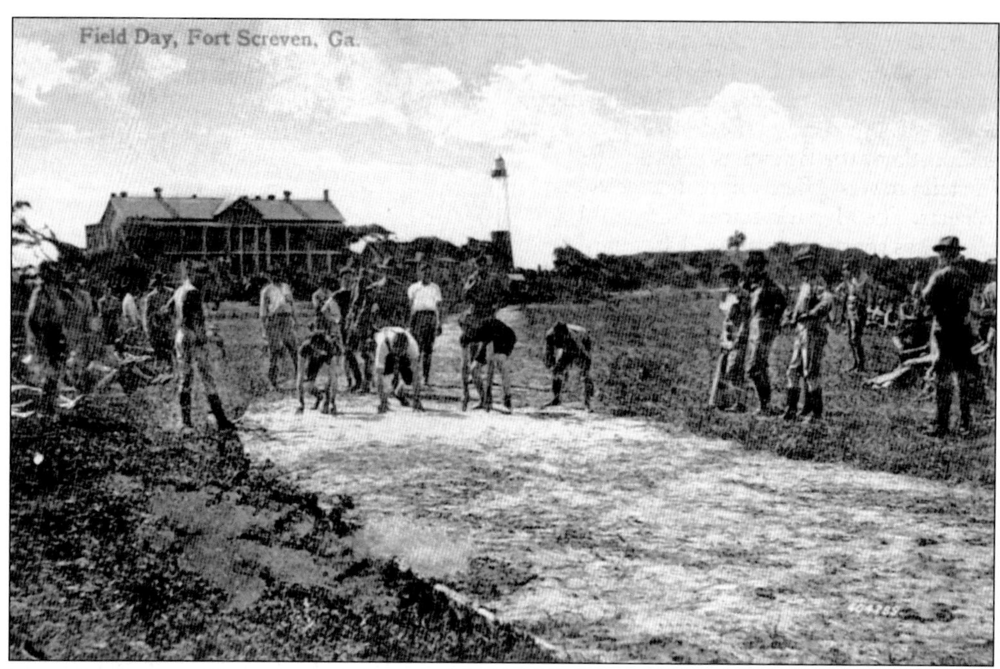

Field Day, 1912. This postcard shows a field day running event about to begin. The day was popular at Fort Screven. (Courtesy of Tybee Island Historical Society.)

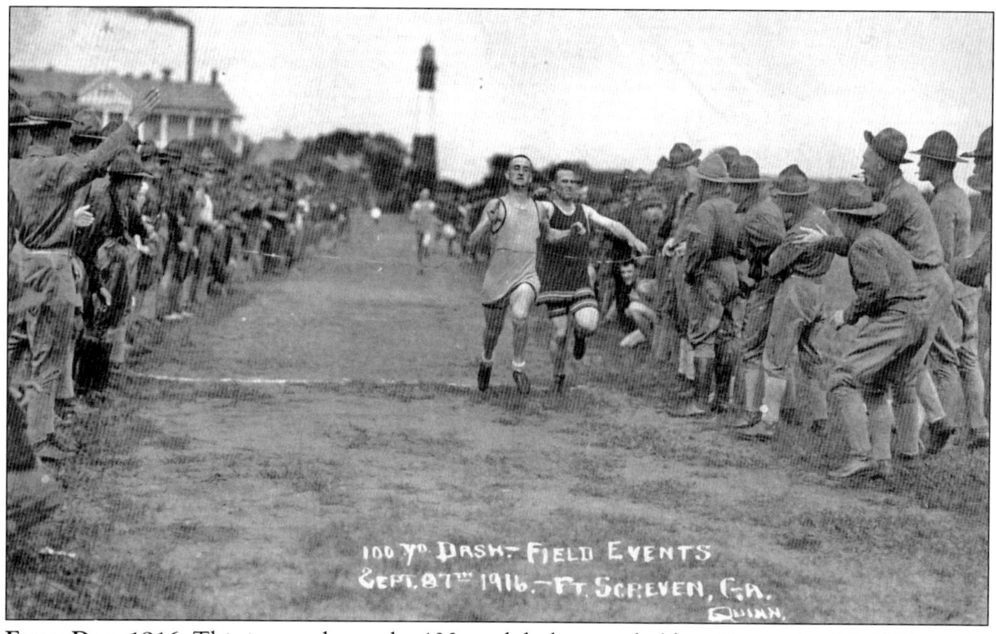

Field Day, 1916. This image shows the 100-yard dash event held on September 27, 1916, at the Fort Screven field day. (Courtesy of Tybee Island Historical Society.)

MARTELLO TOWER, C. 1907. Several Martello towers were built in various locations in the United States. Although the design was copied from the towers erected in Canada by the British, the American Martello towers differed in some significant respects. The Martello tower built at Tybee Island was constructed around 1815 using wood and tabby, a common local building material at the time. Also, unlike the British towers, the Tybee tower featured gun loops on the garrison floor that enabled muskets to be fired through the walls. It was never tested in battle. (Courtesy of Tybee Island Historical Society.)

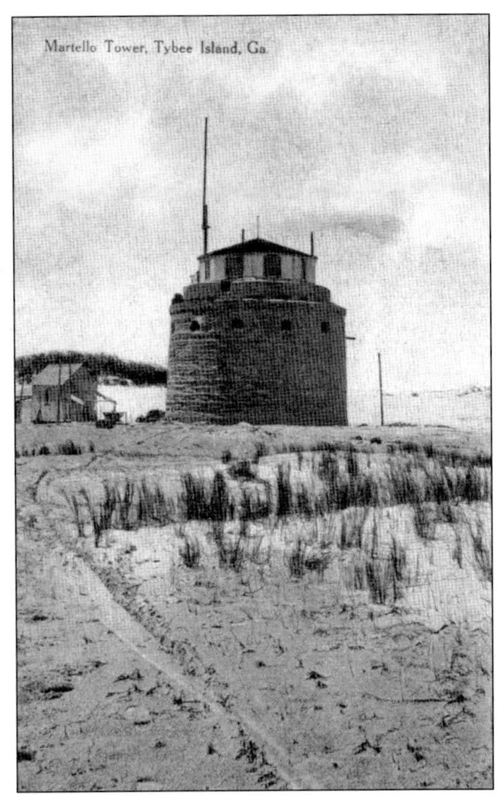

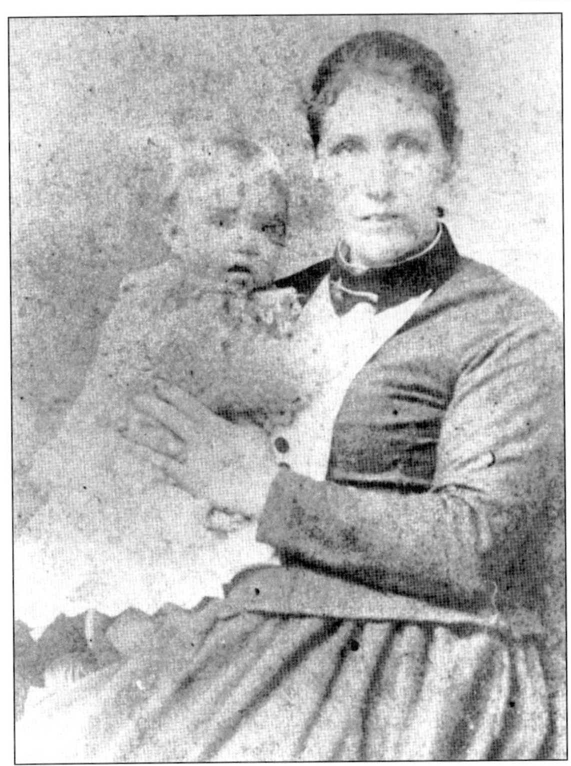

ELIZABETH LOCKWOOD WORTHAM. Elizabeth Wortham lived in the Martello tower around the beginning of the 20th century and was the postmistress. The tower was also used as a telegraph station. (Courtesy of Tybee Island Historical Society.)

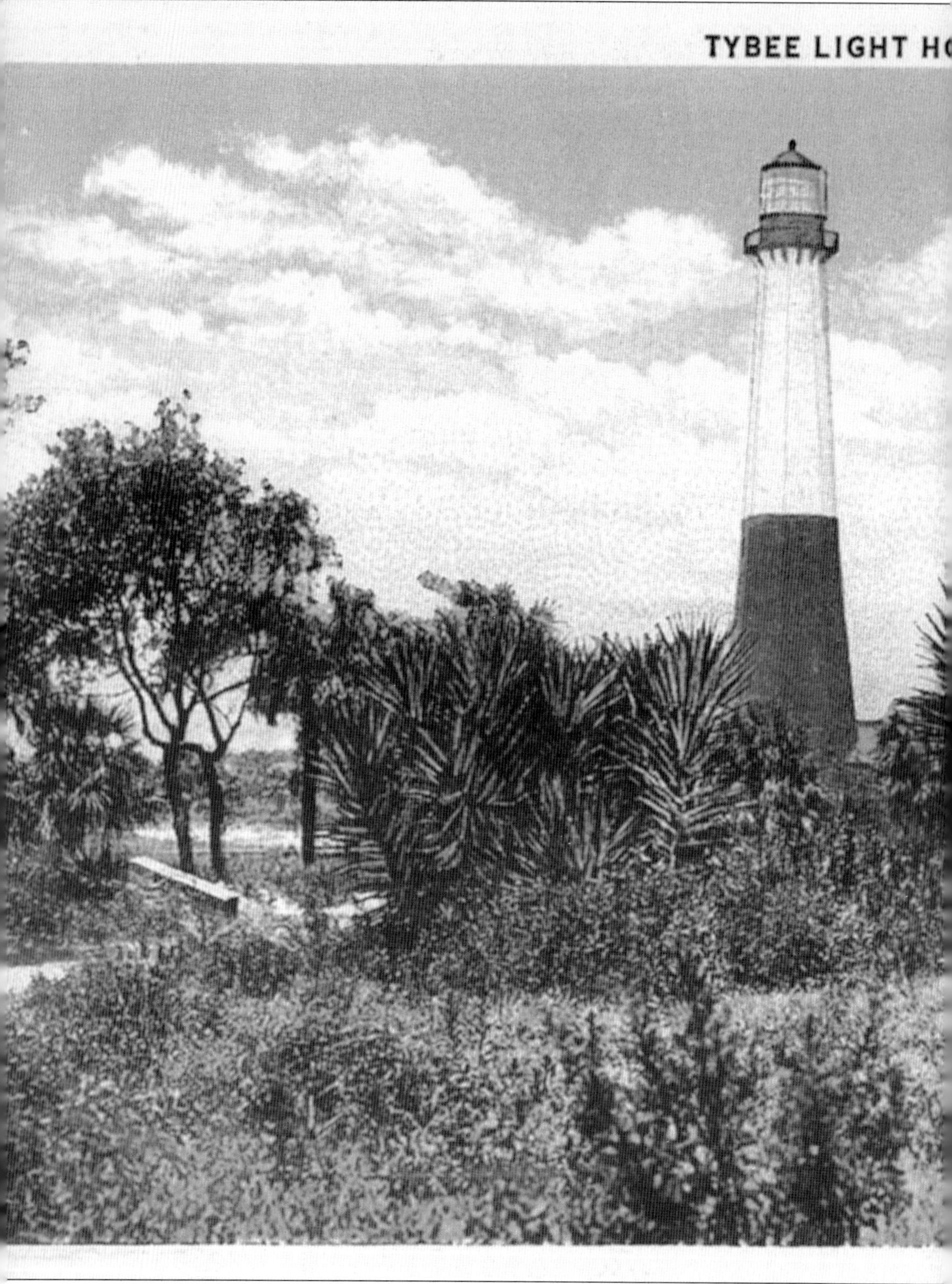
TYBEE LIGHT HO

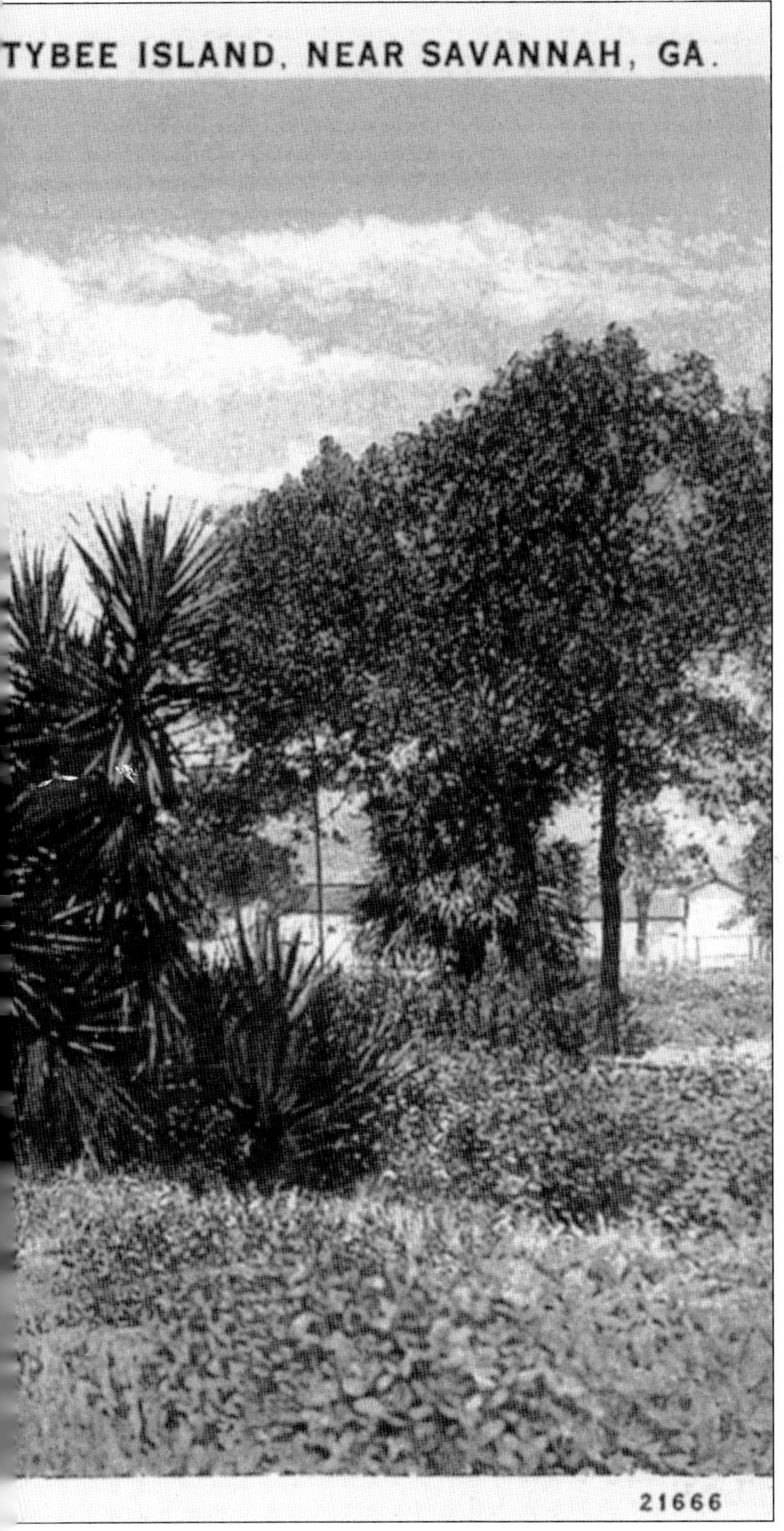

TYBEE LIGHT POSTCARD, 1914. Every lighthouse comes in a distinctive size, shape, and color, and each have what is known as a day mark and a night signature. The day mark, also known as the color scheme or paint pattern, is used so that during the day ships can tell one lighthouse from another. The Tybee Light has had at least six distinctive day marks. (Courtesy of Tybee Island Historical Society.)

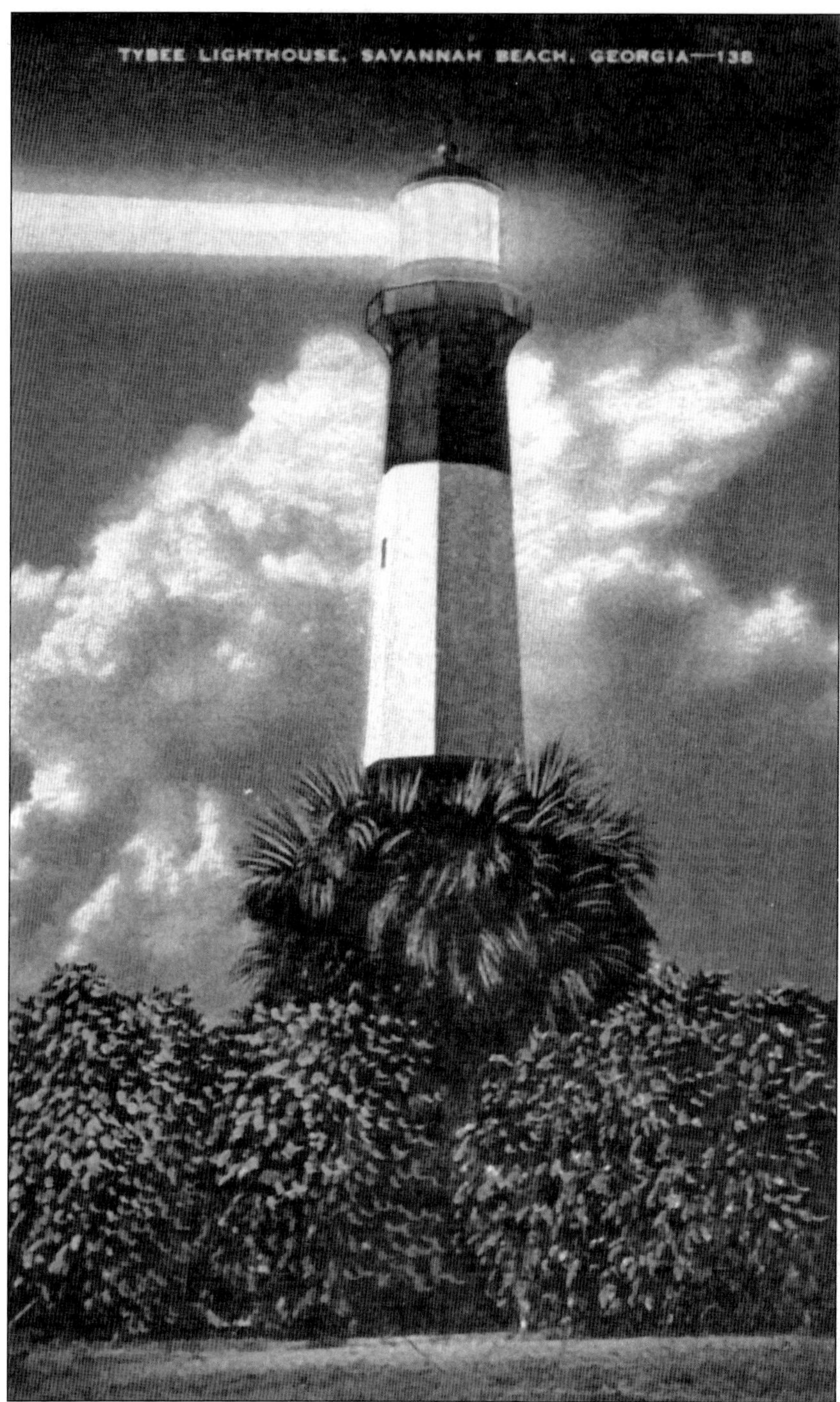

TYBEE LIGHT STATION, 1916–1965. This image shows the Tybee Light's fourth day mark. To identify a lighthouse at night, ships use a night signature or light pattern. Each pattern is different. The Tybee lighthouse has a constant beam shining 18 miles out to sea, while the St. Simons Lighthouse has a flash pattern of one rotation per minute. (Courtesy of Tybee Island Historical Society.)

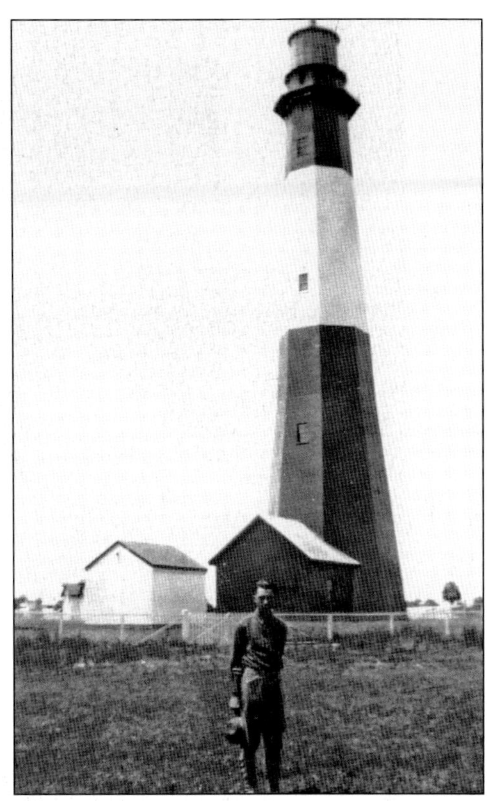

Unidentified Soldier, 1914–1918. The lighthouse has its fourth day mark during the World War I years. The U.S. Coast Guard occupied the light and maintained its operation until 1987. (Courtesy of Tybee Island Historical Society.)

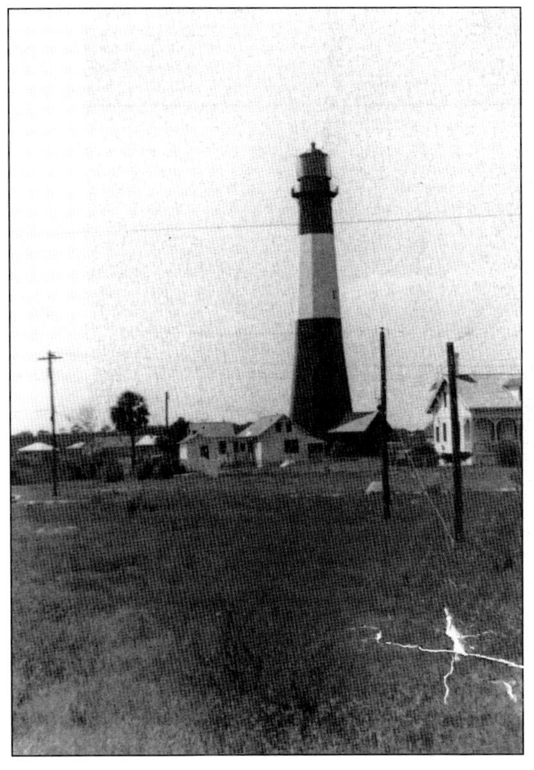

Across the Field. This lighthouse, the fourth built on Tybee, is the one standing today. (Courtesy of Tybee Island Historical Society.)

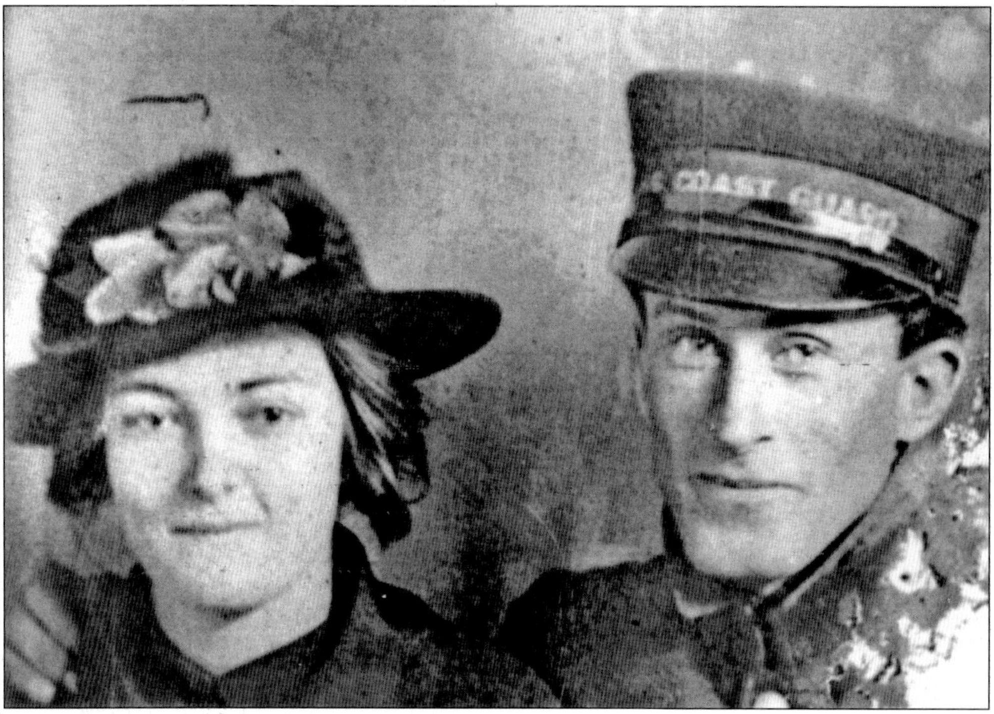

HEAD KEEPER AND HIS WIFE, 1933–1945. George Jackson was Tybee's head keeper between 1933 and 1945. He is shown here with and his wife, Laura. (Courtesy of Tybee Island Historical Society.)

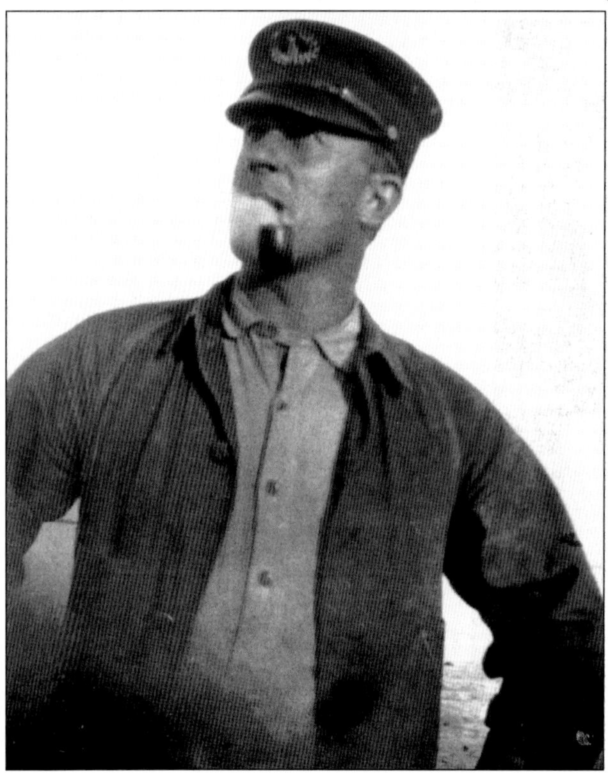

GEORGE JACKSON, 1933–1945. U.S. Lighthouse Service–trained George Jackson was the lighthouse's head keeper between 1933 and 1945. He was Tybee's last keeper. The U.S. Coast Guard took over the operation and maintenance of the lighthouse in 1939, but Jackson stayed on as keeper. He died in 1948. (Courtesy of Tybee Island Historical Society.)

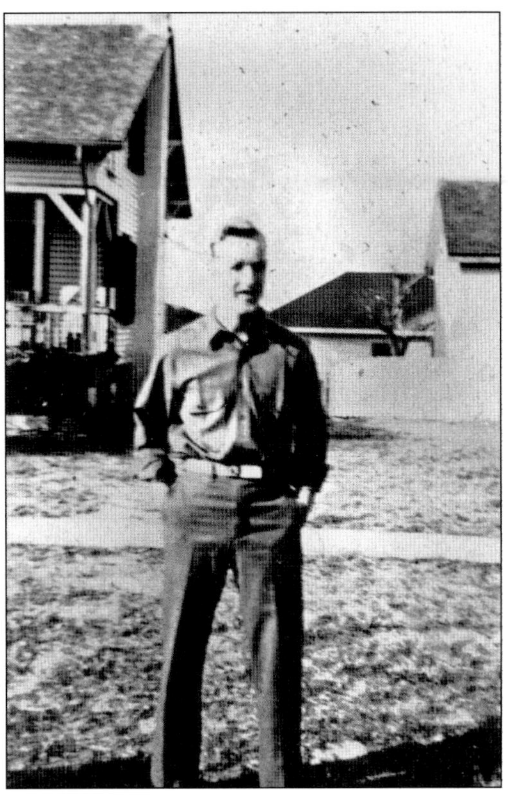

Bernie Knapp, 1933–1945. This photograph shows Bernie Knapp, a friend of the Jackson family. In the background, the first assistant keeper's house and summer kitchen can be seen. (Courtesy of Tybee Island Historical Society.)

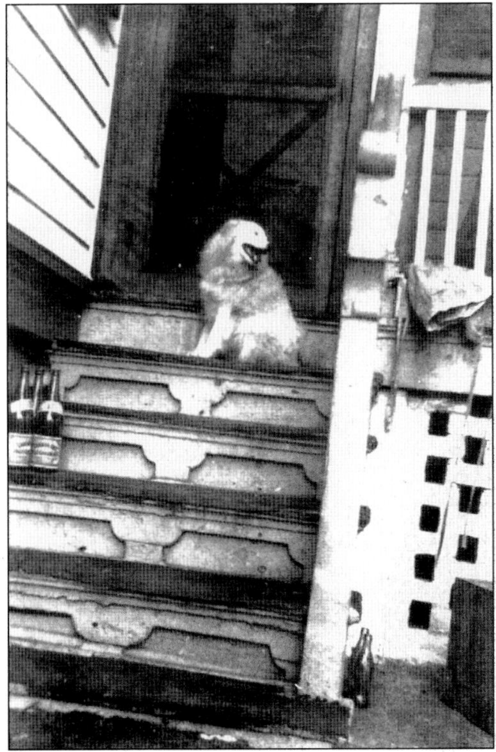

Taffy. Taffy, the Jackson family dog, sits on the head keeper's home steps. This photograph helped staff with the restoration of the head keeper's house in 2000. (Courtesy of Tybee Island Historical Society.)

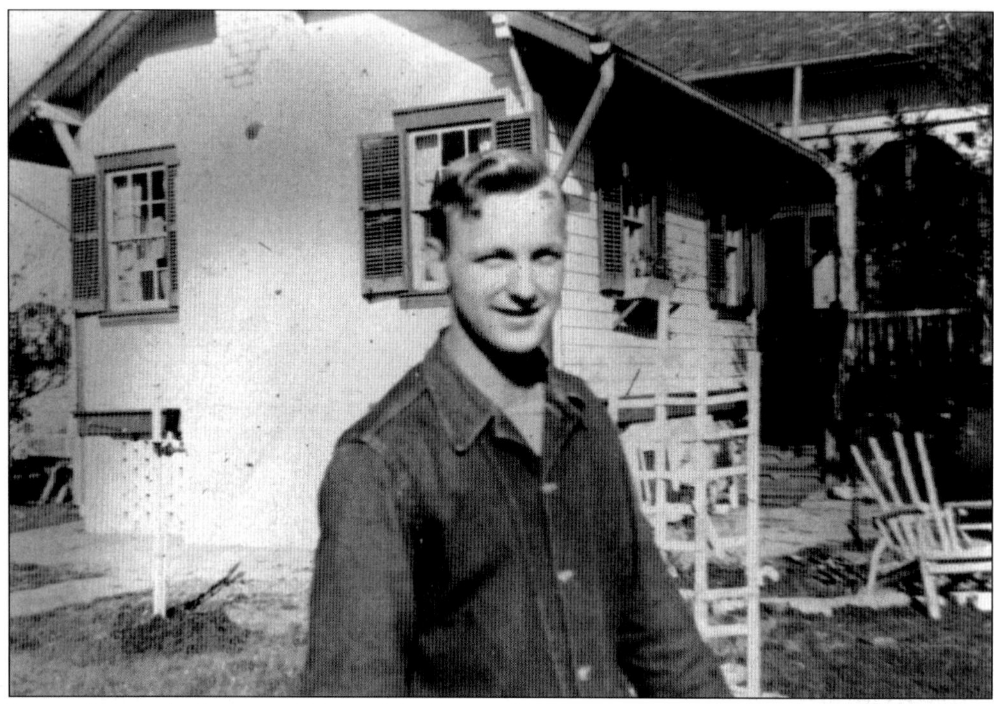

Light Keeper's Friend, 1933–1945. Bernie Knapp was Grace Jackson's boyfriend. He is pictured here with the head keeper's house in the background. (Courtesy of Tybee Island Historical Society.)

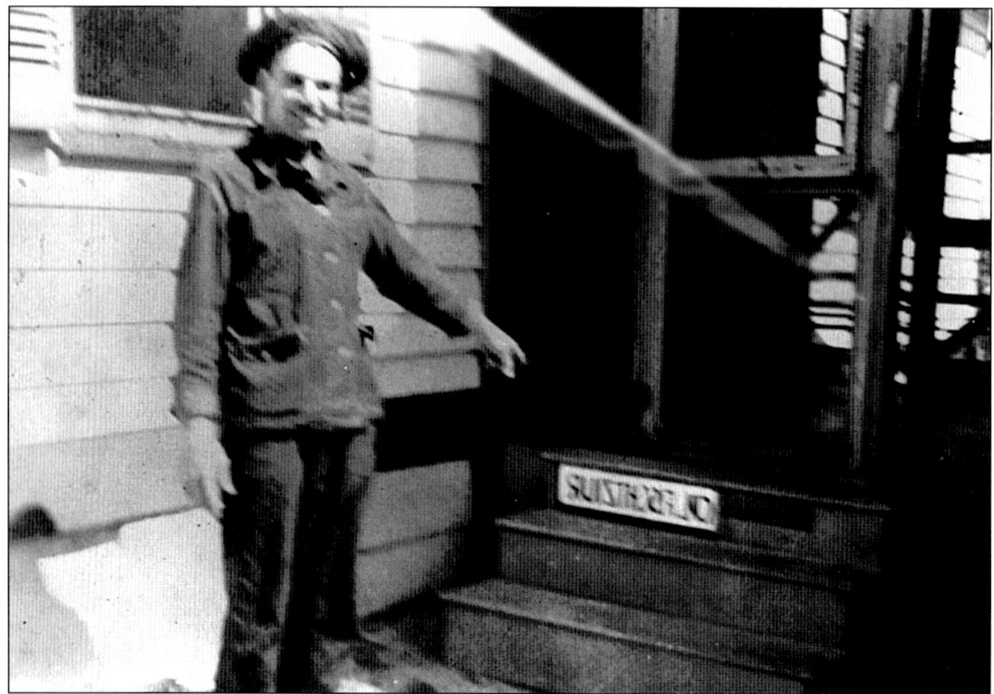

Unidentified Coast Guard Artilleryman. An unidentified man points at the steps leading to the porch of the second assistant keeper's house. (Courtesy of Tybee Island Historical Society.)

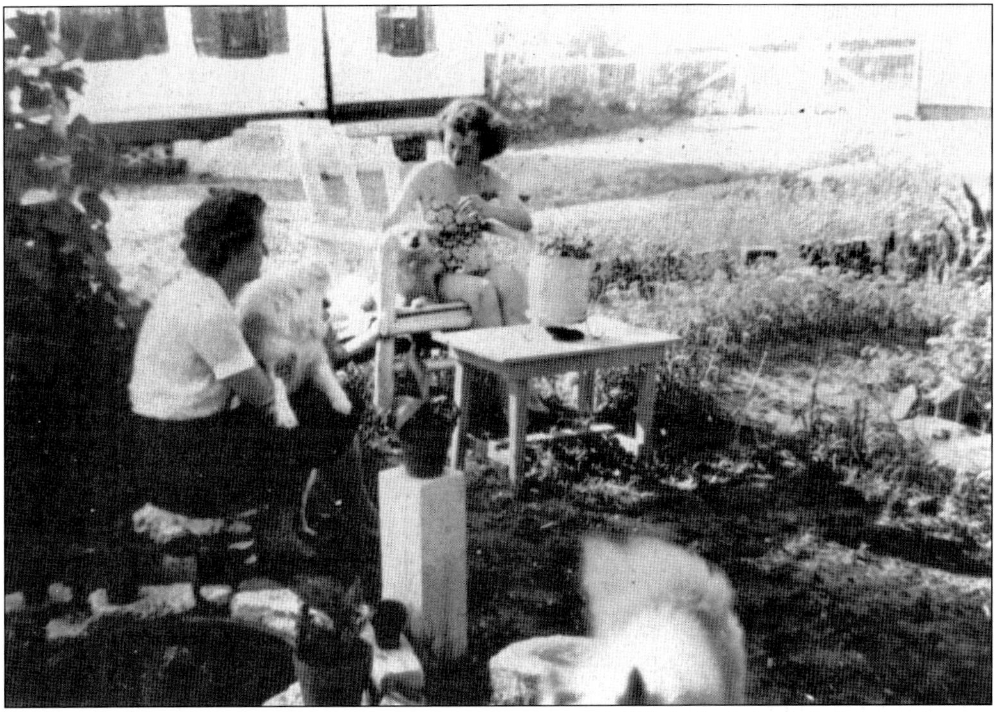

LAURA JACKSON AND FRIEND NELL BREWER, 1933–1945. While the life of a lighthouse keeper and his family might be isolated at times, family and friends were important. (Courtesy of Tybee Island Historical Society.)

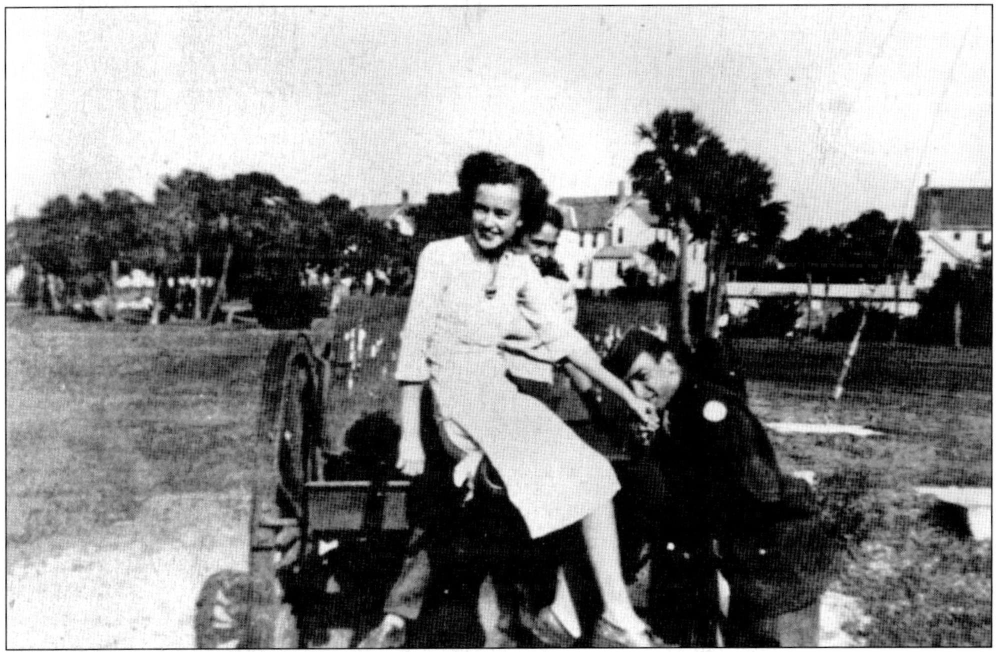

GRACE JACKSON, JOY EAST, AND OMER "FRENCHY," 1940–1945. Here on the parade grounds of Fort Screven, Grace Jackson is being wooed by a suitor, known only as Frenchy, as Joy East takes a peek. (Courtesy of Tybee Island Historical Society.)

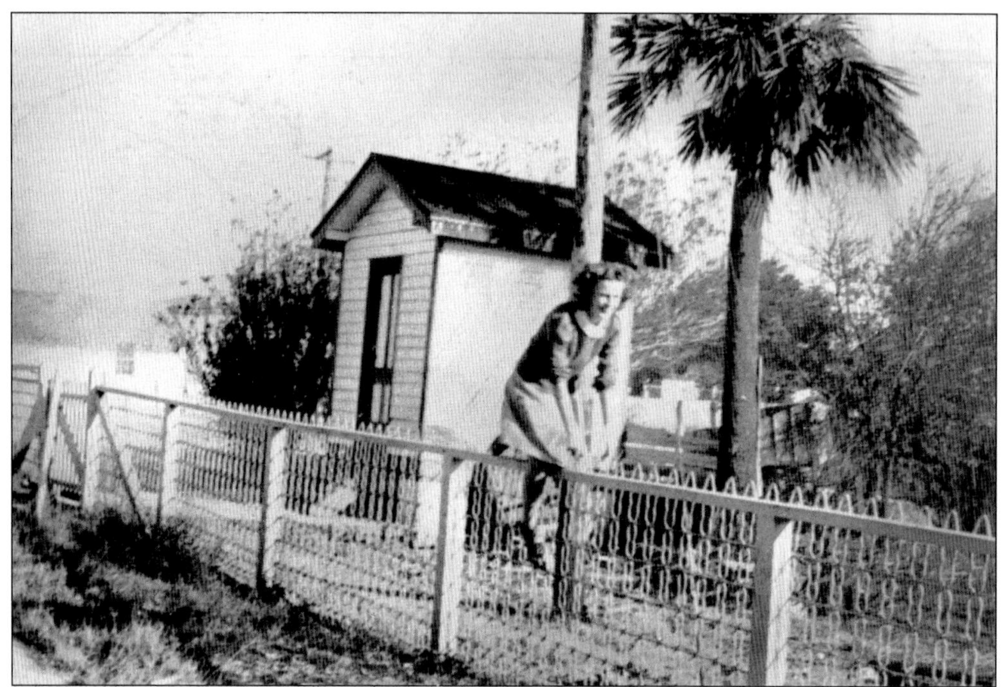

Grace Jackson Jumps Fence, 1933–1945. Often the lighthouse keeper's job was routine and monotonous. The family often had to make their own fun. (Courtesy of Tybee Island Historical Society.)

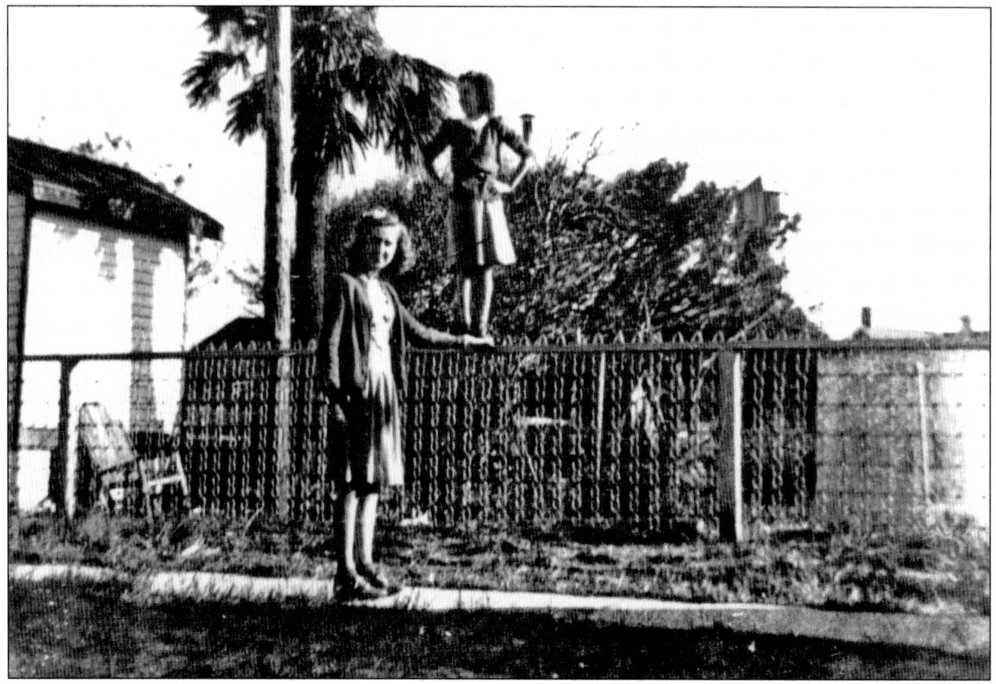

Gloria East and Grace Jackson (on Fence), 1933–1945. Because most lighthouses were isolated until World War I, education of the lighthouse keeper's children could be problematic. Often their only playmates were other siblings. (Courtesy of Tybee Island Historical Society.)

LAURA AND GEORGE JACKSON. Today the descendants of the Jackson family still reside on Tybee Island. (Courtesy of Tybee Island Historical Society.)

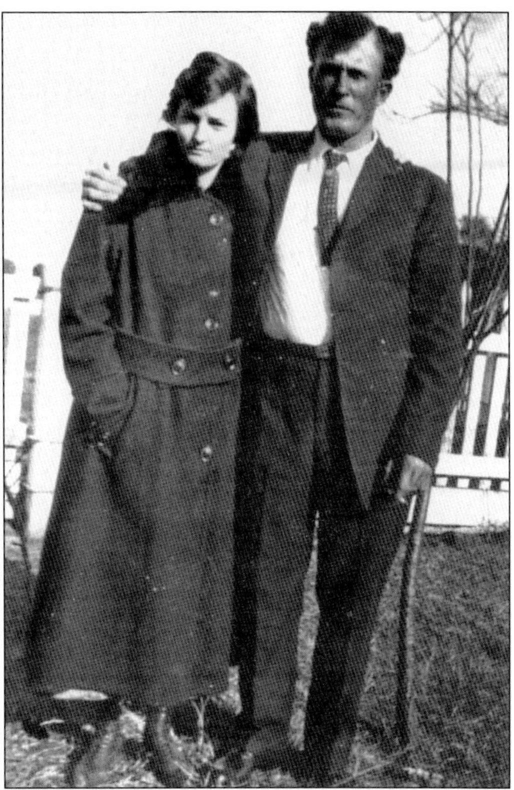

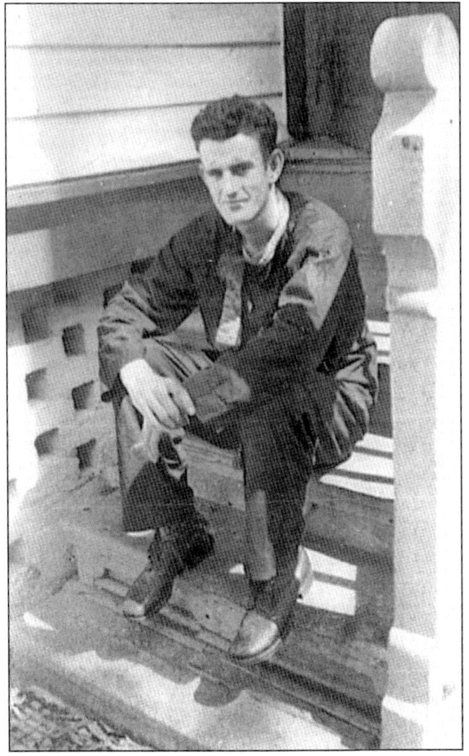

RALPH JACKSON, 1943. Ralph Jackson is shown here sitting on the stoop of the head keeper's house. He was the son of George and Laura Jackson. (Courtesy of Tybee Island Historical Society.)

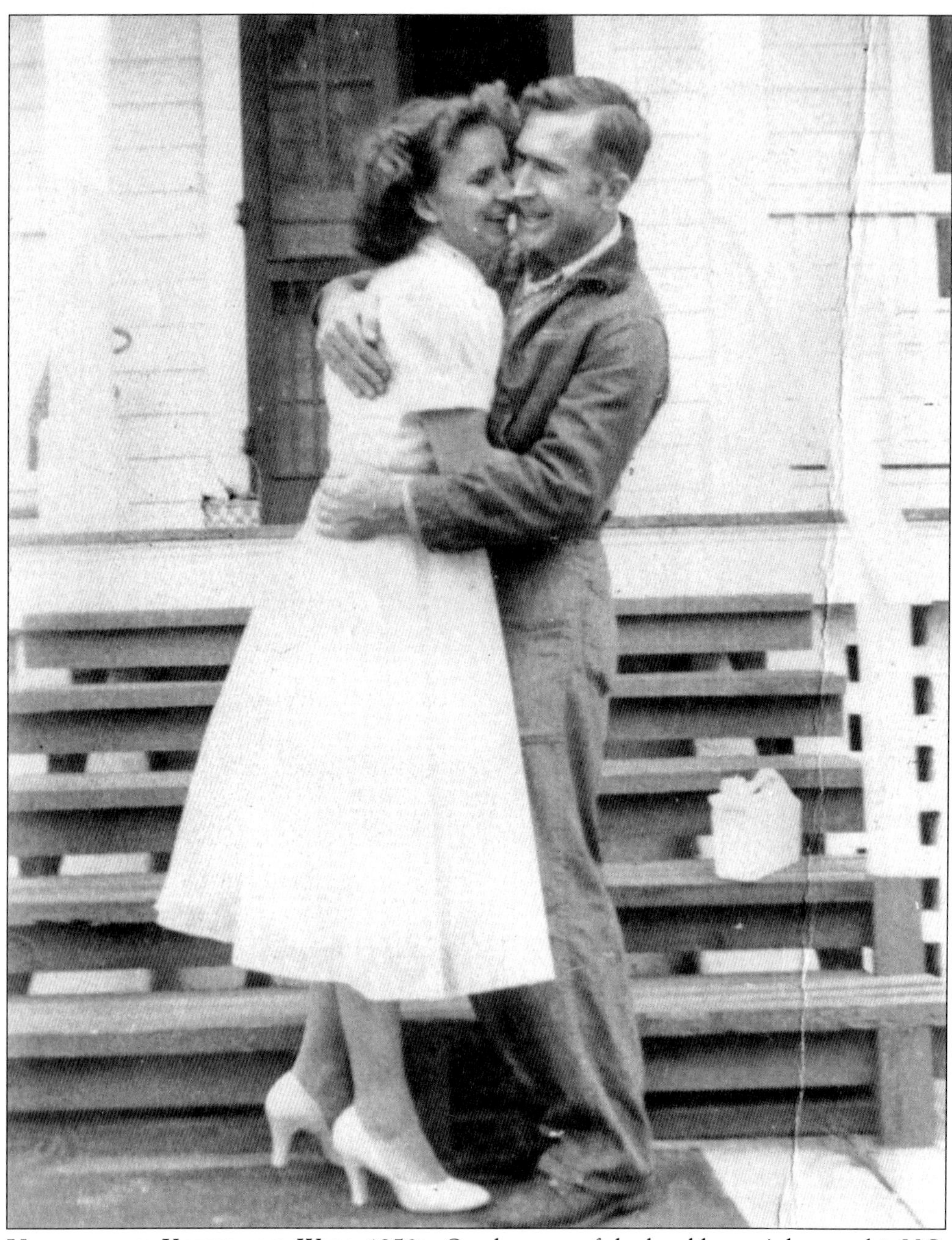

UNIDENTIFIED KEEPER AND WIFE, 1950S. On the steps of the head keeper's house, this U.S. Coast Guard keeper and his wife are all hugs. After 1947, Coast Guard personnel were stationed at the lighthouse until 1987, when they moved to Cockspur Island. (Courtesy of Tybee Island Historical Society.)

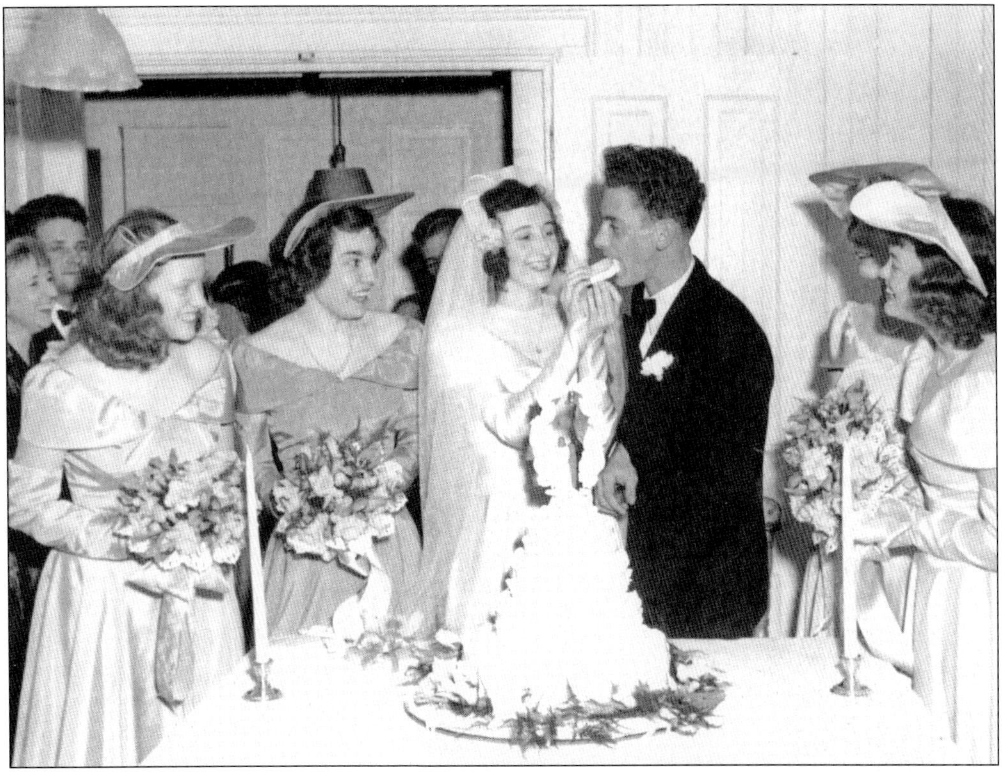

WEDDING RECEPTION, 1949. This wedding reception was held in the kitchen of the head keeper's house. The bride was Mildred Voigt and her groom was Clayton Jolley. (Courtesy of Tybee Island Historical Society.)

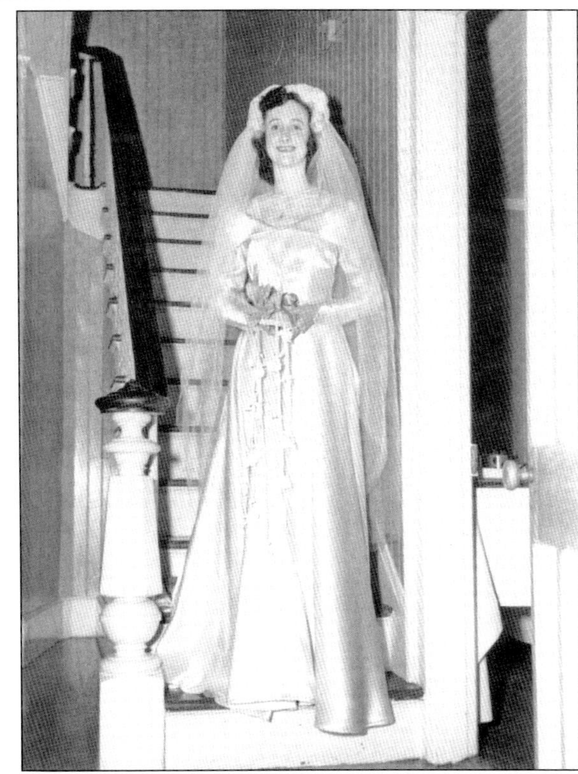

HERE COMES THE BRIDE, 1949. Mildred Voigt is pictured here on the steps of the keeper's house. This photograph was used to help the restoration of the stairs. (Courtesy of Tybee Island Historical Society.)

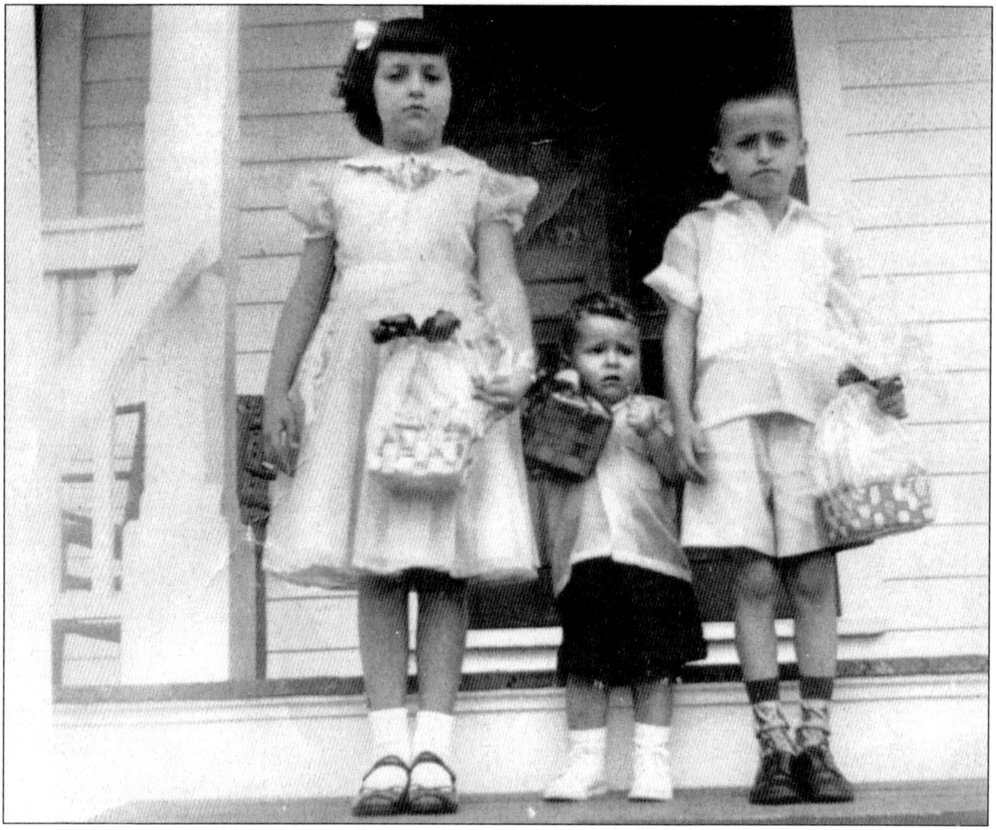

UNIDENTIFIED CHILDREN, C. 1950. These unidentified children are pictured with the keeper's son Mike L. O'Dell Brown holding their Easter baskets. (Courtesy of Tybee Island Historical Society.)

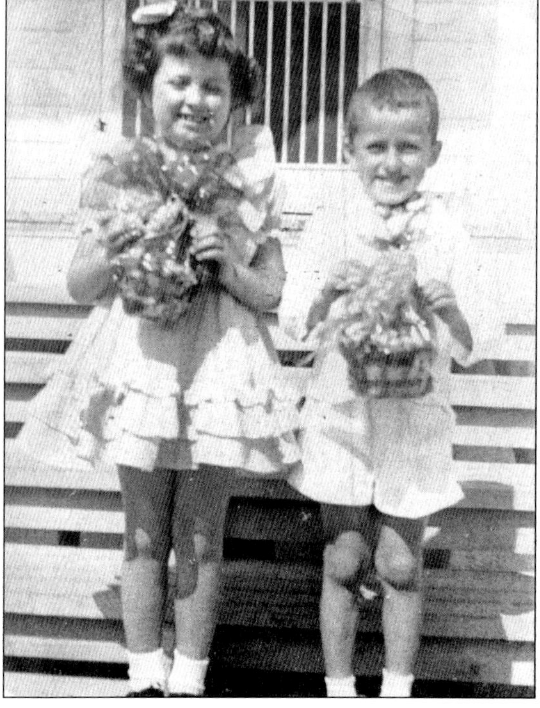

EASTER ON TYBEE, C. 1950. These children are excited about their Easter treats. (Courtesy of Tybee Island Historical Society.)

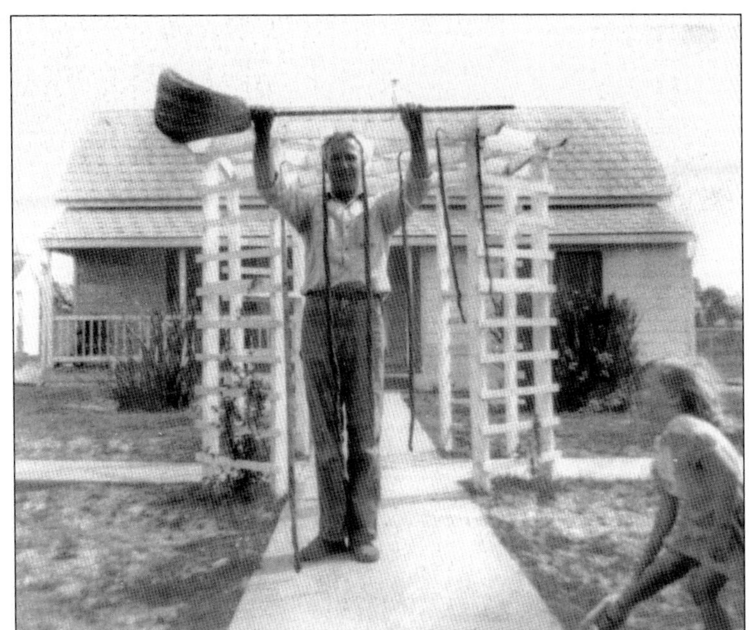

SNAKES, 1961–1963. O'Dell, keeper for the U.S. Coast Guard from 1961 to 1963, holds up a broom with snakes attached. (Courtesy of Tybee Island Historical Society.)

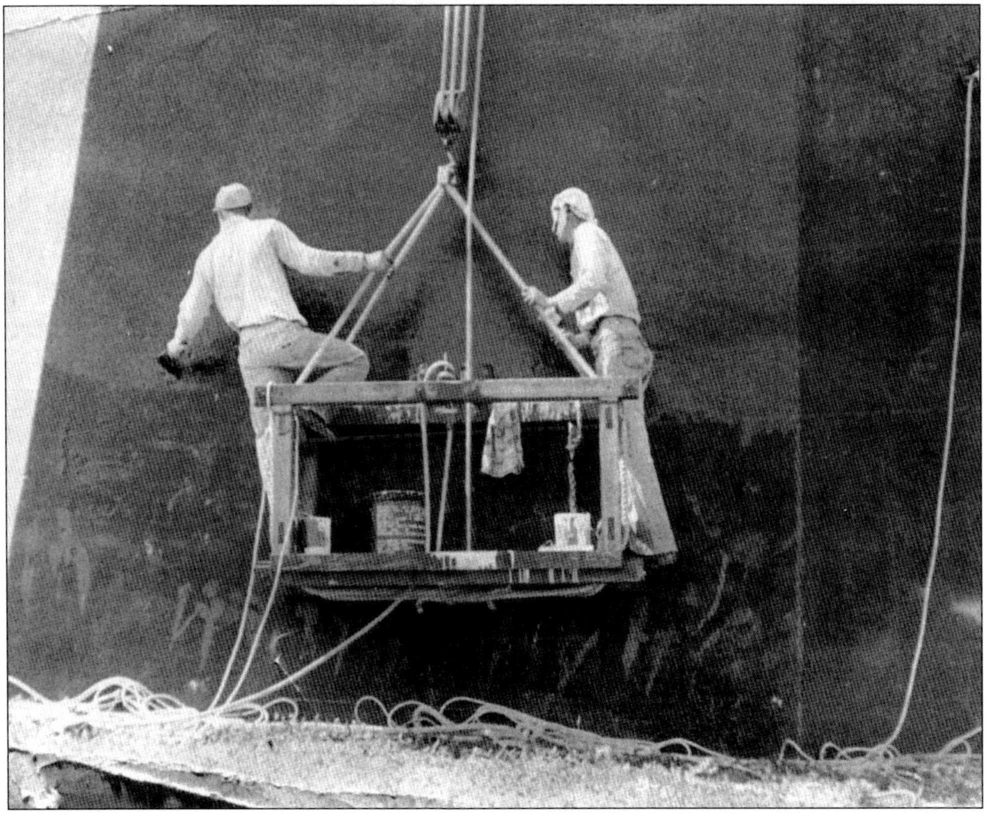

PAINTING THE LIGHTHOUSE, 1961–1963. Lighthouse maintenance was a constant. Coasties Bennett and Johnson use a hanging basket along the side of the lighthouse to paint it in the 1960s. (Courtesy of Tybee Island Historical Society.)

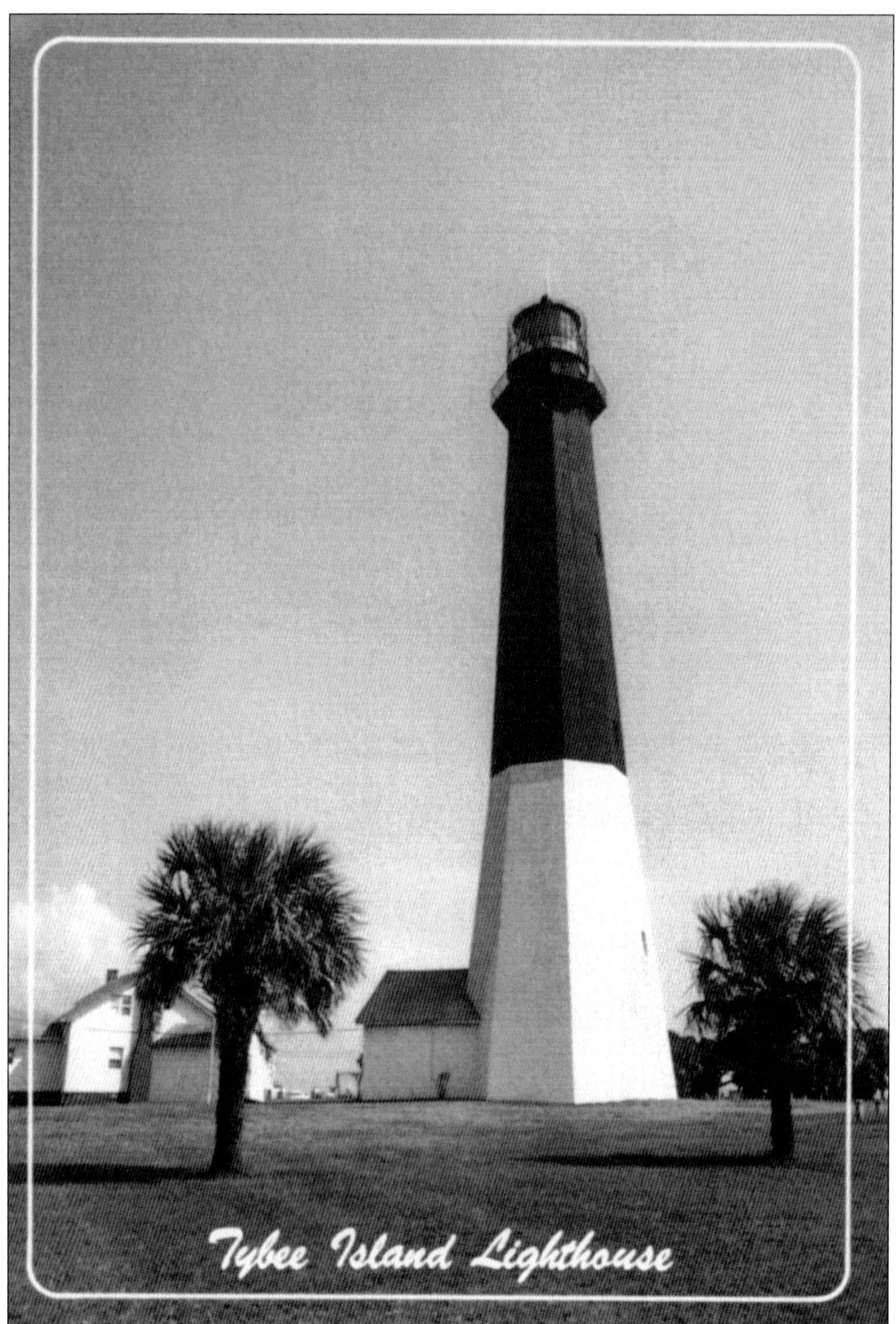

POSTCARD, 1970–1998. The Tybee Island Light had its sixth day mark between 1970 and 1998. No two lighthouses are the same. Each is built for its specific location to provide the best possible message about a particular geographic location. (Courtesy of Tybee Island Historical Society.)

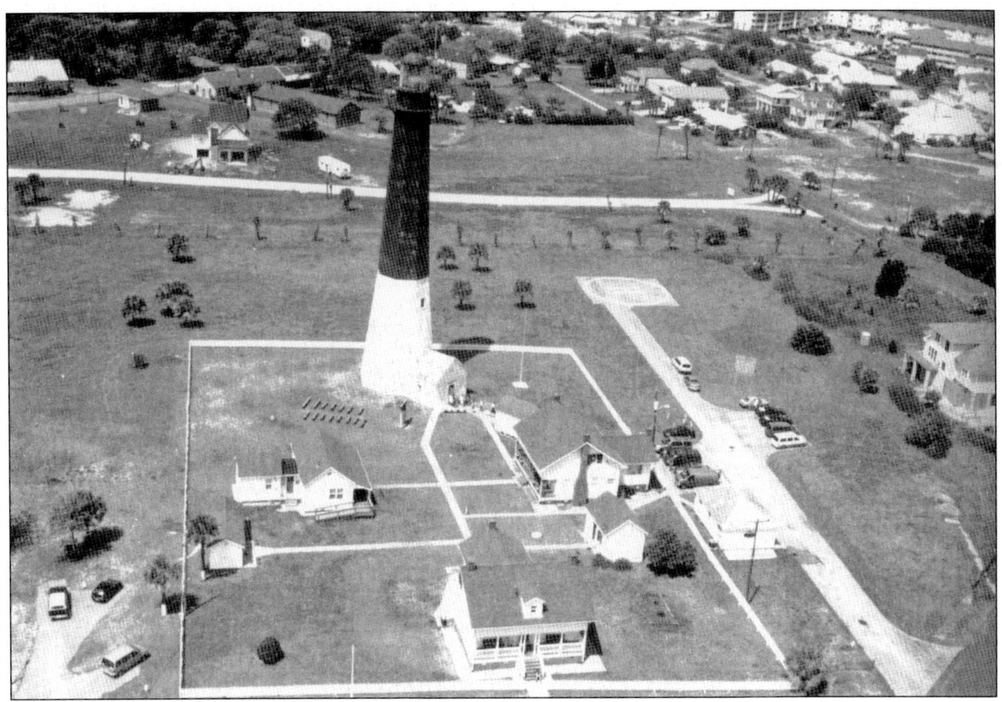

Aerial View, 1996. An aerial view of Tybee Island Light Station shows how complete the station is today. (Courtesy of Tybee Island Historical Society.)

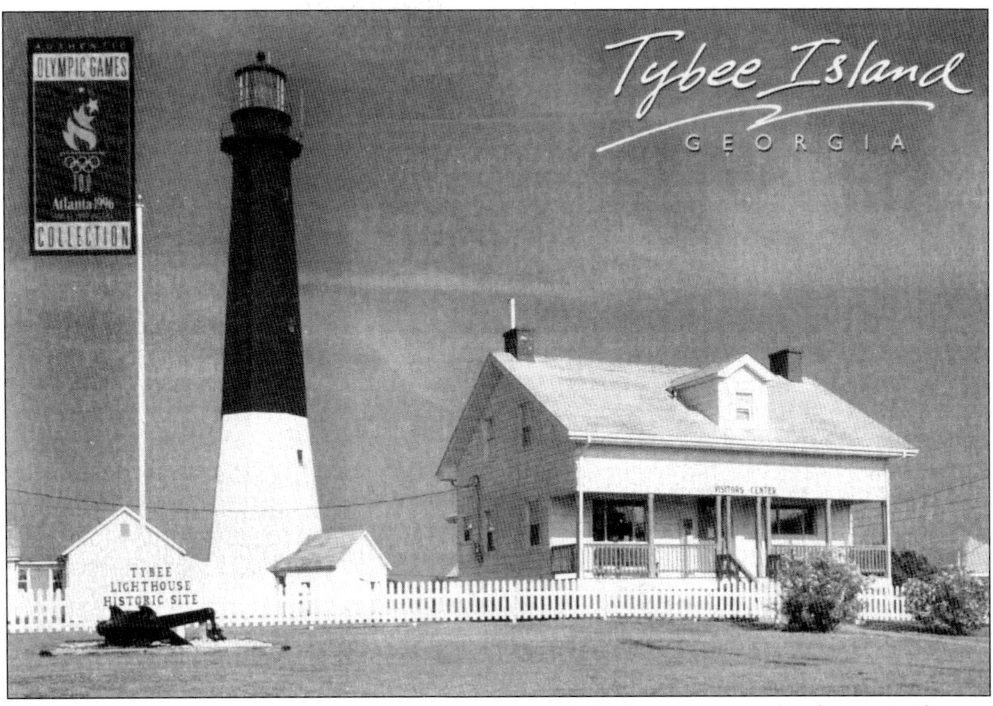

Postcard, 1996. Tybee Island was the site of the volleyball competition for the 1996 Olympic Games. (Courtesy of Tybee Island Historical Society.)

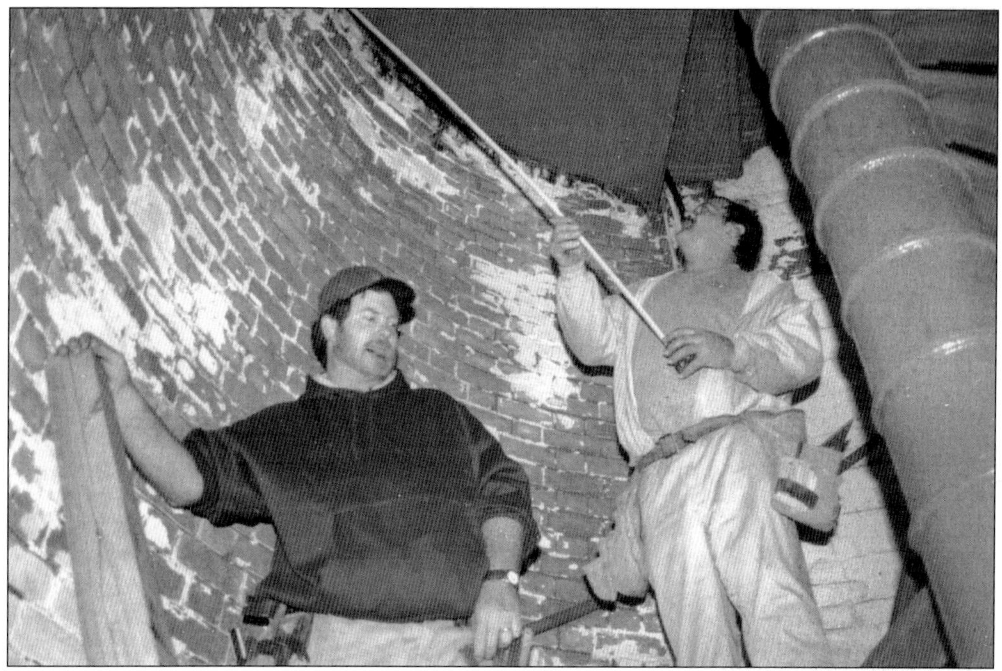

Lighthouse Preservation, 1996. This view shows the coating failure of the masonry walls within the lighthouse. (Courtesy of Tybee Island Historical Society.)

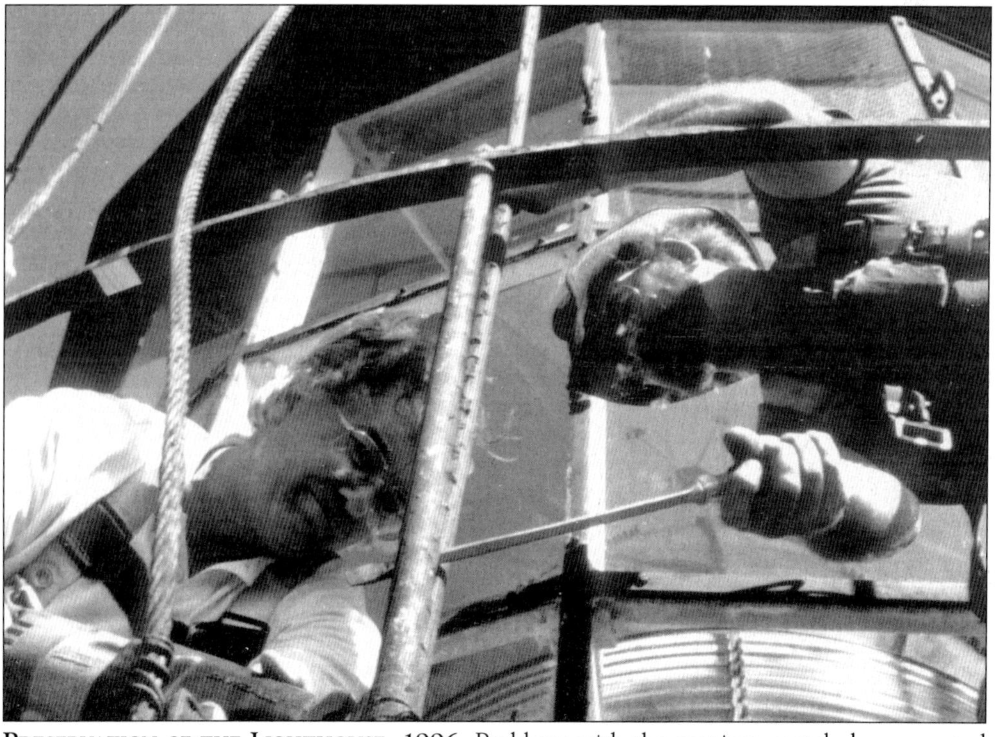

Preservation of the Lighthouse, 1996. Problems with the cast-iron metal also presented itself during the preservation process. During restoration, new protective coatings were applied over cleaned and repaired metal work. (Courtesy of Tybee Island Historical Society.)

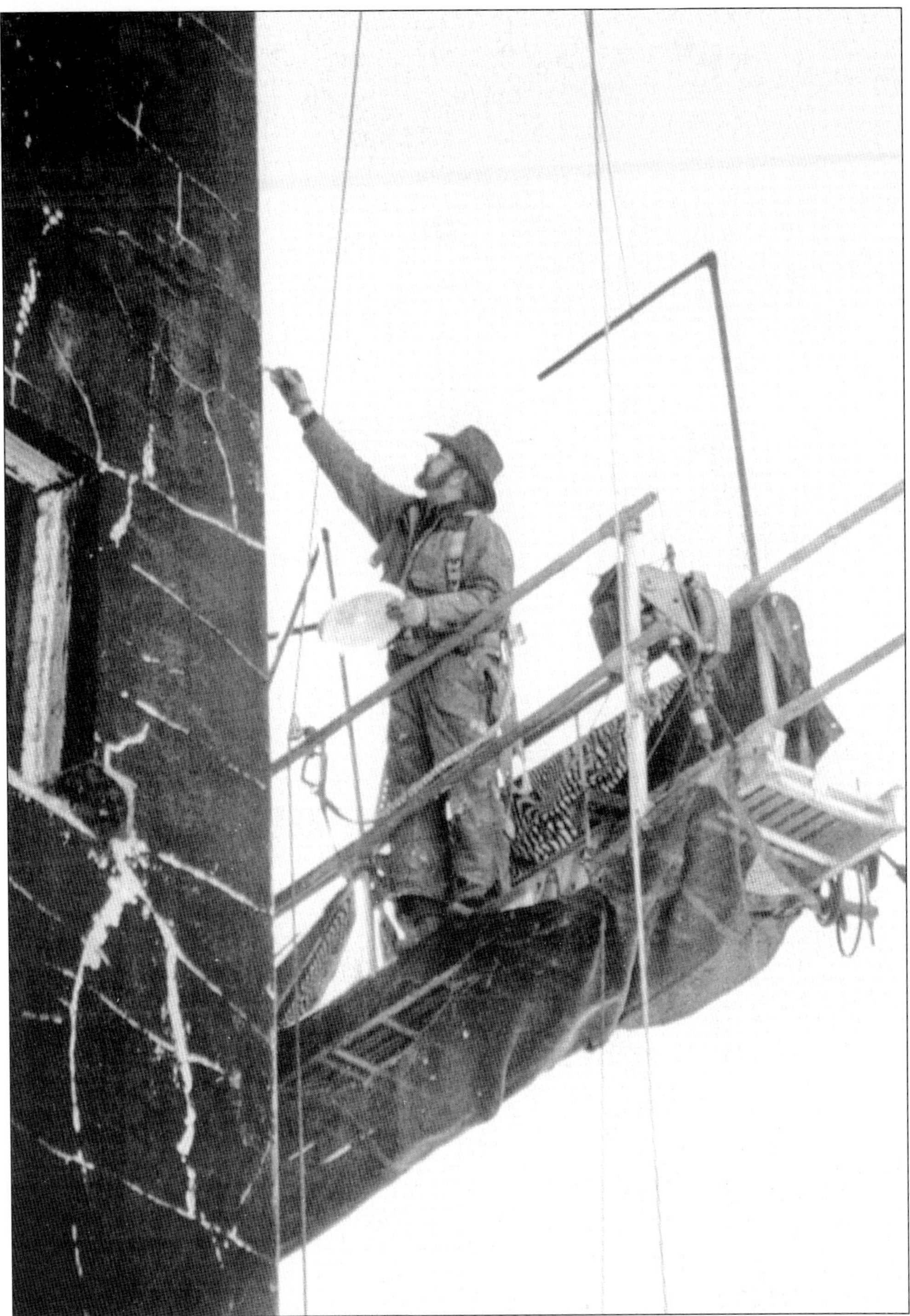

Lighthouse Restoration, 1996. Crews worked both inside and out to make sure that the lighthouse was returned to its original, pristine condition. Here years of decay are being stripped away. The end result returned the lighthouse to its former glory. (Courtesy of Tybee Island Historical Society.)

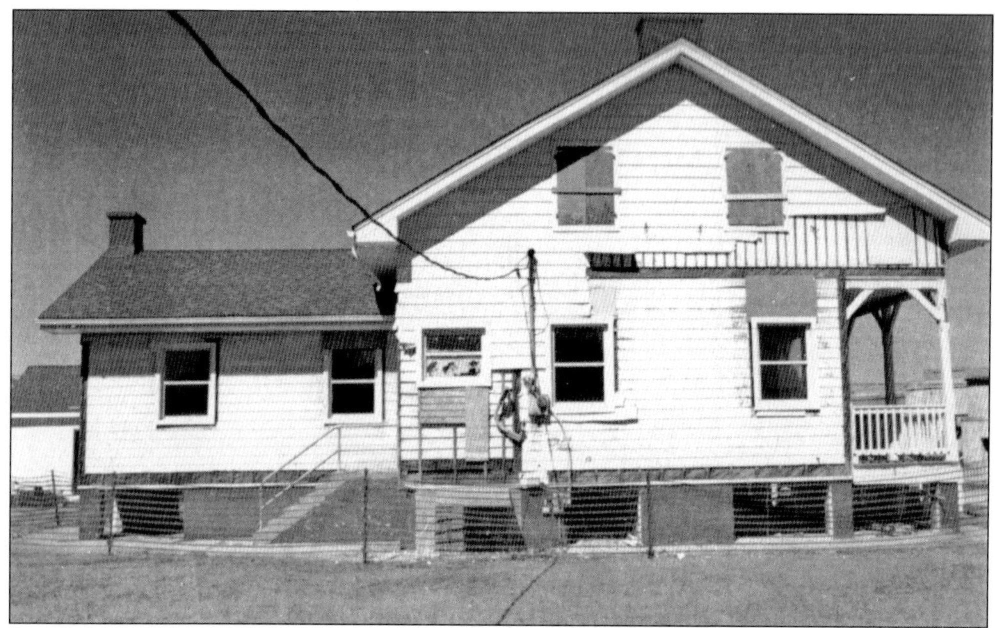

PRESERVATION OF THE HEAD KEEPER'S HOUSE, 2000–2001. The head keeper's dwelling, constructed in 1881, has been restored. The two-story wood-frame building served as the residence for the head keeper and his family from 1881 until 1947. One of the oldest buildings on Tybee Island, the home is a wonderful example of a bygone era. (Courtesy of Tybee Island Historical Society.)

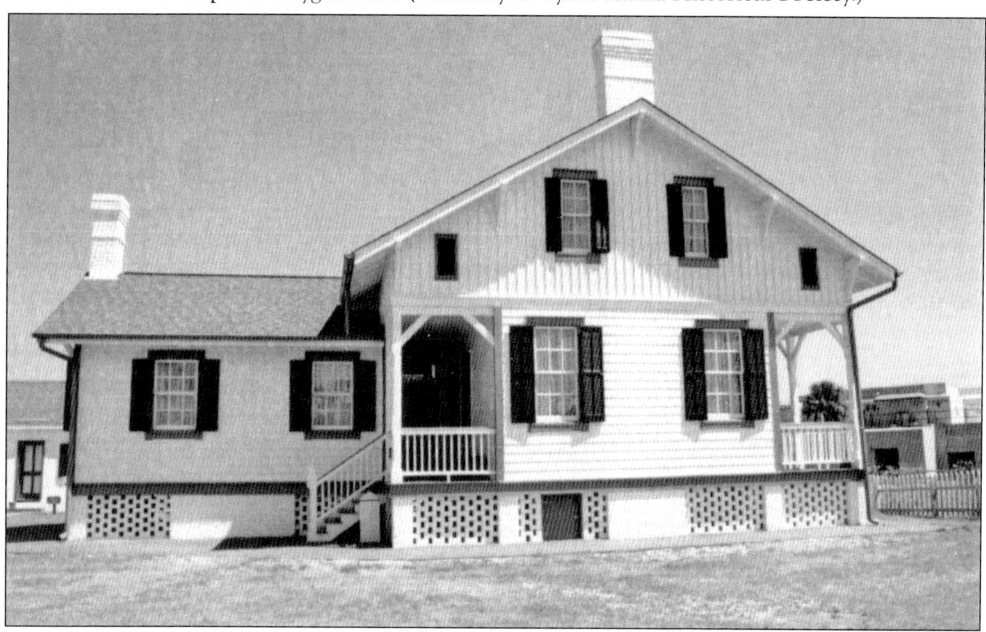

HEAD KEEPER'S HOUSE RESTORATION, 2000–2001. This image shows the completed restoration of the head keeper's house. Though modified over the decades, the house remains mostly intact, and an early investigation uncovered a large amount of historic wood fabric that was used in the restoration. The completed structure reflects the 1916–1939 character of the interior. The oldest building on Tybee Island, this structure is a shining example of a head light keeper's home. (Courtesy of Tybee Island Historical Society.)

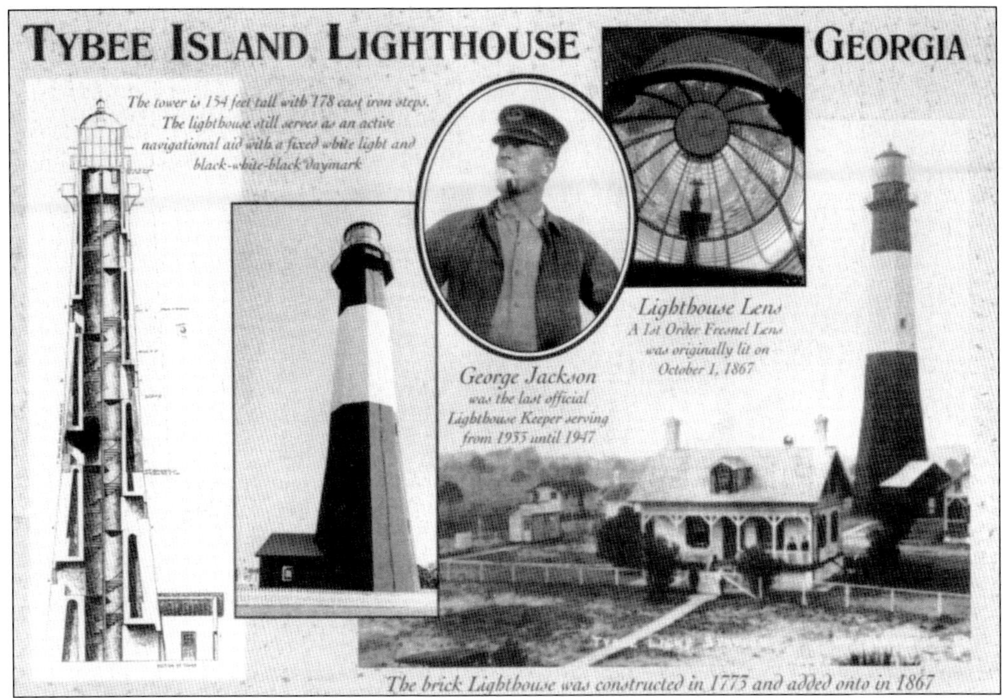

POSTCARD, 1999–PRESENT. This image shows the Tybee Island Lighthouse's seventh day mark. The Tybee Light Station is now a museum and is open to the public. The public can still climb the 178 steps to the top. (Courtesy of Tybee Island Historical Society.)

LIGHTHOUSE RELIGHTING CEREMONY, 1999. Today the Tybee Island Historical Society has full responsibility for the maintenance and restoration of the lighthouse site. The U.S. Coast Guard still maintains the light as a navigational aid. The lighthouse held a relighting ceremony in February 1999. (Courtesy of Tybee Island Historical Society.)

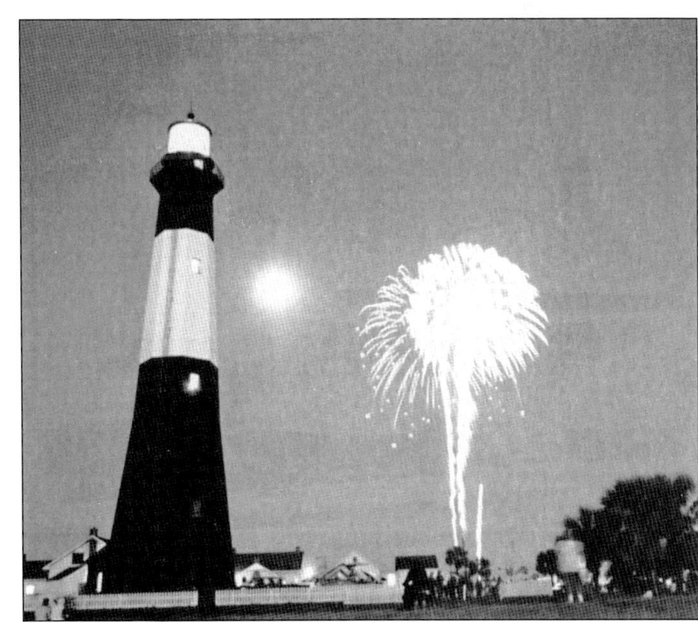

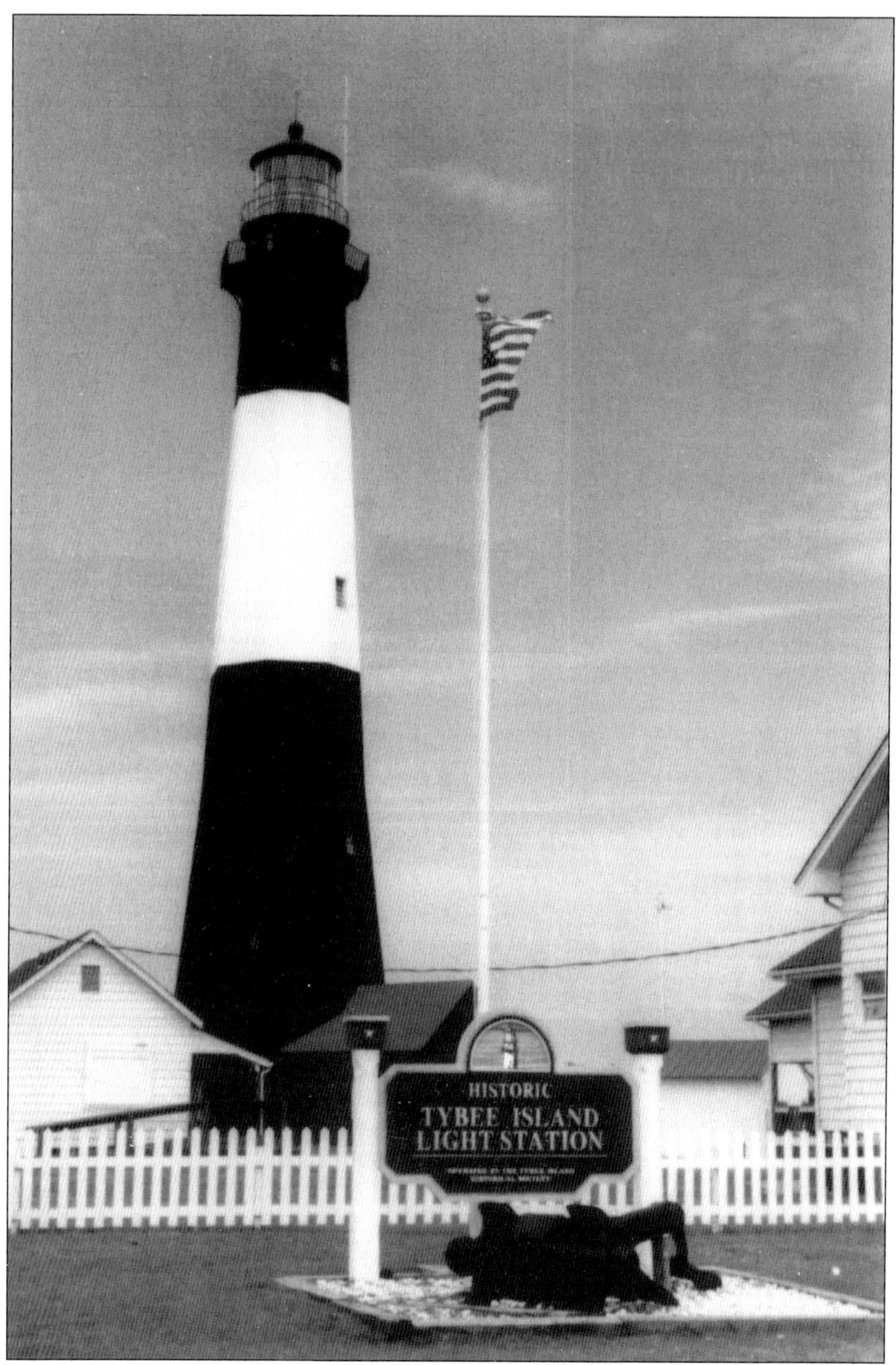

TYBEE LIGHTHOUSE TODAY. Under the staff's watchful eye, the Tybee Island Light Station stands today as an outstanding example of one of the most beautifully restored light stations in America. In addition, the lighthouse, the first keeper's house, and the second keeper's house (still under renovation) provide one of the most complete looks into the life of a light keeper. (Courtesy of Amelia Island Images.)

Two

SAPELO LIGHT

First built to guide ships through the estuaries of tidewater Georgia to the port of Darien, the Sapelo Lighthouse was built on 5 acres sold to the federal government by Thomas Spalding for $1. Because of its ideal position at the mouth of the Altamaha River, which flows to the coast from the interior, the port of Darien became an active shipping town between 1820 and 1915 for exporting timber, cotton, and rice.

The lighthouse operated, more or less, from 1820 to 1933. Built by Winslow Lewis of Boston, the 65-foot tower was topped by a 15-foot iron lantern. In 1854, a fourth-order Fresnel lens was installed, but during the Civil War, the retreating Confederate troops removed the lens and destroyed the reflector system, leaving the tower intact. Following the war, the tower was repaired and reactivated, and by 1877, a 25-foot cast-iron range beacon was constructed.

By 1905, because of the erosion of land around the lighthouse and the 1898 hurricane, the structure was declared unsafe. A new, 100-foot, steel pyramid lighthouse was built a few hundred feet north of the brick tower.

Over the years, the Darien port was being used less and less. Finally, in 1933, the skeletal tower was dismantled and shipped to Fox Island on Lake Michigan, where it remains standing today.

For 65 years, the old tower stood as a silent testament to history; however, this is a story of its rebirth. In 1994, the Georgia Department of Natural Resources began the long process of restoration. Once in ruins, the 1820 tower now features its distinctive red-and-white stripes marking the entrance once again to the port of Darien.

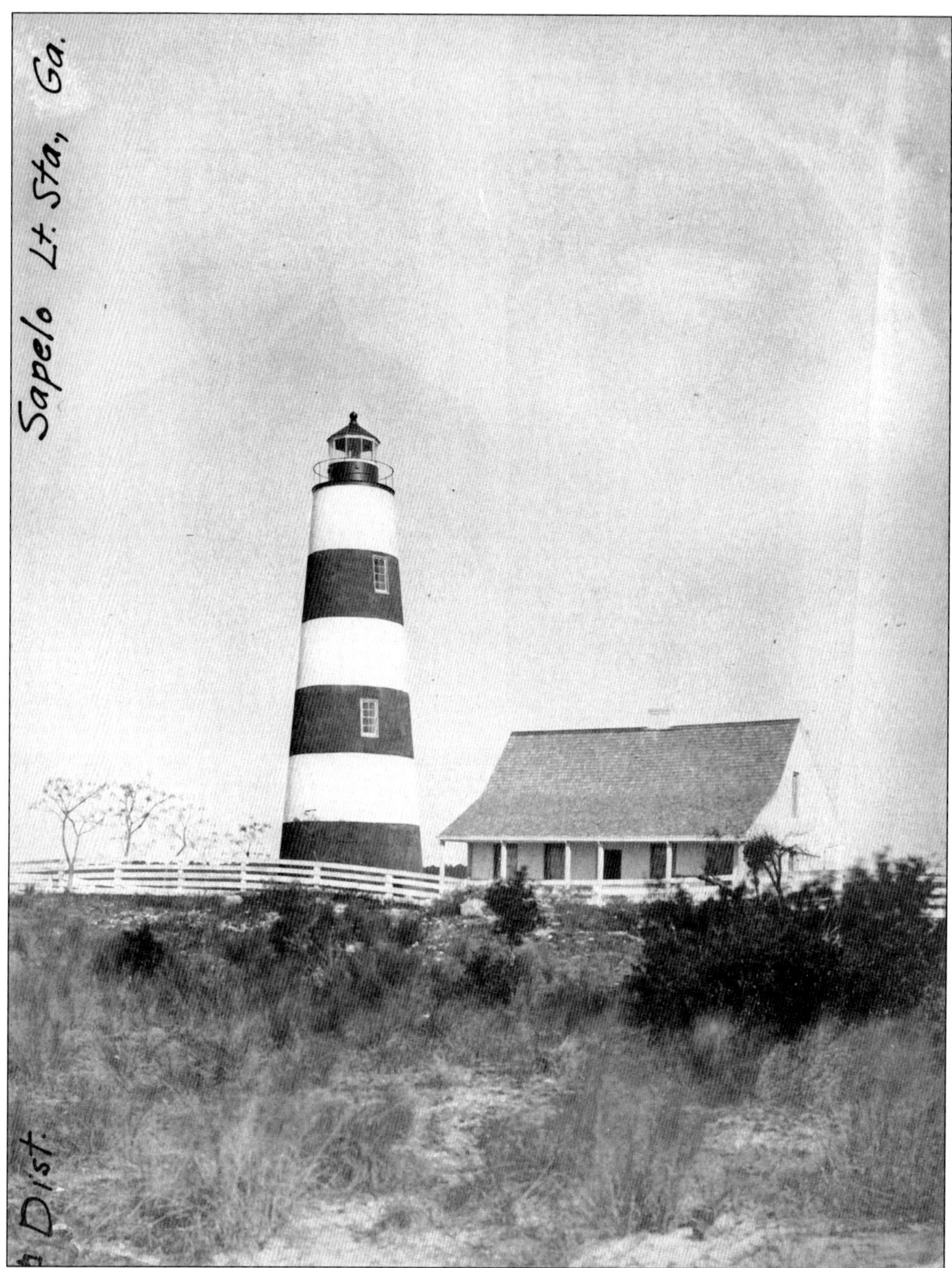

SAPELO LIGHT AND KEEPER'S HOUSE, C. 1915. Winslow Lewis of Boston received a contract to build an 80-foot lighthouse and keeper's quarters on Sapelo Island in 1820. A 65-foot circular brick tower topped with a 15-foot iron lantern room was built. (Courtesy of National Archives.)

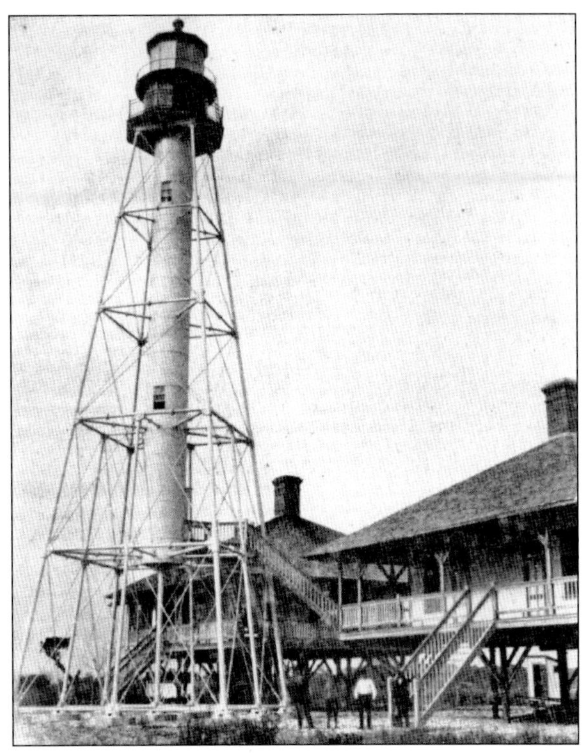

Replacement, 1913. During a hurricane in 1898, water covered the lower 18 feet of the lighthouse tower resulting in serious damage to the foundation. Failed attempts were made to stabilize the tower's foundation. A steel tower was placed just north of the original tower in 1905. Note the keeper and assistant keeper's houses. (Courtesy of National Archives.)

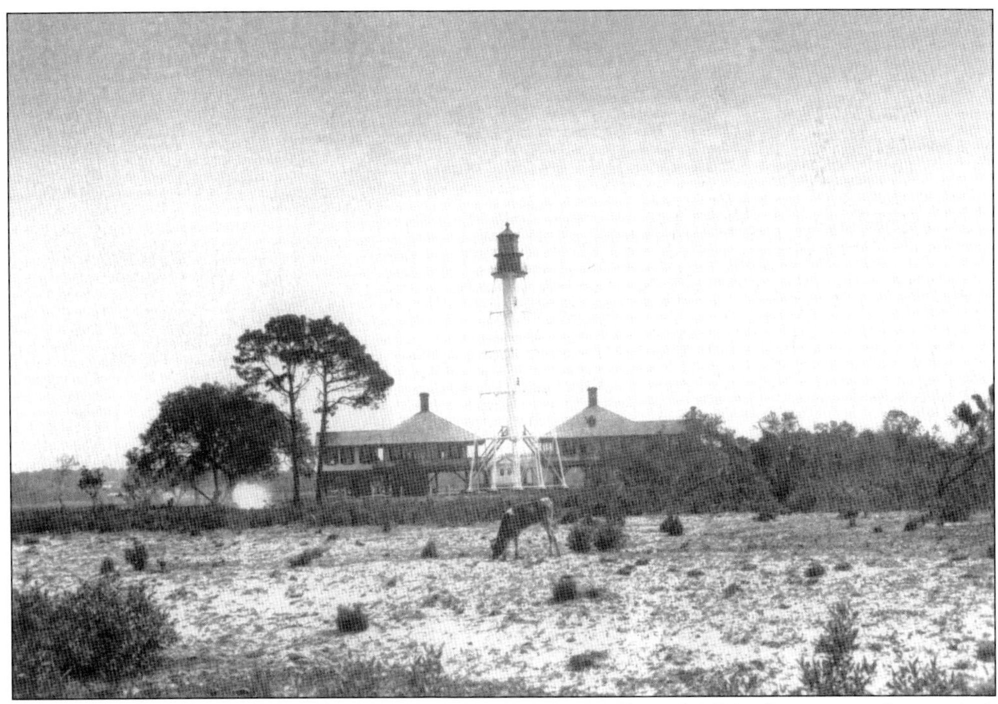

Steel Tower, 1913. The replacement steel tower operated until 1933 when it was dismantled. It was then shipped to Michigan, where is stands today. (Courtesy of National Archives.)

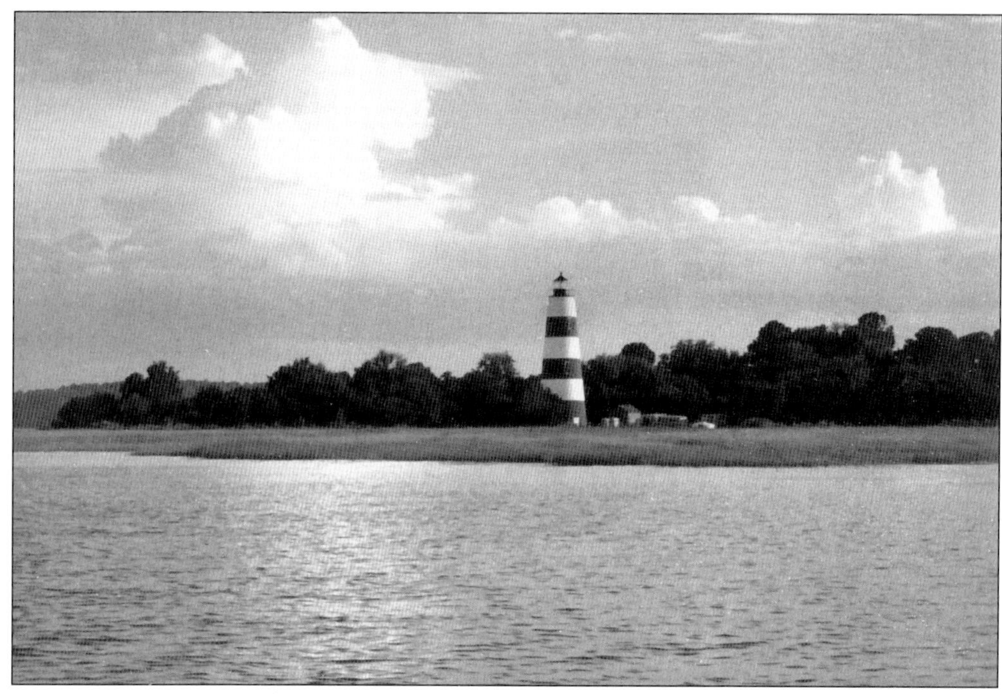

Doboy Sound. Approaching Sapelo Island across Doboy Sound, the Sapelo Light serves as a monument to the former glory days of waterborne commerce in the region. (Courtesy of Georgia Department of Natural Resources.)

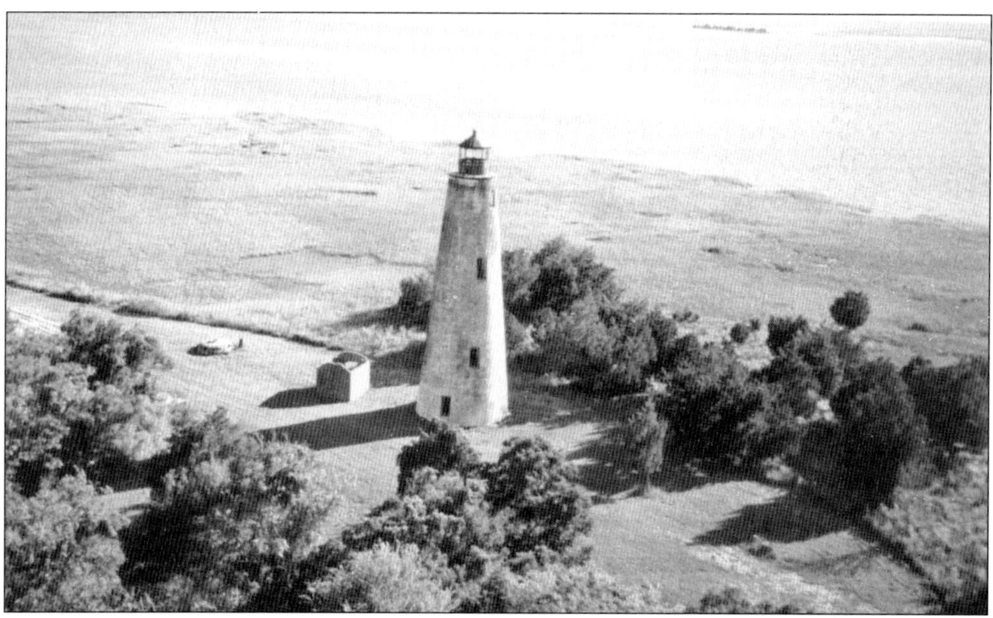

Sapelo Island. Surrounded by 16,000 acres of pristine marsh, Sapelo Island has a quiet solitude and is one of Georgia's barrier islands. (Courtesy of Georgia Department of Natural Resources.)

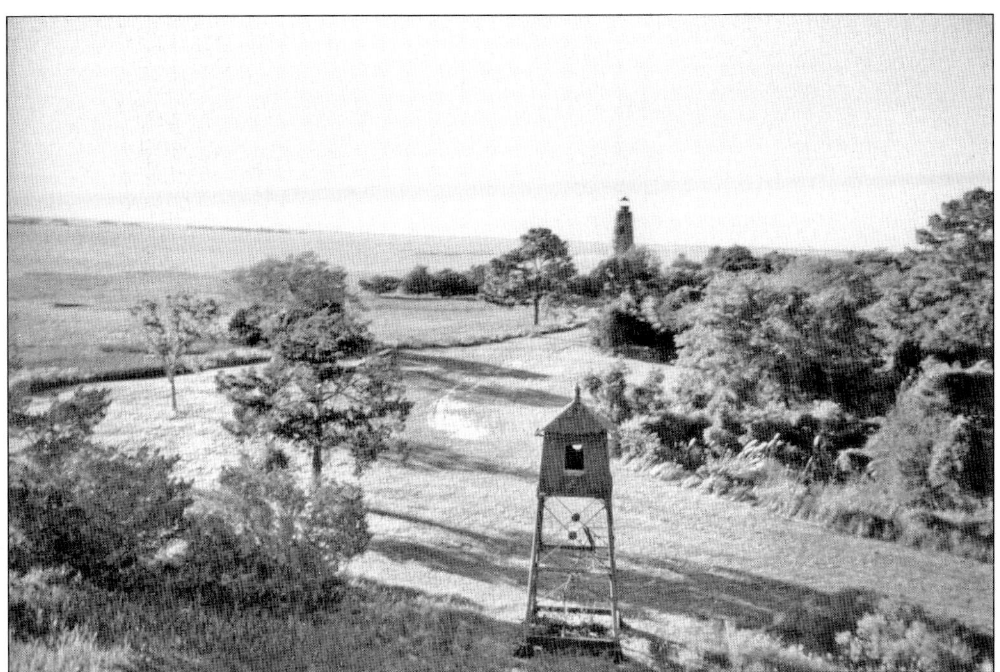

SAPELO LIGHT AND RANGE LIGHT, C. 1970. Today most of Sapelo Island is owned by the state of Georgia. (Courtesy of Georgia Department of Natural Resources.)

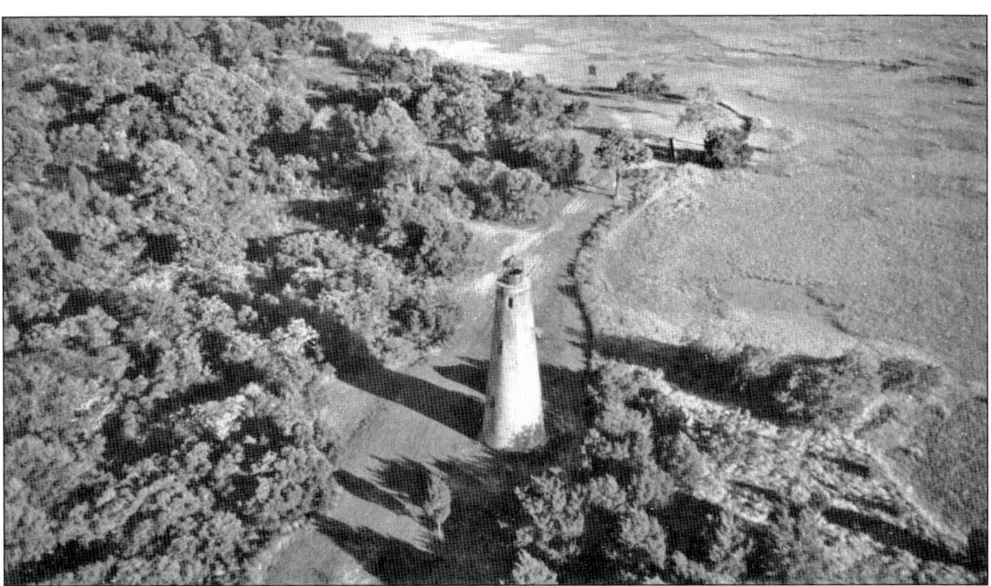

SAPELO LIGHT. For 65 years, the Sapelo Light remained dark and in need of repair. (Courtesy of Georgia Department of Natural Resources.)

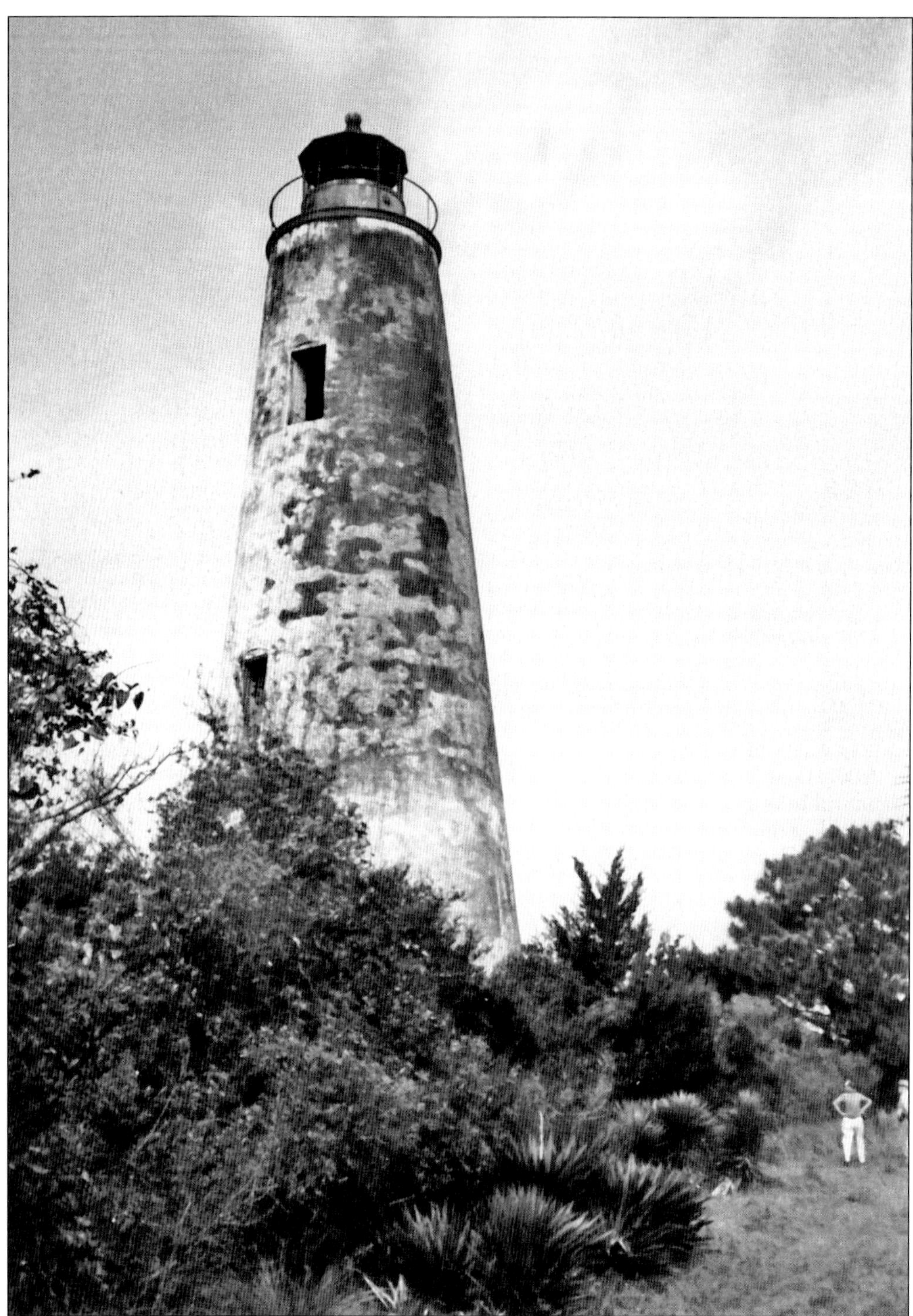

SAPELO LIGHT DAMAGED. During the Civil War, retreating Confederate troops removed the Fresnel lens and destroyed the reflector system. In 1868, the tower was repaired and reactivated, and the tower was painted with wide, alternating red-and-white horizontal bands. (Courtesy of Amelia Island Images.)

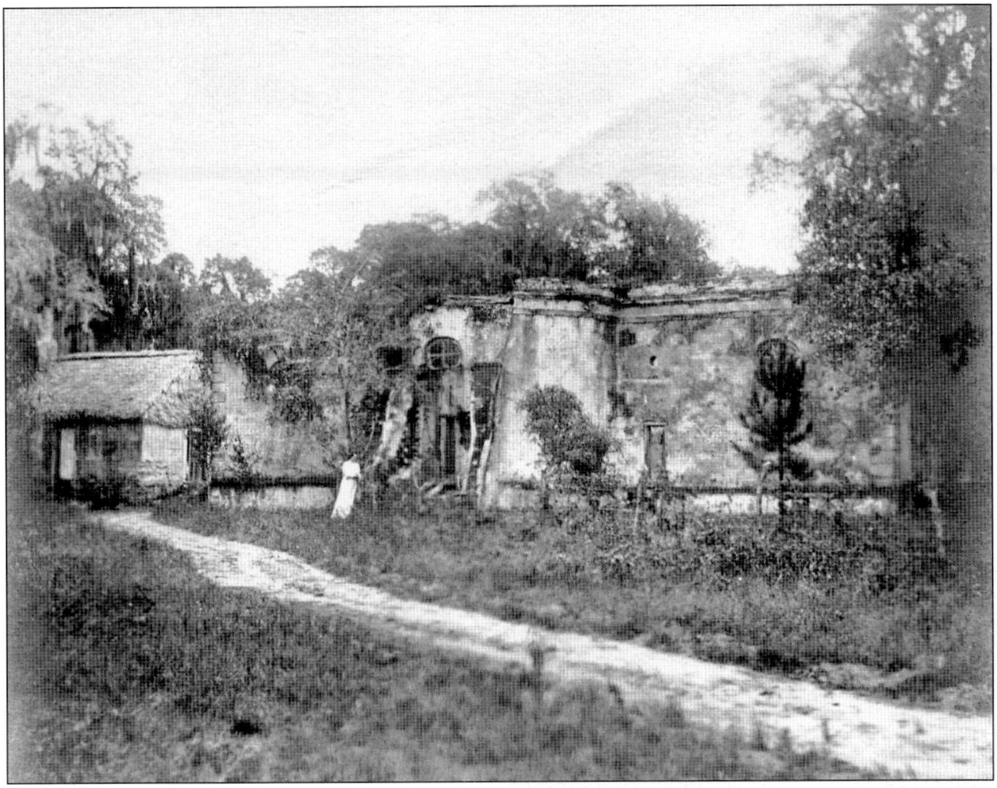

Ruins of the Spalding Plantation, c. 1900. About one percent of Sapelo Island still belongs to the residents of Hog Hammock, a small community on the south end. (Courtesy of Coastal Georgia Historical Society.)

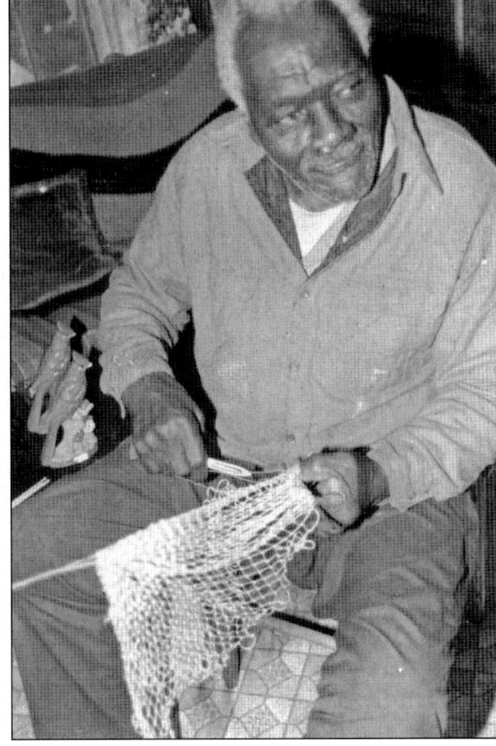

Man Working on Fish Net, 1995. Descendants of slaves who worked the island's plantations 200 years ago still live on Sapelo today. Here a fish casting net is being handcrafted. (Courtesy of Coastal Georgia Historical Society.)

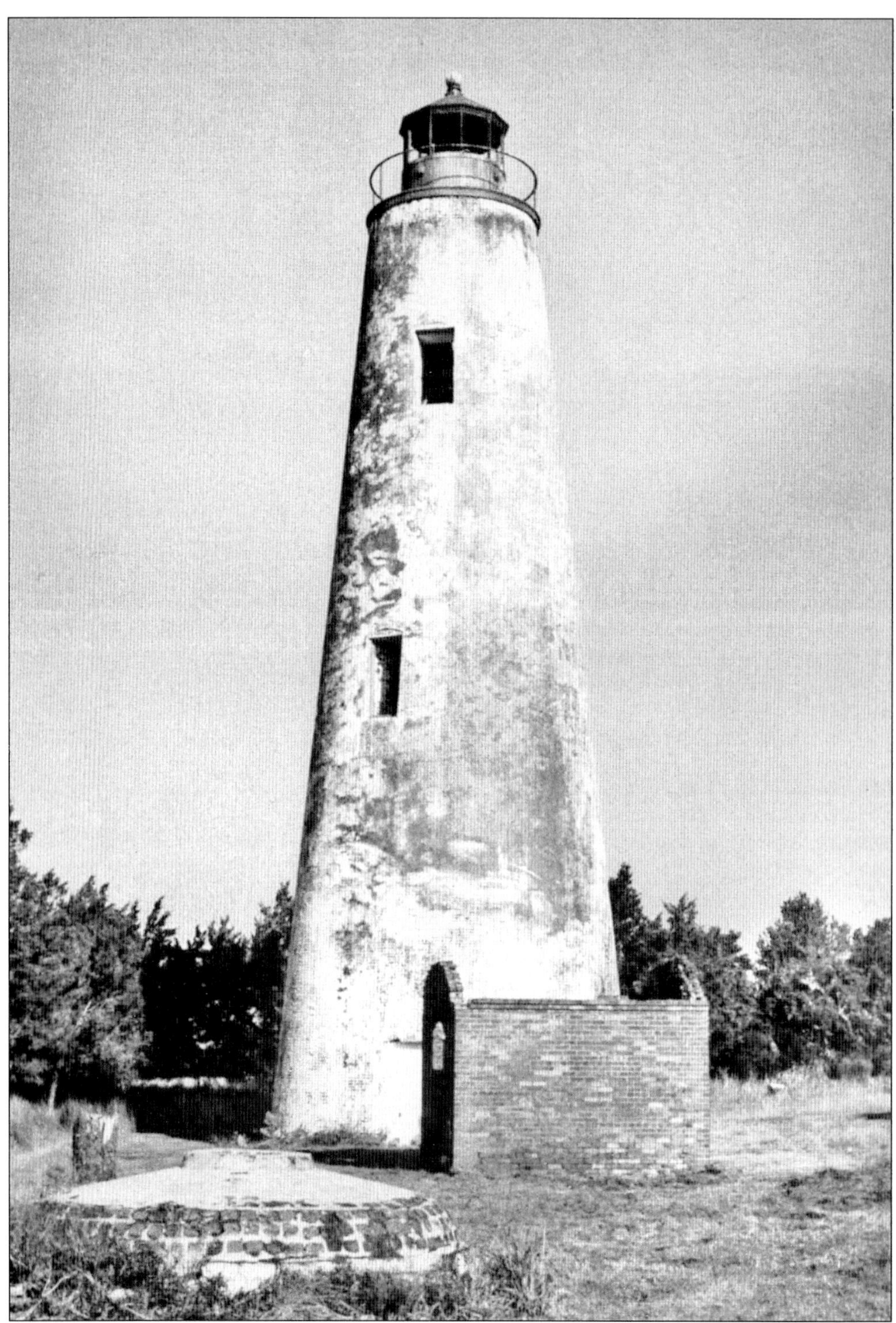

SAPELO LIGHT AND OIL HOUSE. In 1994, the Georgia Department of Natural Resources (DNR) submitted a grant, which was subsequently awarded, and work began to transform the derelict light to its original proud state. (Courtesy of Georgia Department of Natural Resources.)

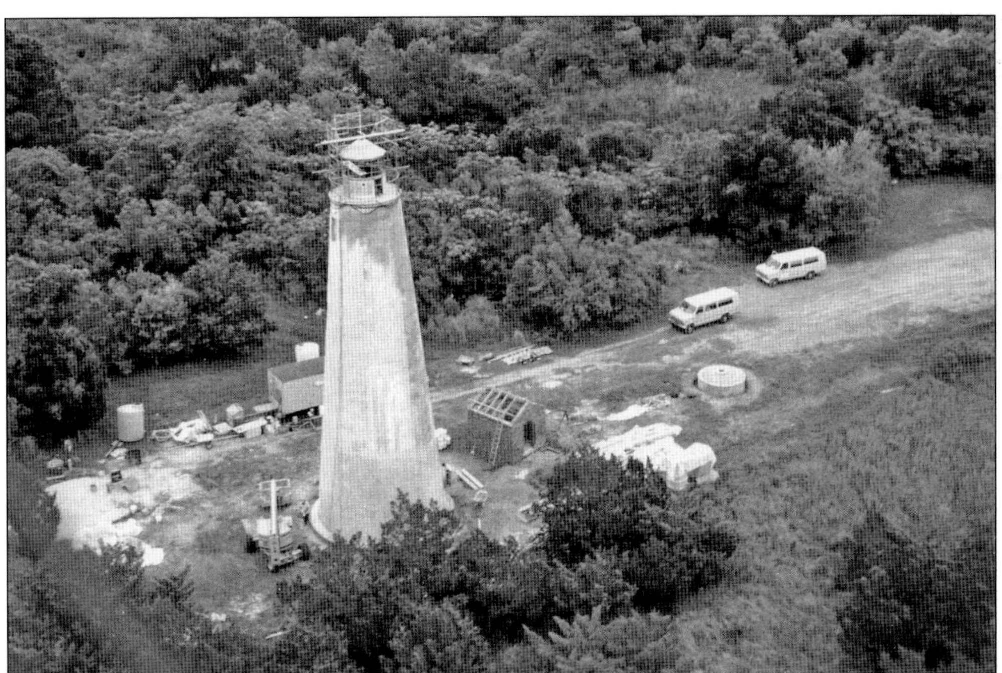

WORK BEGINS, 1995. Before construction could begin, a substantial amount of research needed to be completed. An archeological investigation was conducted to verify the lighthouse foundation. (Courtesy of Georgia Department of Natural Resources.)

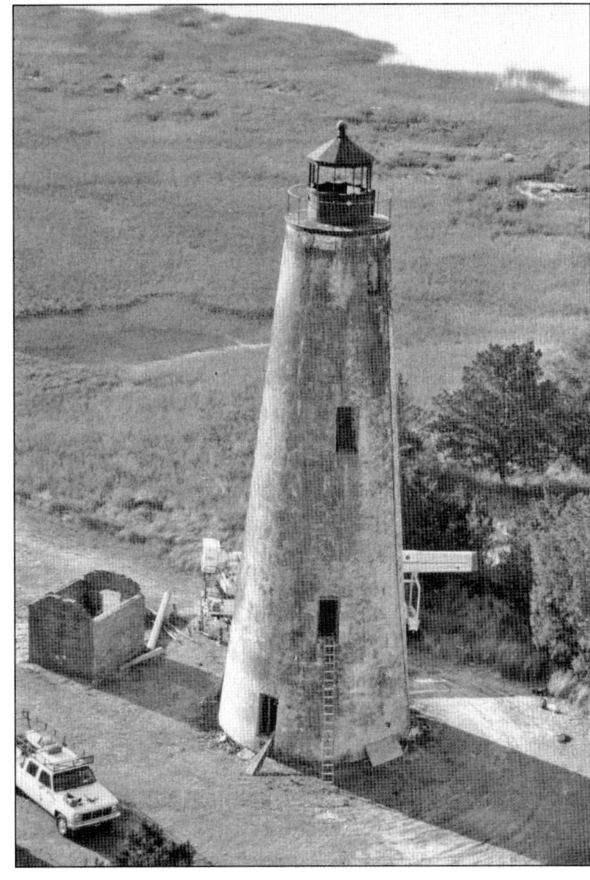

AERIAL VIEW, 1995–1997. Since the staircase was in such bad repair, a Georgia DNR helicopter was used to conduct an aerial inspection of the lighthouse remains. (Courtesy of Georgia Department of Natural Resources.)

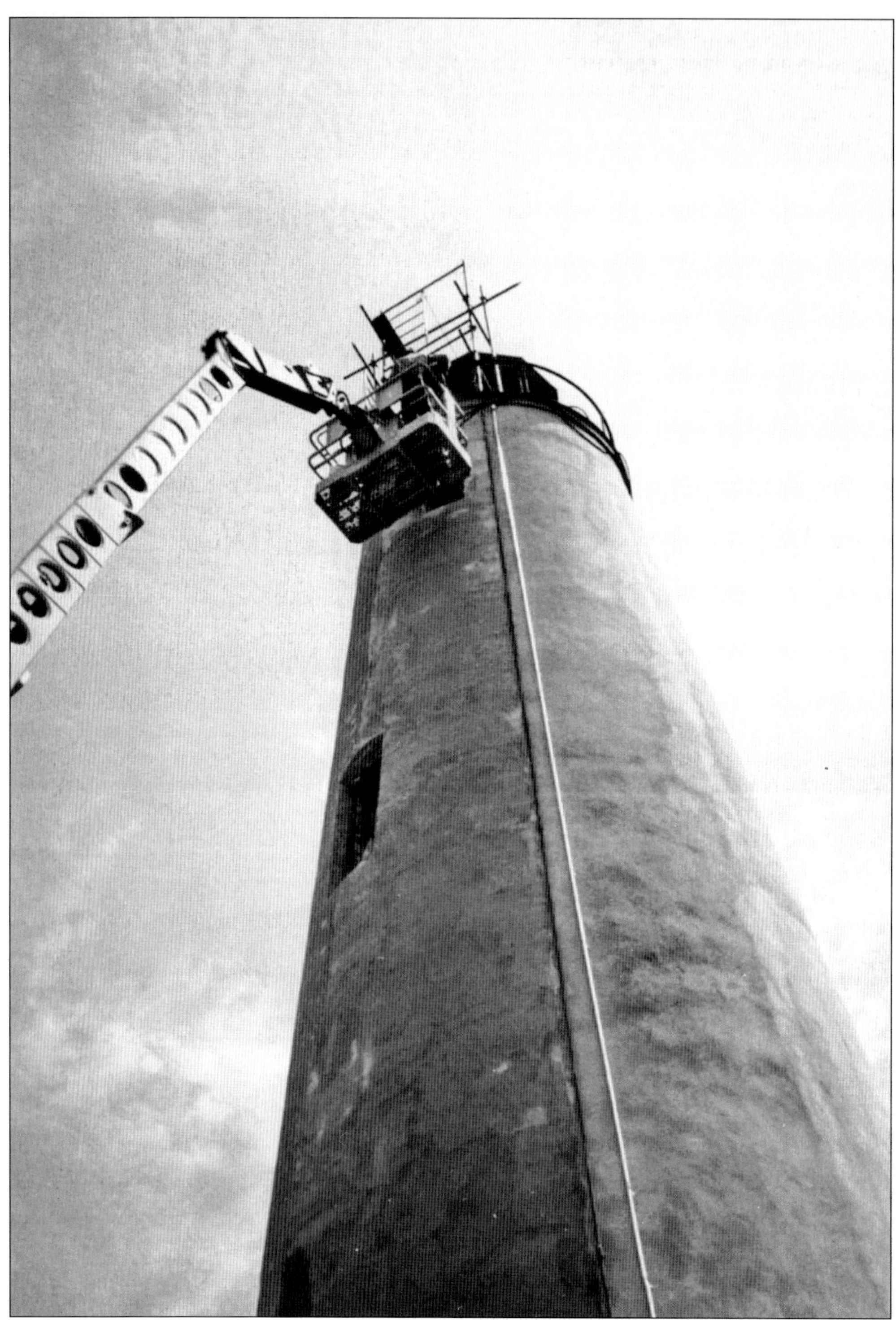

Reaching the Top, 1995–1998. Once it was determined that the top was structurally sound, the Georgia Power Company provided a bucket truck to access the peak of the light. (Courtesy of Georgia Department of Natural Resources.)

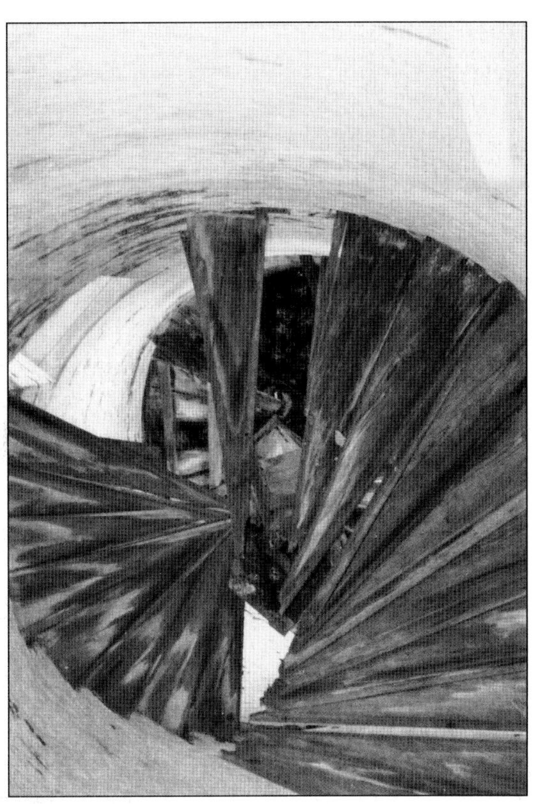

STAIRCASE. Before the restoration process began, no one had accessed the top of the Sapelo Light in more than 20 years. (Courtesy of Georgia Department of Natural Resources.)

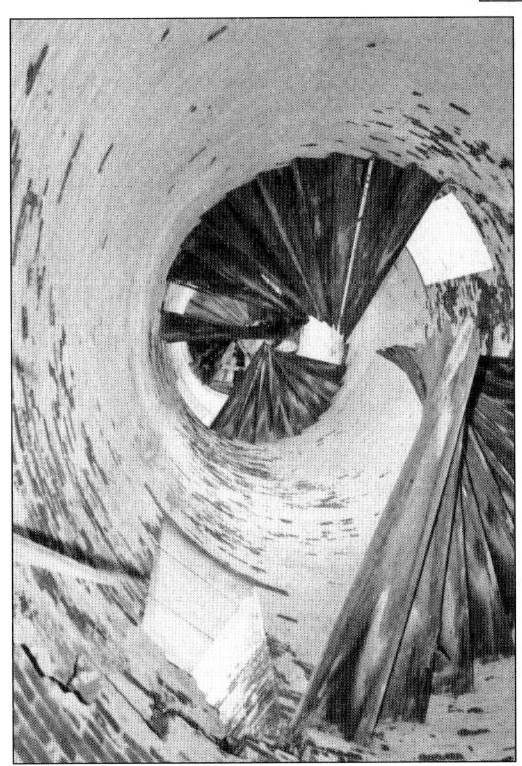

INSIDE THE LIGHTHOUSE, C. 1995. The dilapidated staircase was removed by a DNR Search and Rescue Repel Team. (Courtesy of Georgia Department of Natural Resources.)

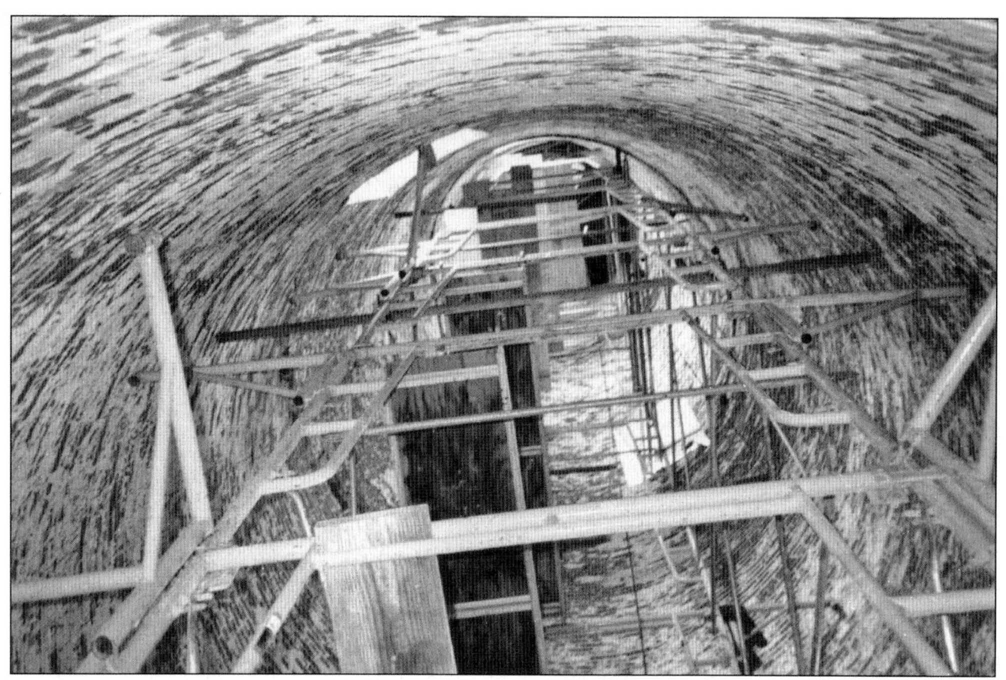

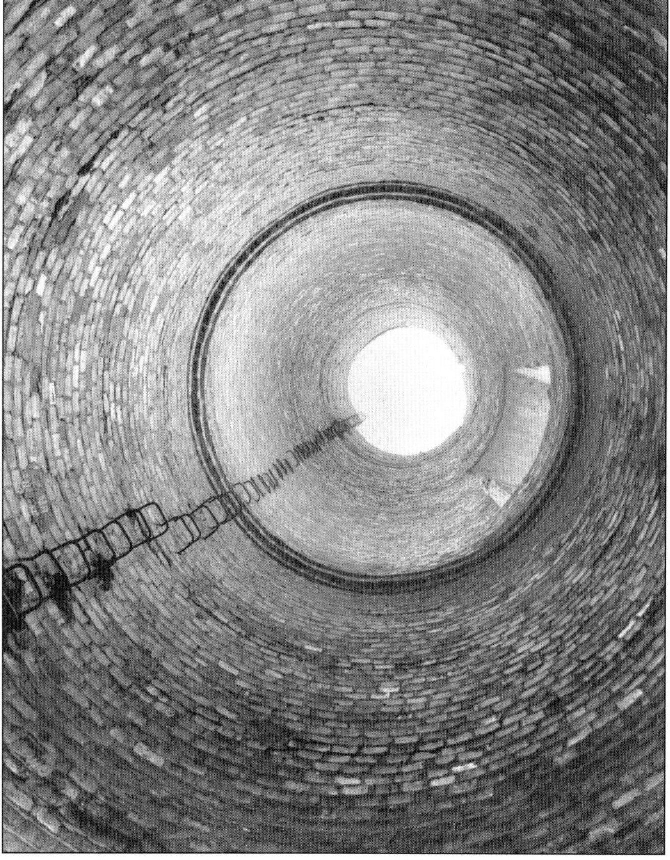

Scaffolding, 1995–1997. After the old staircase was removed, then a restoration architect took detailed measurements of the entire structure. (Courtesy of Georgia Department of Natural Resources.)

Looking Up, 1995–1997. Once measurements were taken, detailed construction plans for the restoration of the lighthouse were developed. (Courtesy of Coastal Georgia Historical Society.)

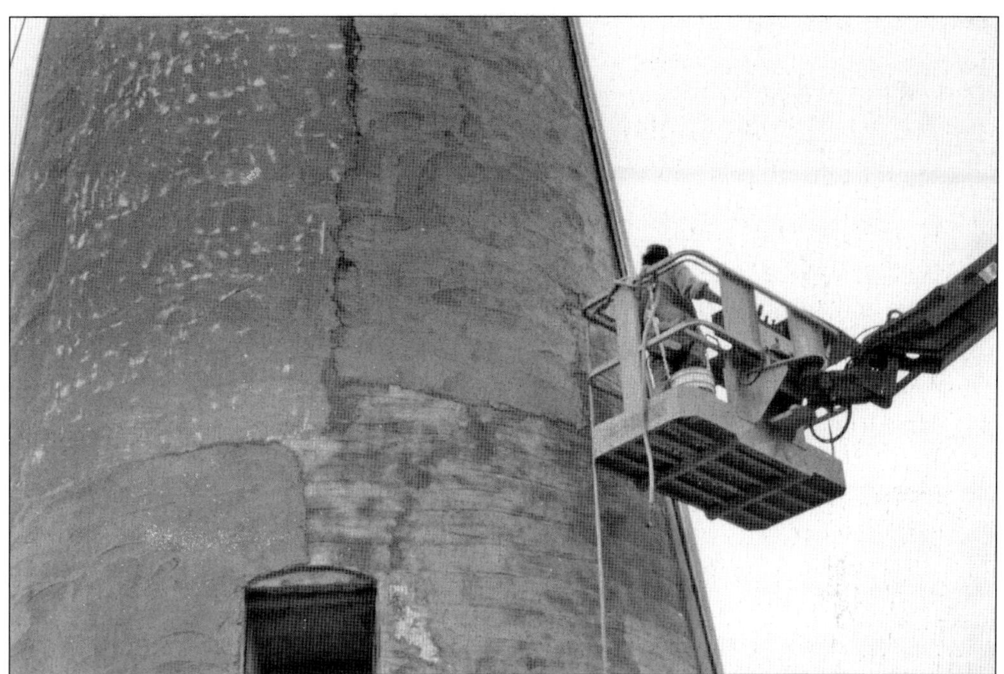

Measurements. Every inch of the original building was analyzed. (Courtesy of Georgia Department of Natural Resources.)

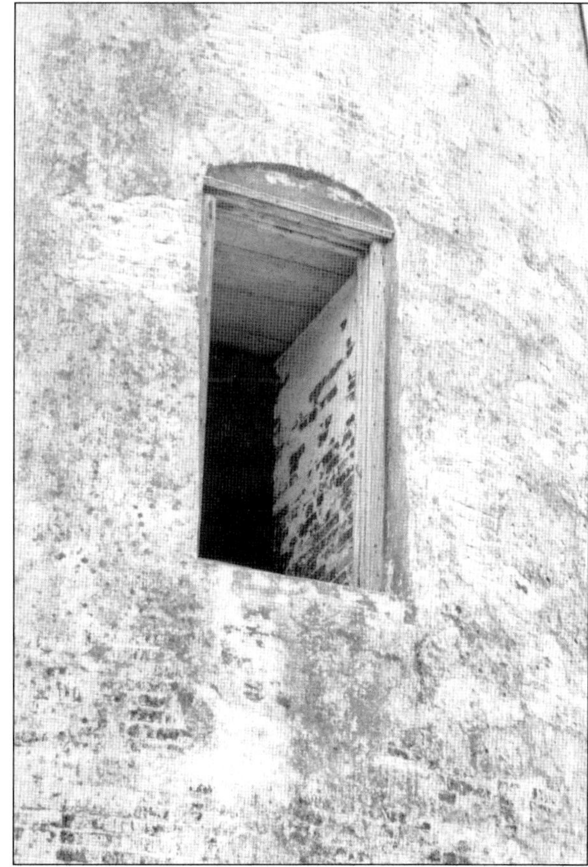

Windows, 1995–1997. The restoration project included repairing the stucco on the exterior and replacing the doors and windows. (Courtesy of Georgia Department of Natural Resources.)

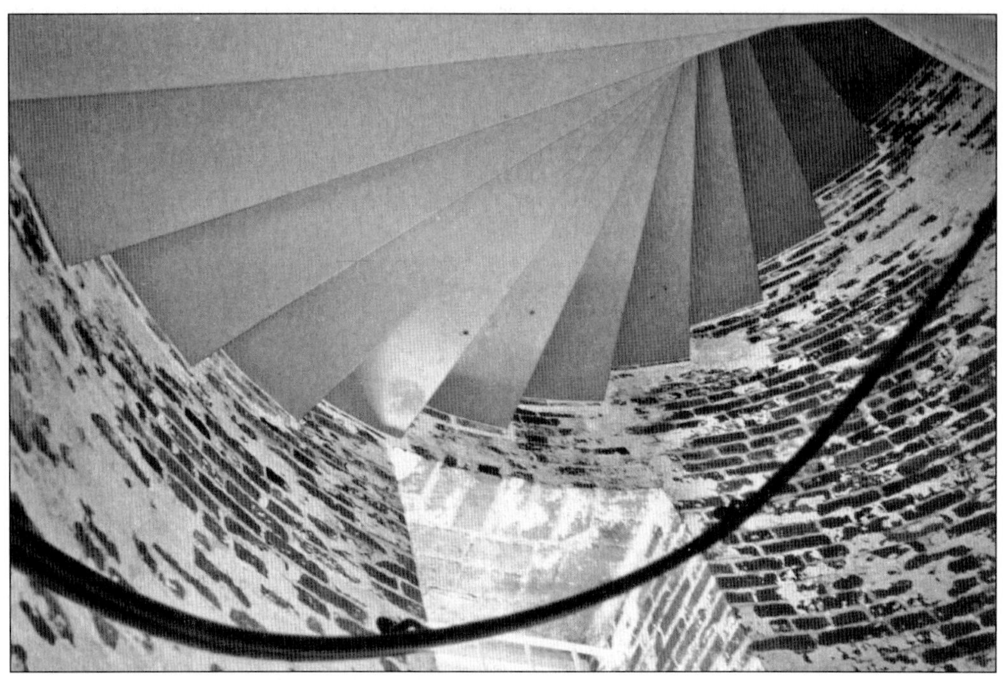

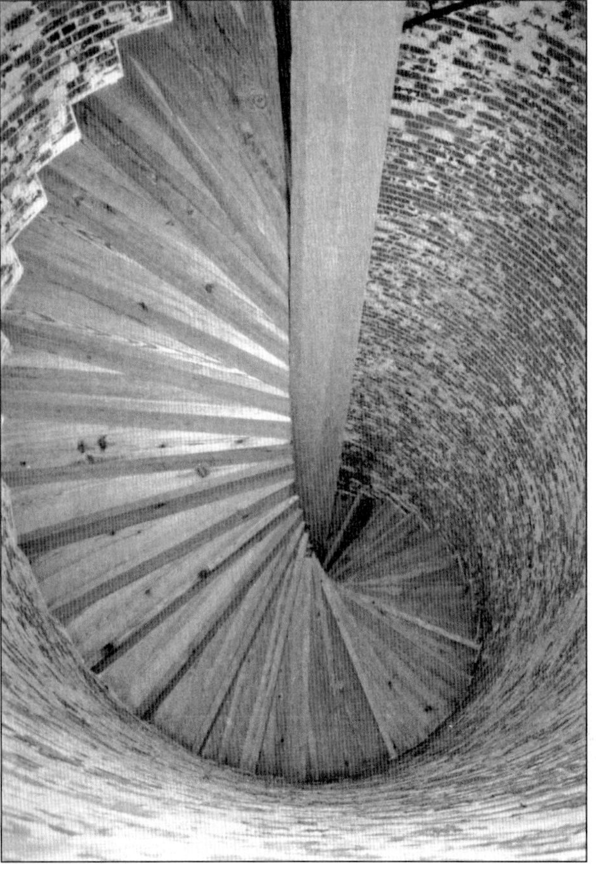

STAIRCASE, 1996–1997. During the restoration, the interior wooden spiral staircase was reconstructed. (Courtesy of Georgia Department of Natural Resources.)

STAIRCASE RESTORED, 1996–1997. The original staircase was believed to have been made of cypress; however, the new stairs are constructed of pine. There are 80 steps to the top. (Courtesy of Georgia Department of Natural Resources.)

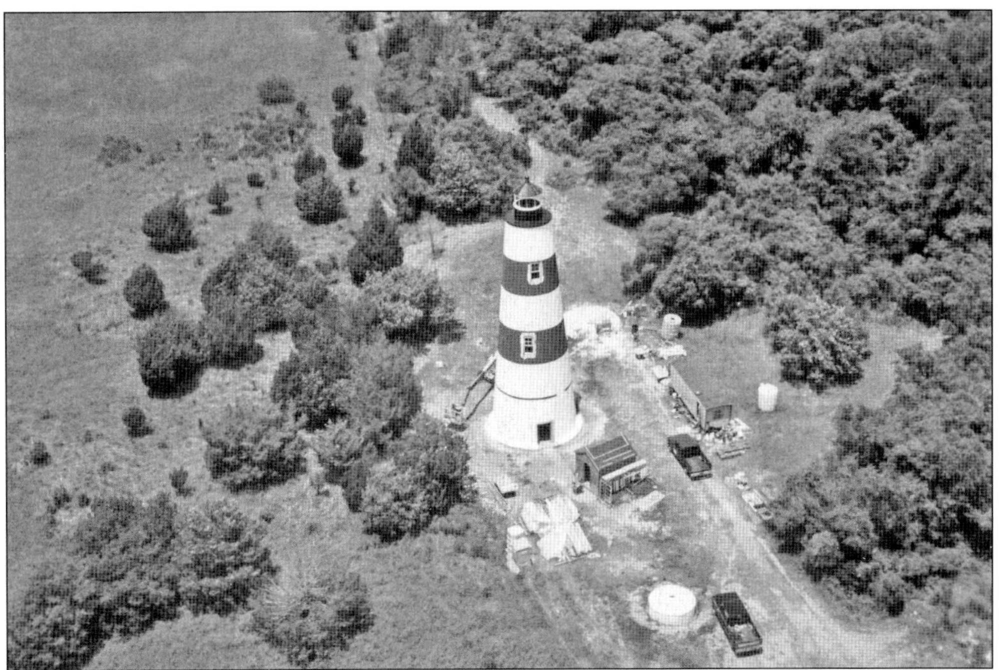

REPAINTING THE LIGHT, 1997–1998. The project called for the lighthouse to be repaired to its original 1890 glory. This included painting the lighthouse with its red-and-white day mark. (Courtesy of Georgia Department of Natural Resources.)

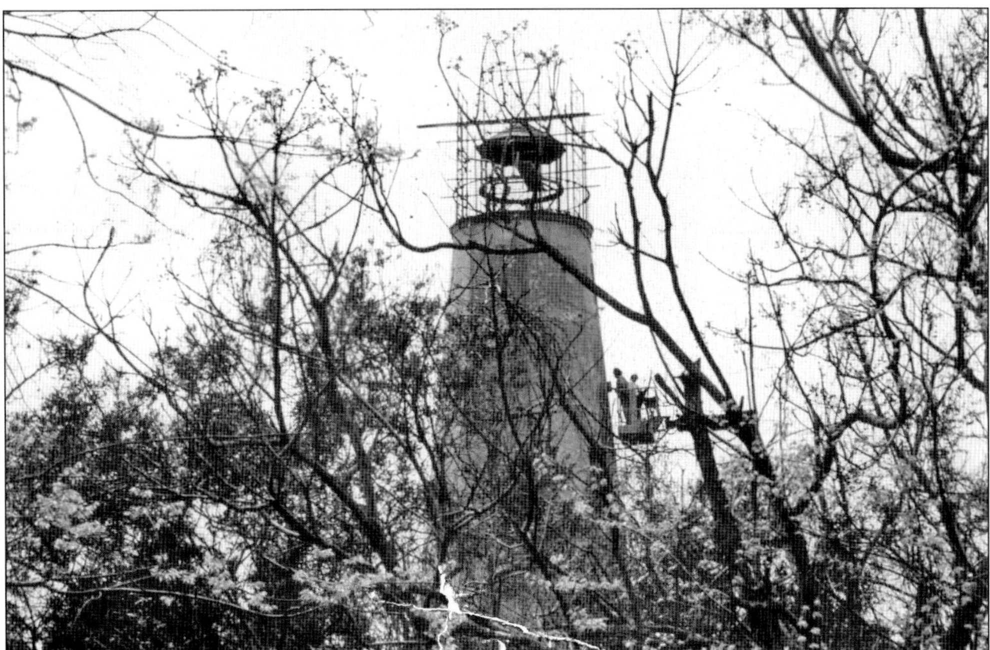

TOP OF THE LIGHT, 1995–1997. The preservation team also secured the top of the structure and readied it for repair. (Courtesy of Georgia Department of Natural Resources.)

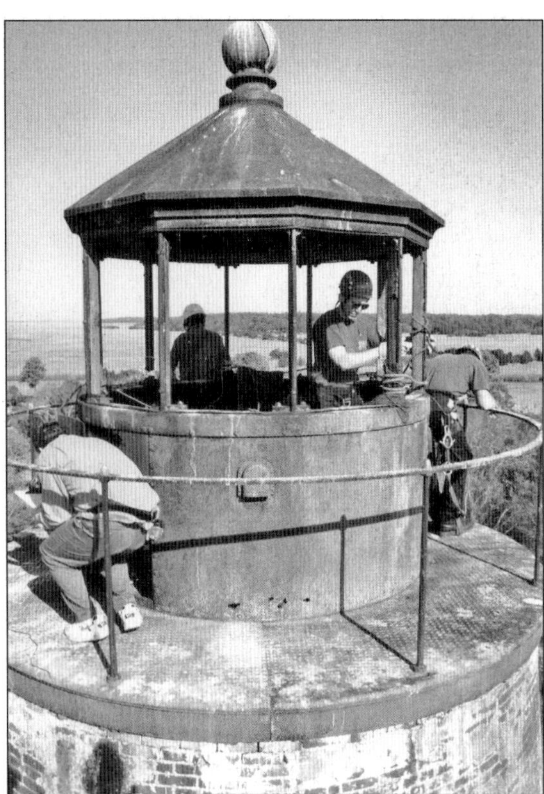

WORKING AT THE TOP, 1997–1998. The metal at the top of the lighthouse was repaired, and new glass was installed in the lantern room. (Courtesy of Georgia Department of Natural Resources.)

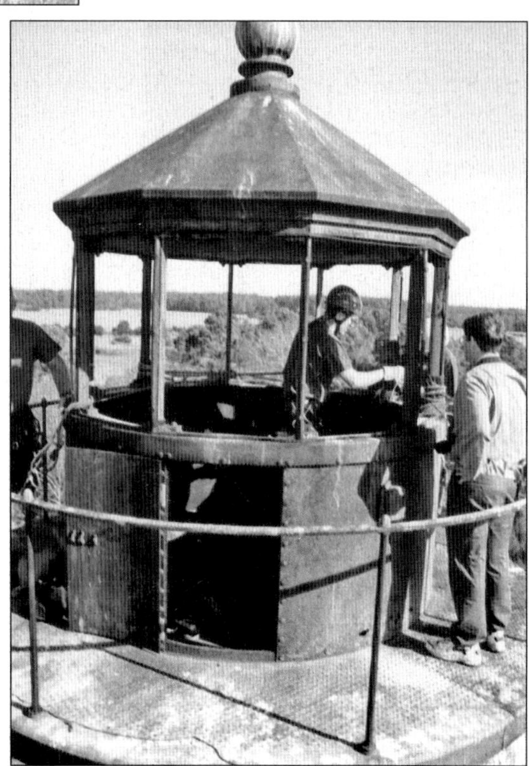

MODERN LIGHT, 1997–1998. A new modern light with the same 45-second flash as the original was also mounted. (Courtesy of Georgia Department of Natural Resources.)

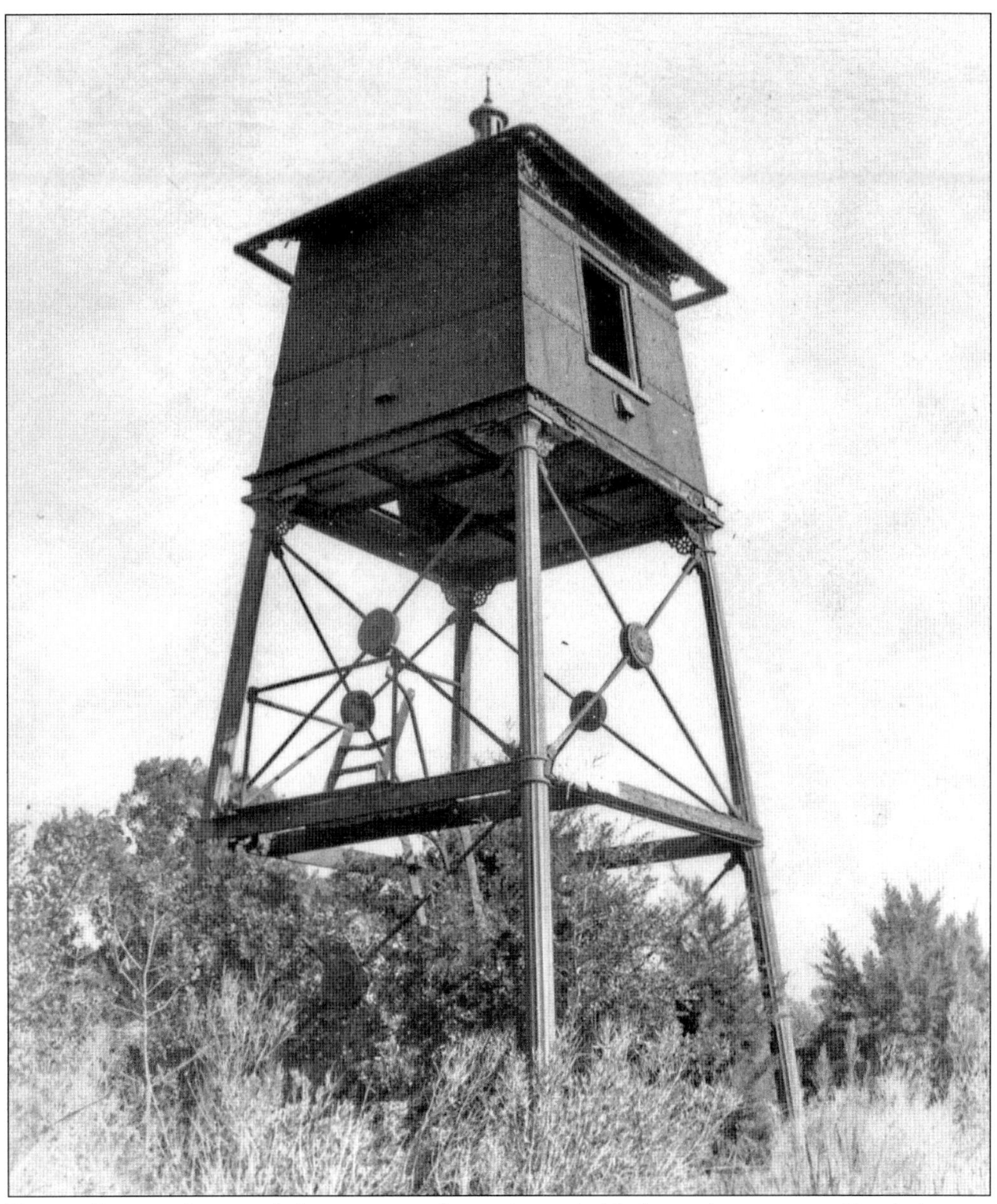

RANGE LIGHT. A range light can provide much needed help to the mariner. Two lights are used; one is named the front range, and the other is called the rear range. (Courtesy of Georgia Department of Natural Resources.)

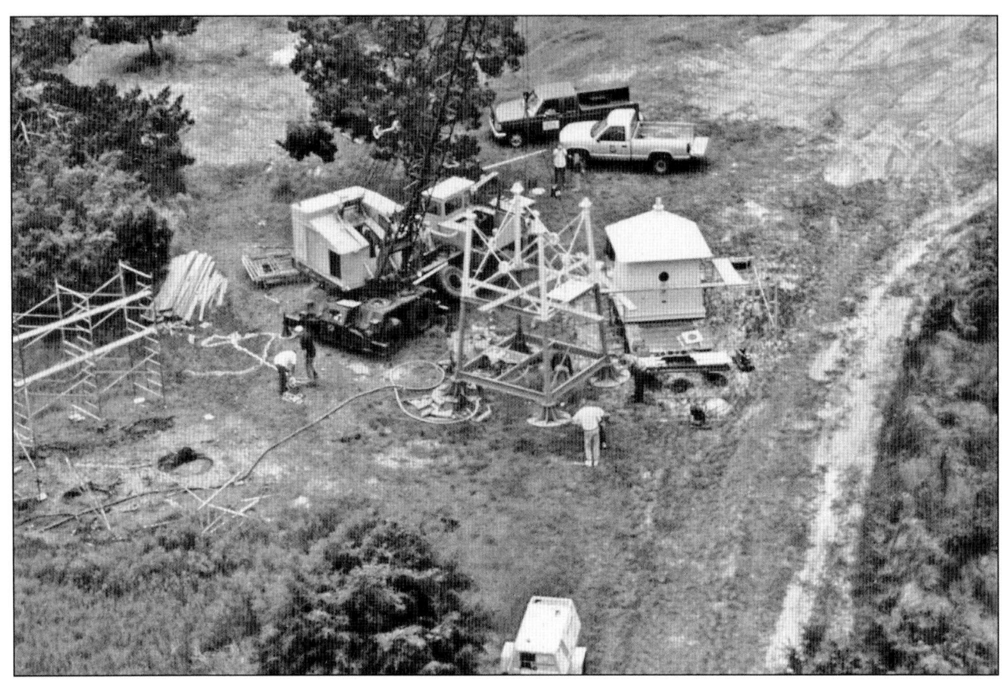

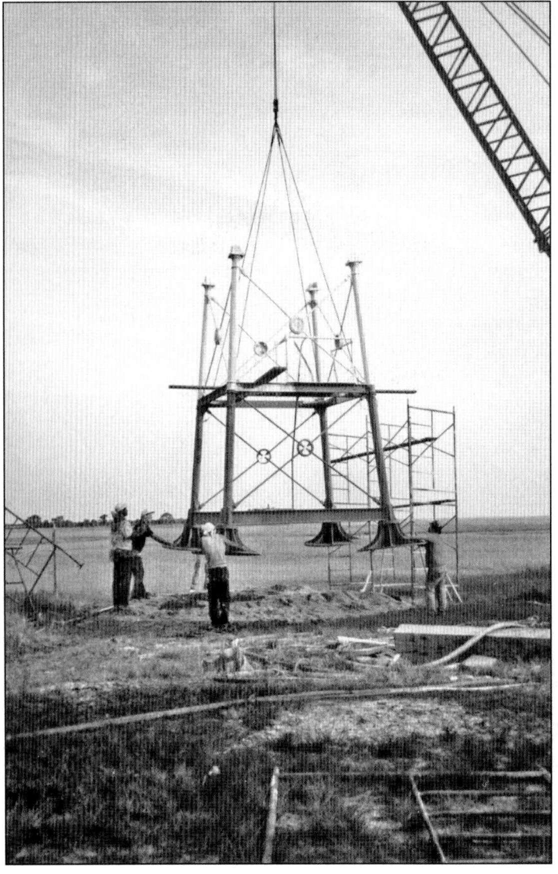

Range Light Repairs. A 25-foot, cast-iron range beacon was constructed in 1877. (Courtesy of Georgia Department of Natural Resources.)

Range Light Dismantled. Scheduled for repairs as part of the total project, the range light was completely dismantled and repaired during the restoration of the lighthouse. (Courtesy of Georgia Department of Natural Resources.)

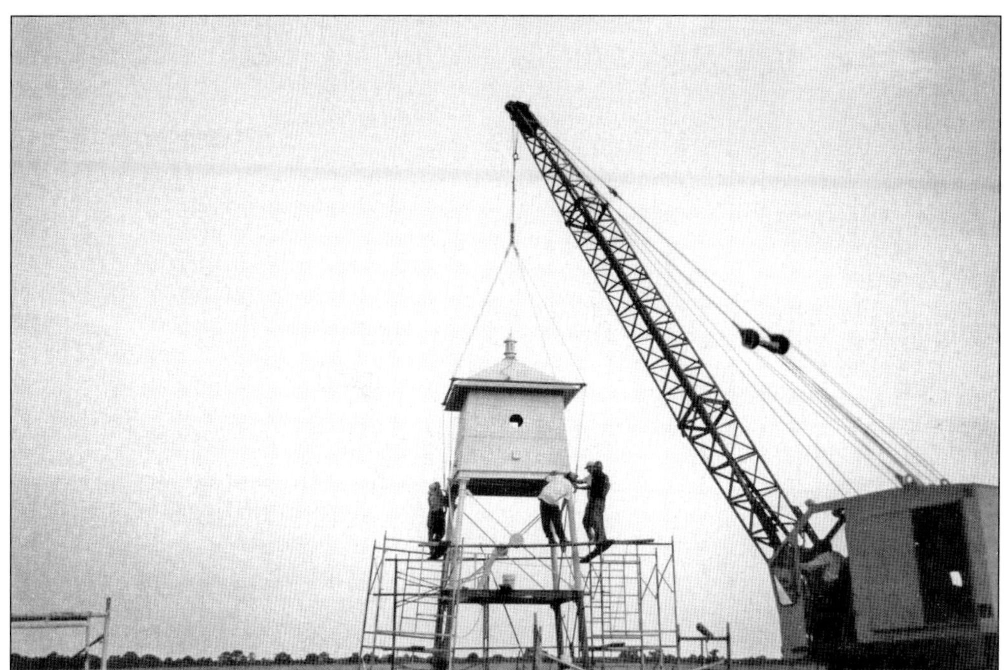

RANGE LIGHT RESTORED. The beacon was then placed back at its original site. A single lighthouse can provide only a single point of light. For many navigation problems, this is sometimes insufficient. (Courtesy of Georgia Department of Natural Resources.)

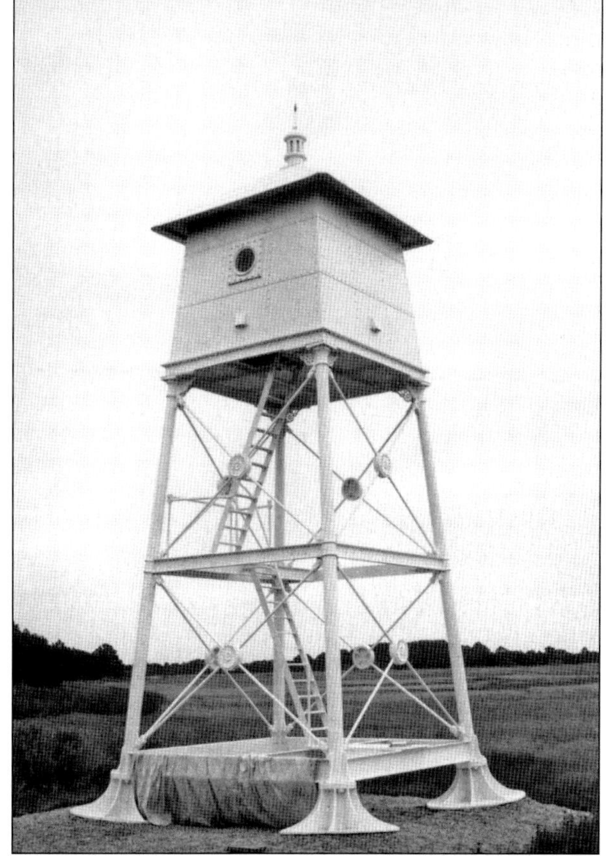

RANGE LIGHT, 1998. The rear range light is always taller than the front range light. The Sapelo Light is considered the rear range. When traveling on the path into the river, the two lights line up, one on top of the other. This provides the sailor with the information needed to travel the channel. (Courtesy of Georgia Department of Natural Resources.)

SAPELO RANGE LIGHT. The range beacon sits 660 feet east of the main tower. (Courtesy of

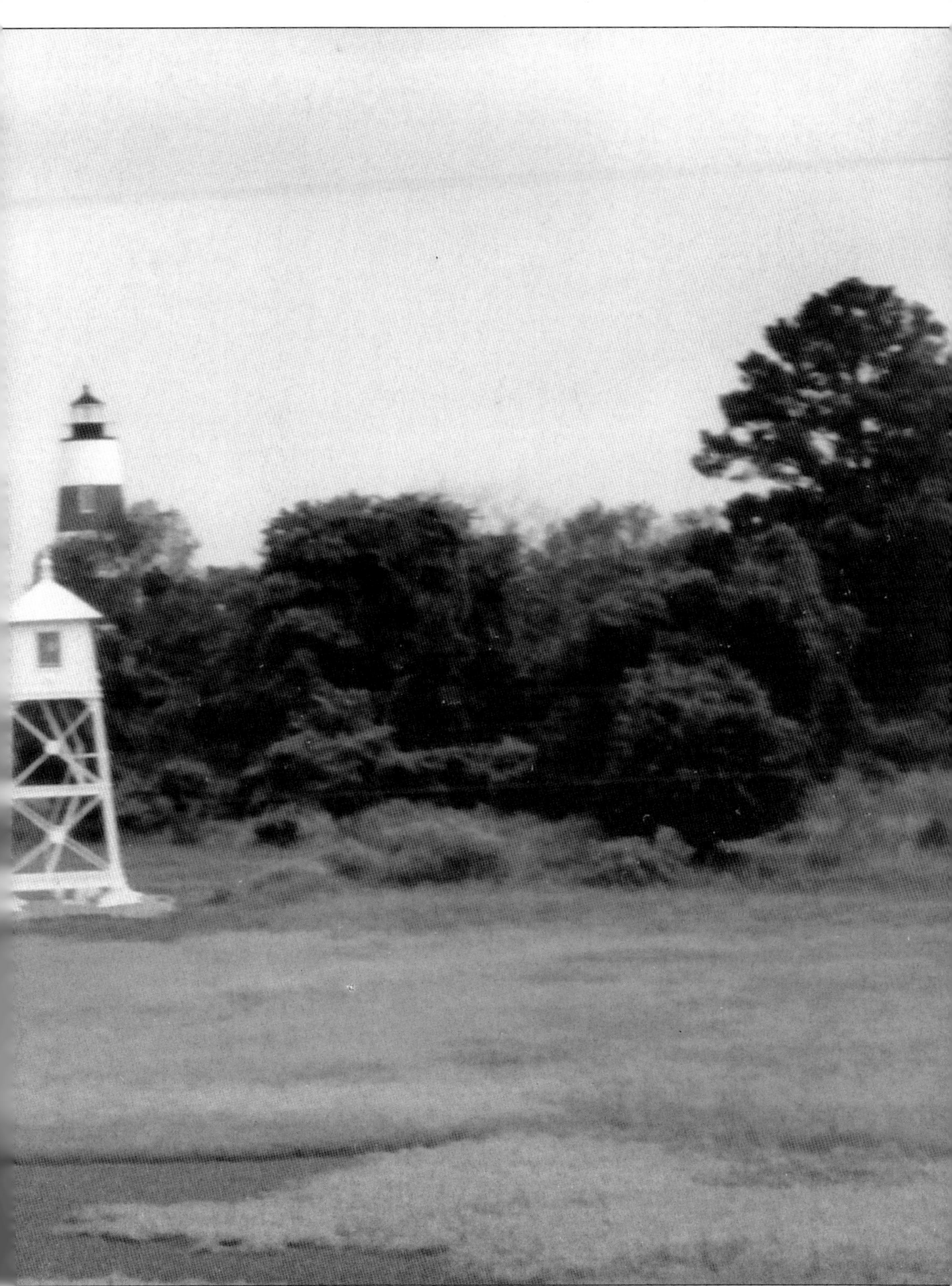

Georgia Department of Natural Resources.)

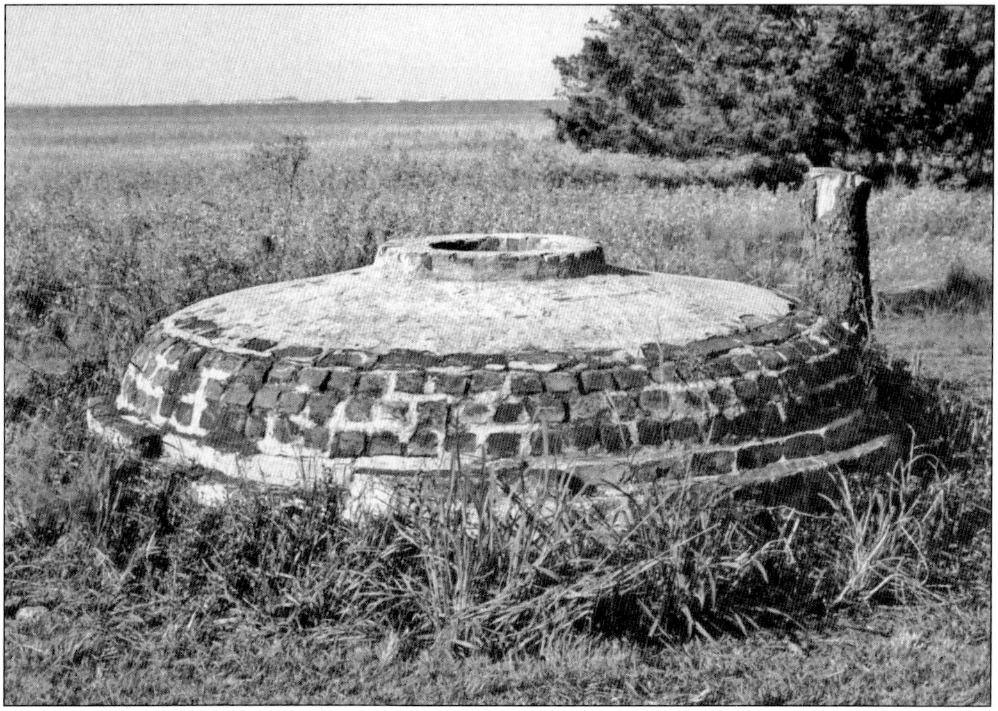

WATER CISTERN. The post–Civil War water cistern was also restored. A cistern is a receptacle for holding liquids, usually water. (Courtesy of Georgia Department of Natural Resources.)

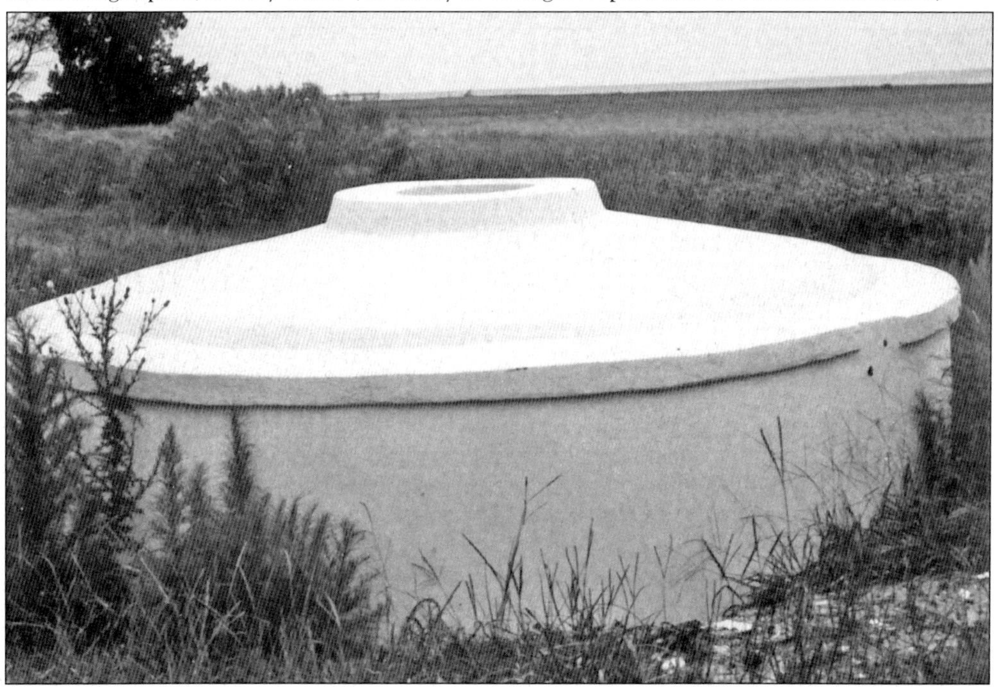

RESTORED WATER CISTERN, 1998. Often cisterns are built to catch and store rainwater, as was the one on Sapelo Island by the lighthouse. Cisterns are commonly used in areas where drinking water is scarce. (Courtesy of Georgia Department of Natural Resources.)

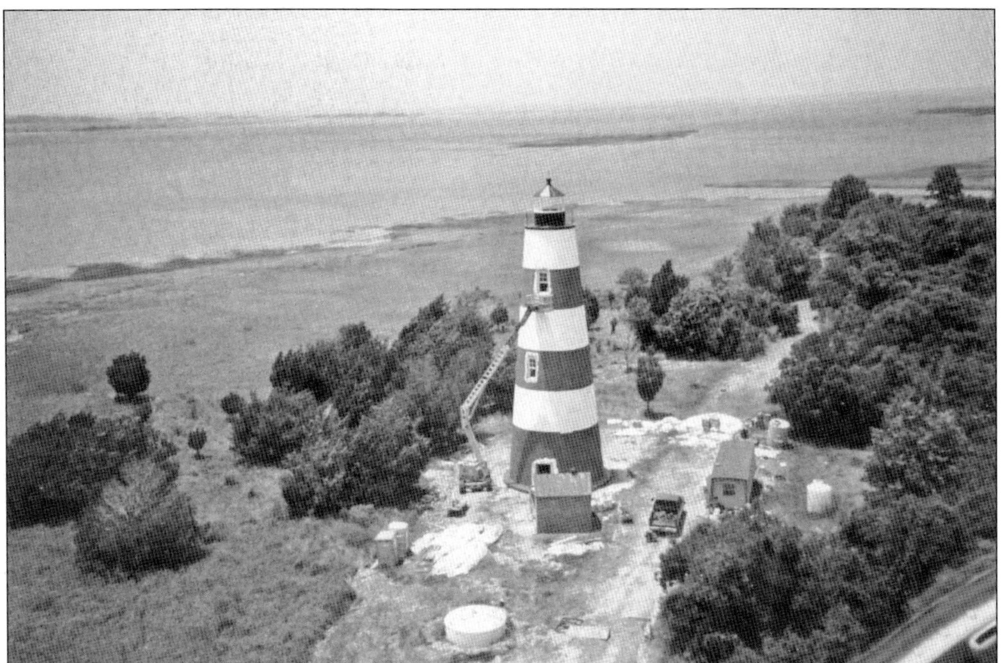

SAPELO LIGHT, 1996–1998. The restoration of the Sapelo Light was a major undertaking. Besides the remote location, the construction team had to also deal with insects and snakes that had taken up residence between the interior and exterior lighthouse walls. (Courtesy of Georgia Department of Natural Resources.)

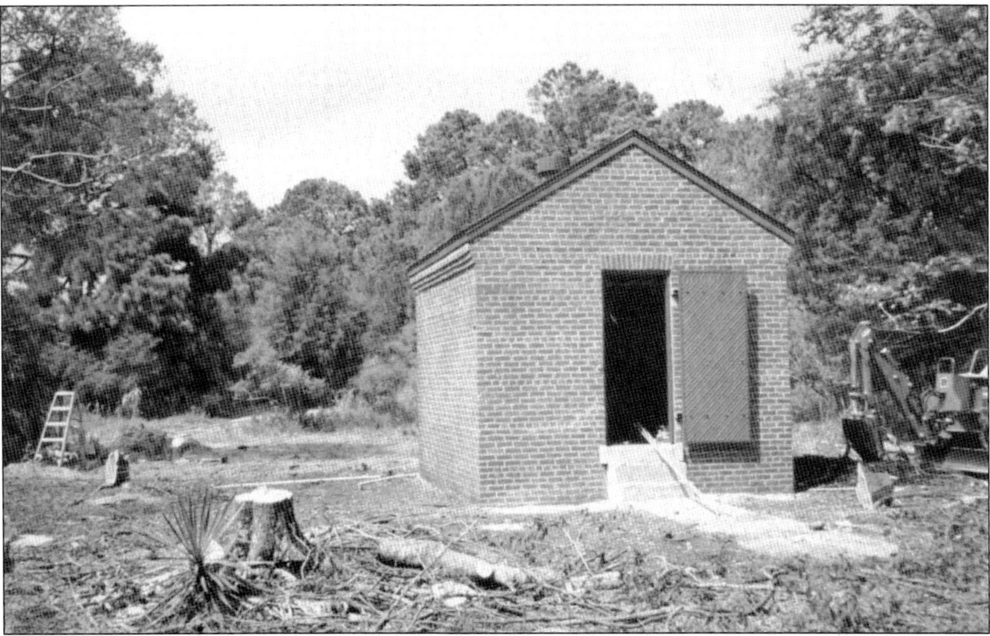

SAPELO LIGHT OIL HOUSE, 1997–1998. The oil house, built in 1890, was also restored. Many lighthouses built during that time had oil houses. These structures were reenforced, double-bricked storage outbuildings used to store large quantities of flammable fuel away from the tower and house. (Courtesy of Georgia Department of Natural Resources.)

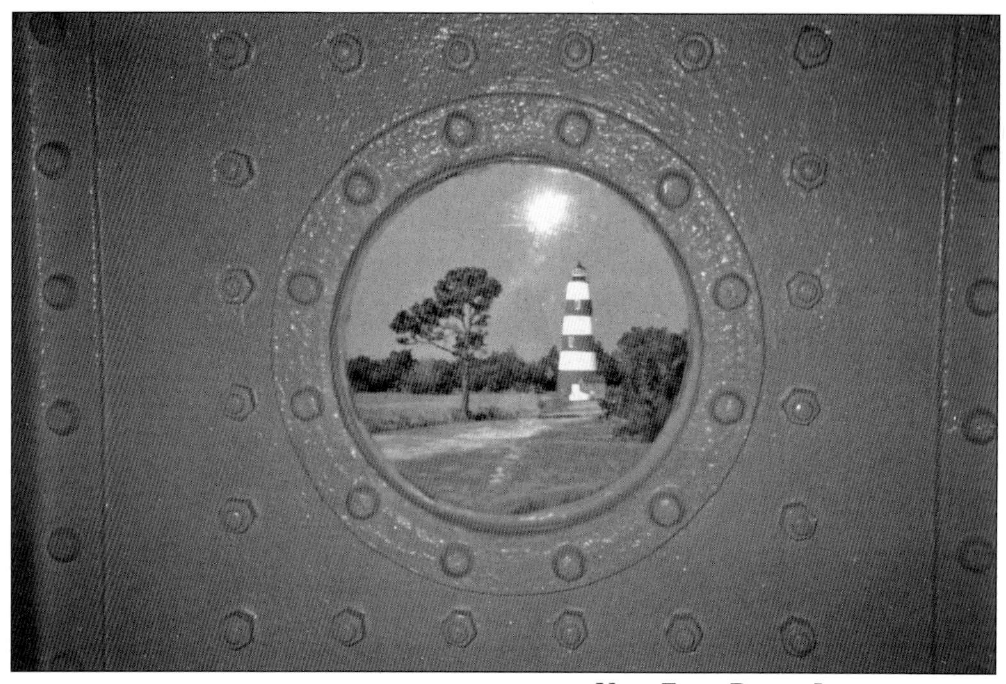

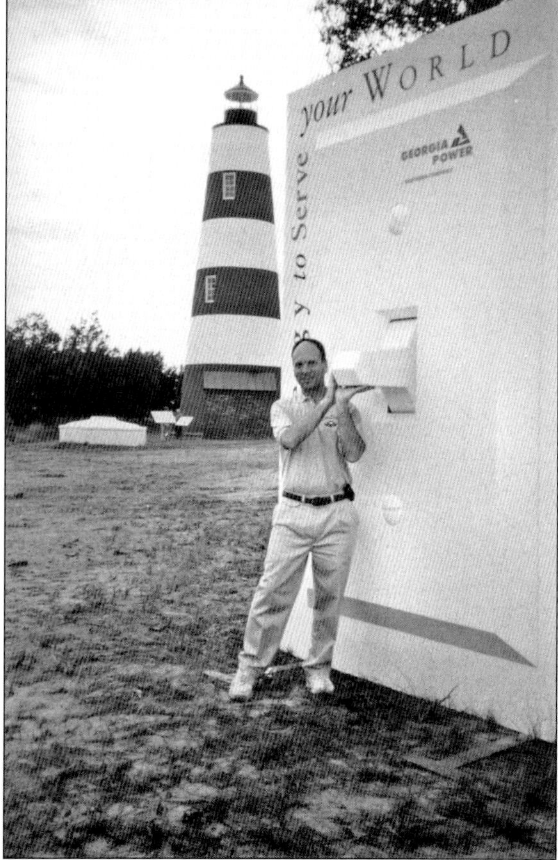

VIEW FROM RANGE LIGHT, C. 1998. Once restored, the Sapelo Light was once again open to the public. (Courtesy of Georgia Department of Natural Resources.)

FLIPPING THE SWITCH, 1998. A dedication and relighting ceremony was held on September 6, 1998. Georgia Power, one of the many partners in this restoration project, ceremoniously flips the switch. (Courtesy of Georgia Department of Natural Resources.)

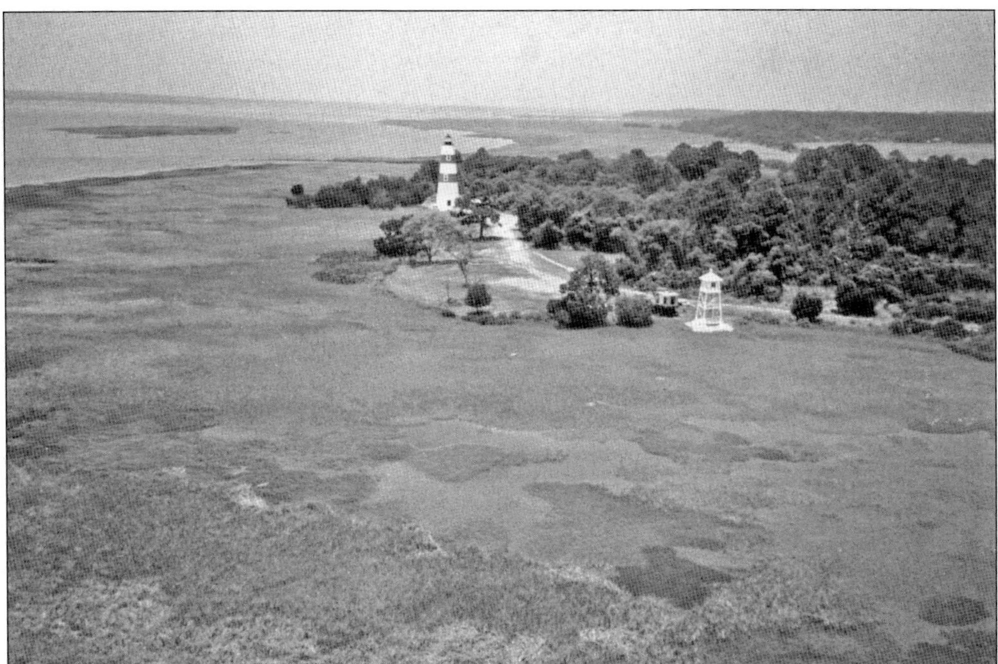

Aerial View. The total cost of the lighthouse restoration project was approximately $494,000. Through partnerships, grants, and private donations, the Sapelo Light was reborn. (Courtesy of Georgia Department of Natural Resources.)

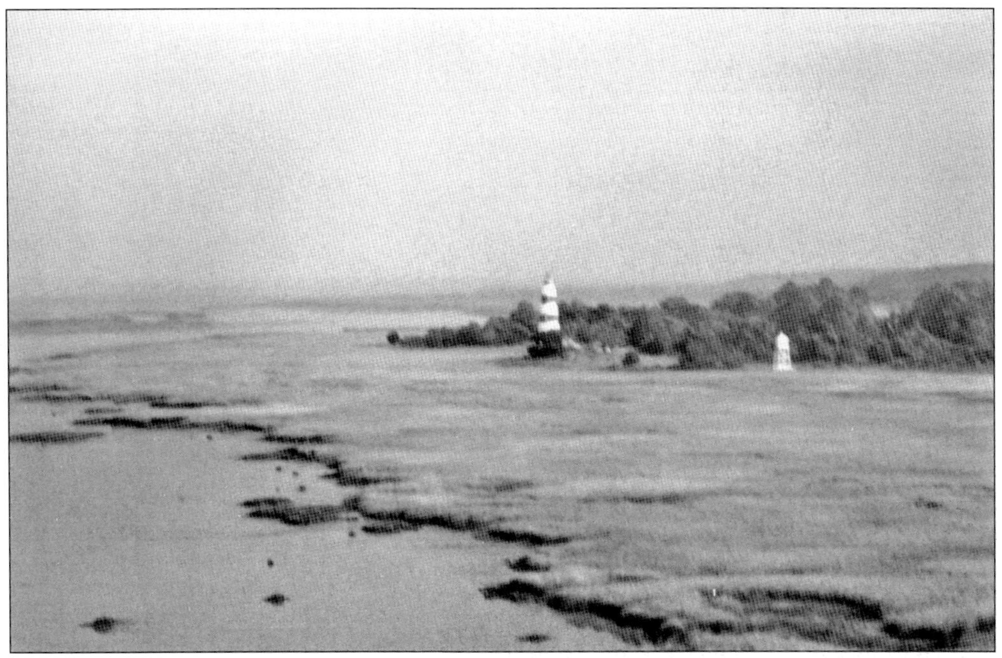

Approach to Sapelo Island. Located on one of Georgia's most pristine barrier islands, the lighthouse is only accessible by boat. Visitors to the island have a unique opportunity to step back in time. (Courtesy of Georgia Department of Natural Resources.)

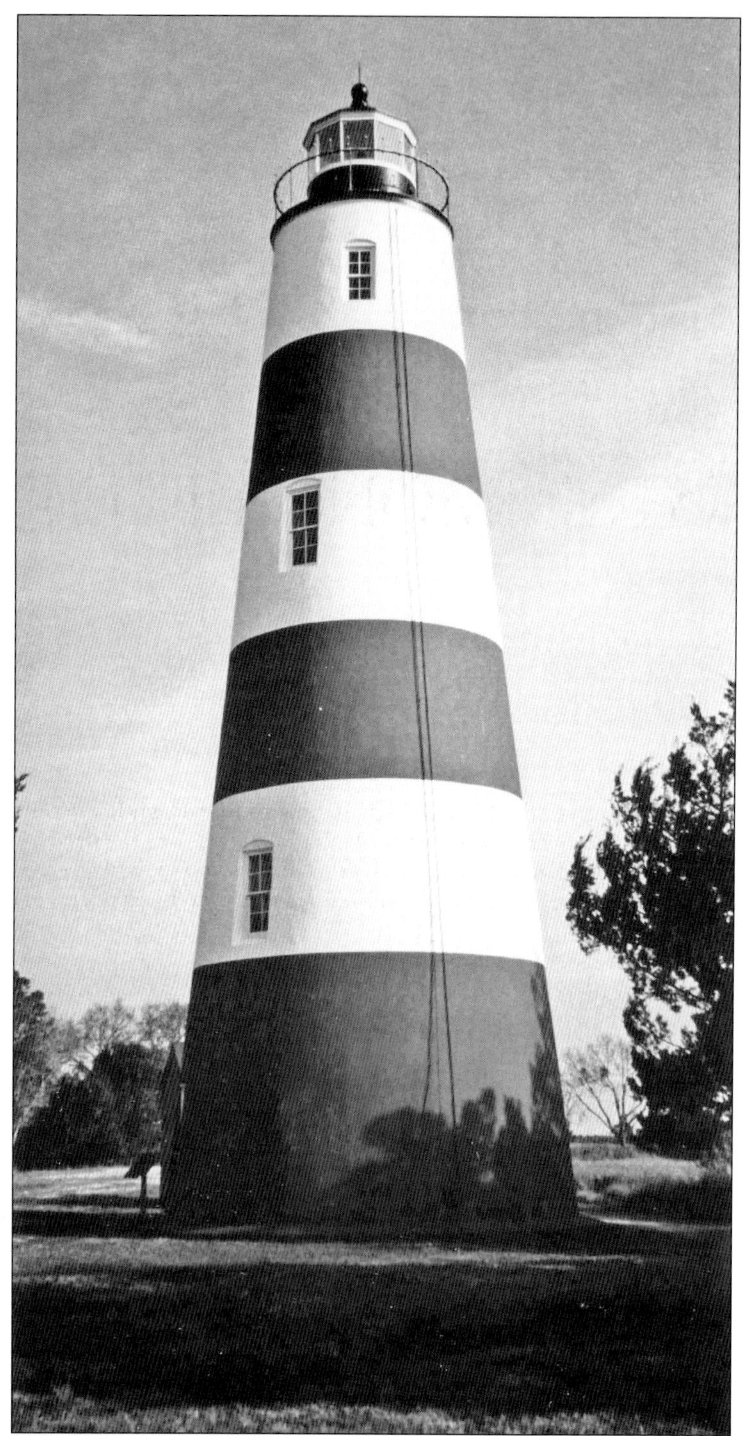

SAPELO ISLAND LIGHT, 1998. Today, fully restored, the Sapelo Lighthouse still functions as an aid to navigation. It is maintained by the Georgia Department of Natural Resources. It stands as a testament to the importance of restoration and preservation of the architectural past. (Courtesy of Georgia Department of Natural Resources.)

Three

St. Simons Light

Truly Georgia's gem of the coast, the 104-foot-high St. Simons Island Lighthouse continues to tower over the port of Brunswick. In the early 1800s, plantation owners saw the need for a lighthouse. For $1, John Couper deeded 4 acres at the south end of the island to the federal government for construction of the lighthouse. James Gould of Massachusetts was hired to design and construct the lighthouse and a one-story frame house. In 1810, the light was lit, and Pres. James Madison appointed Gould as the first lighthouse keeper.

The lighthouse remained in service until the Civil War. When Union ships forced an evacuation of the island in 1862, the Confederate troops destroyed the lighthouse for fear the federal troops would use it as a navigational aid.

The U.S. government ordered the construction of the second lighthouse in 1867. Taking four years to complete, the dwelling and tower were designed by one of Georgia's most noted architects, Charles Cluskey. Cluskey and some of the crew never saw the completion of their work, dying of malaria in 1871, a year before the structures were complete.

Lit in 1872, the St. Simons Island Lighthouse continues to guide ships into the port of Brunswick. While many keepers climbed the 129 steps to the top, the last keeper retired in 1953, when the light was automated. The current light shines from the historic Fresnel lens 23 miles out to sea. Legend has it that ships passing the lighthouse have sounded their horn as a salute to the keeper. This tradition continues today.

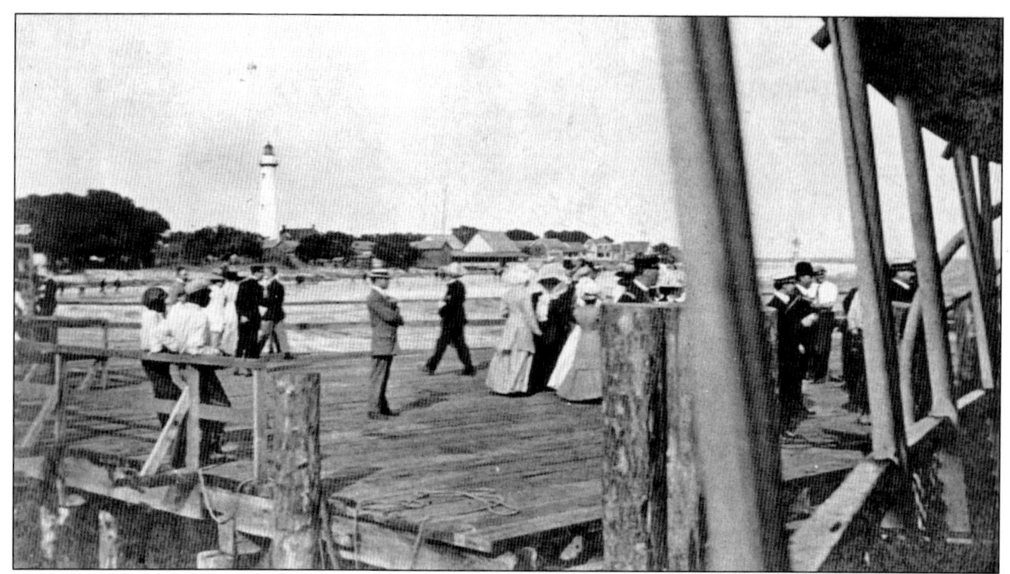

St. Simons Island Village Pier, c. 1910. Looking toward the St. Simons Island Light, visitors arrive on the island. A summer retreat since the 1870s, the St. Simons Island light keeper and his family often welcomed visitors to the lighthouse. (Courtesy of Coastal Georgia Historical Society.)

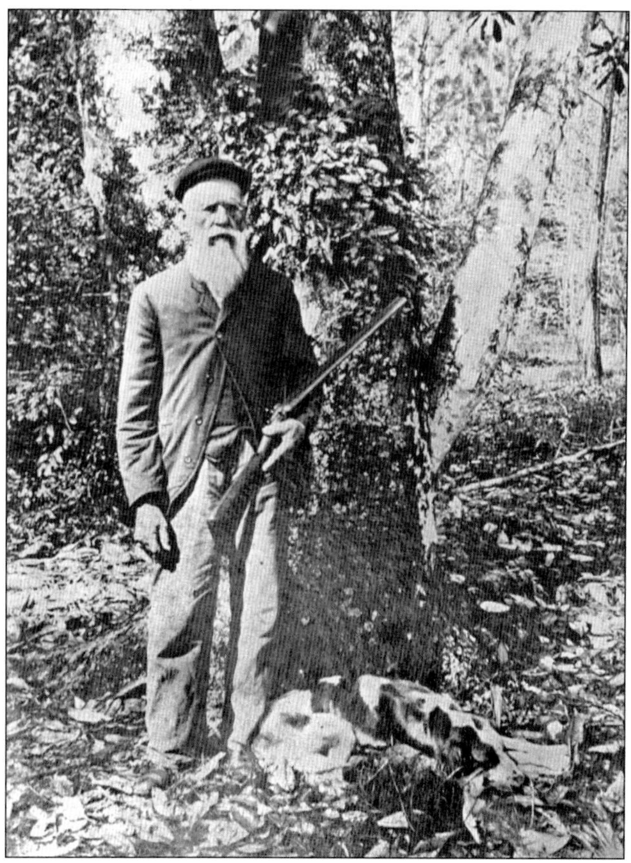

Alexander D. McIntosh, 1852–1855. Alexander D. McIntosh was an early lighthouse keeper. (Courtesy of Coastal Georgia Historical Society.)

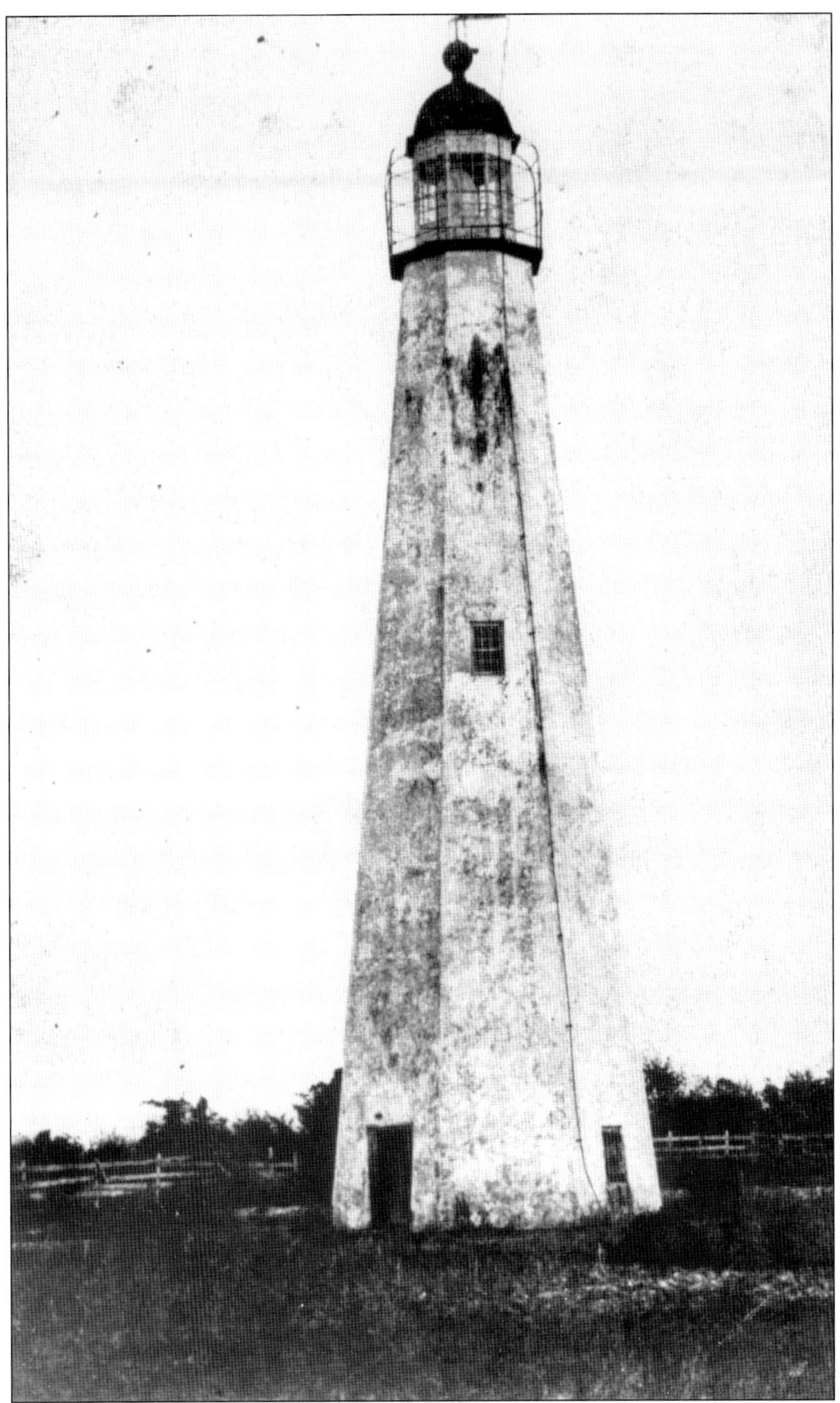

FIRST LIGHTHOUSE. Lit in 1810, the first lighthouse on St. Simons Island was built by James Gould, who also became the first lighthouse keeper. Built of tabby, this lighthouse was destroyed as Confederate troops left the island in 1863. They did not want the Union navy to use it as a navigational aid. (Courtesy of National Archives.)

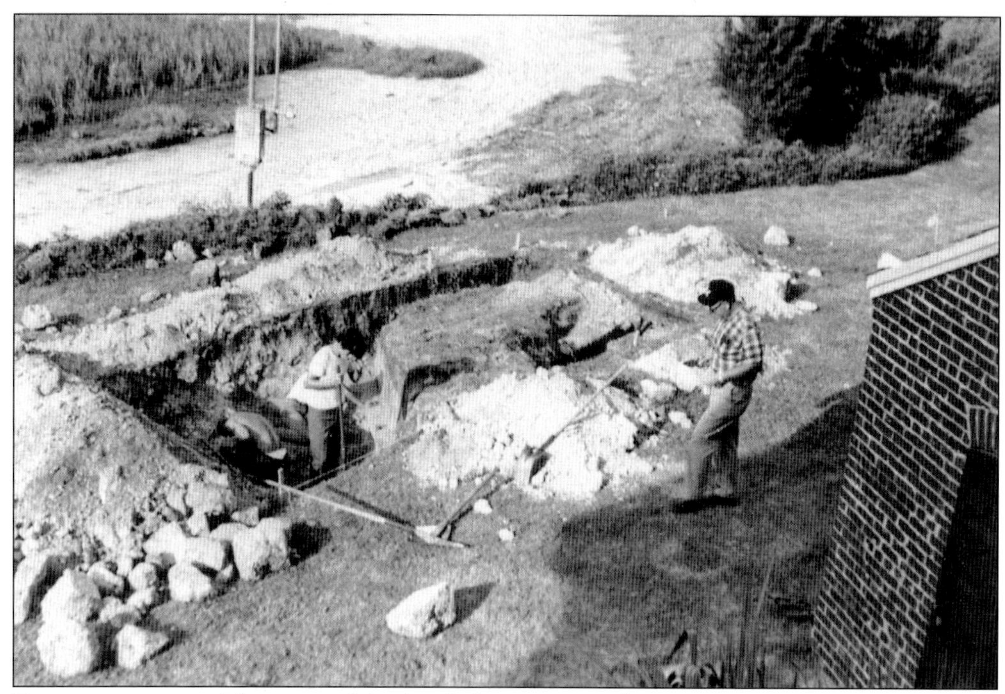

EXCAVATION, 1974. The ruins of the first light were partially excavated by archeologists during August 1974. Dr. Lewis Larson, the Georgia Historical Commission state archeologist, oversaw the project. (Courtesy of Coastal Georgia Historical Society.)

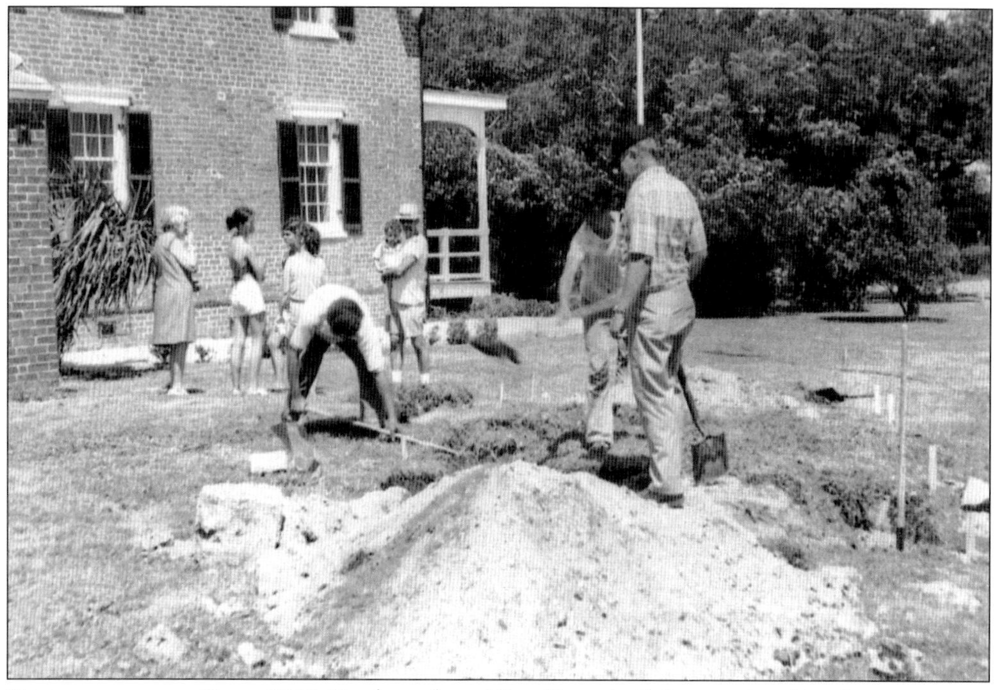

DIGGING FOR THE PAST, 1974. Students from West Georgia College assisted in the excavation. Here the team prepares the site. (Courtesy of Coastal Georgia Historical Society.)

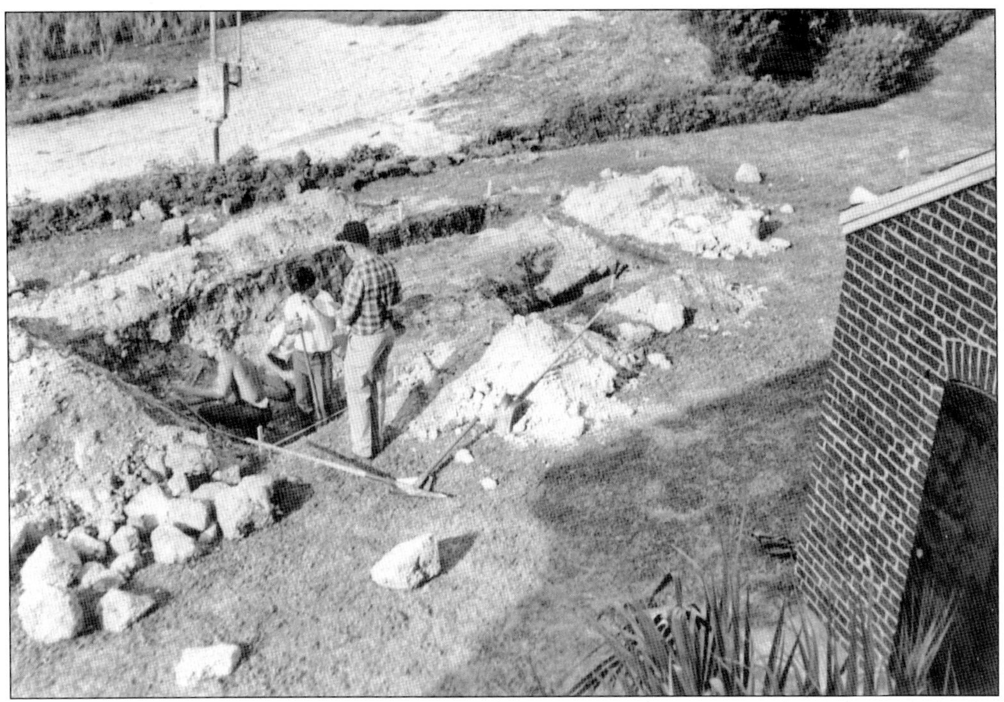

FIRST LIGHT FOUND, 1974. The site of the first lighthouse is just south of the present-day lighthouse. (Courtesy of Coastal Georgia Historical Society.)

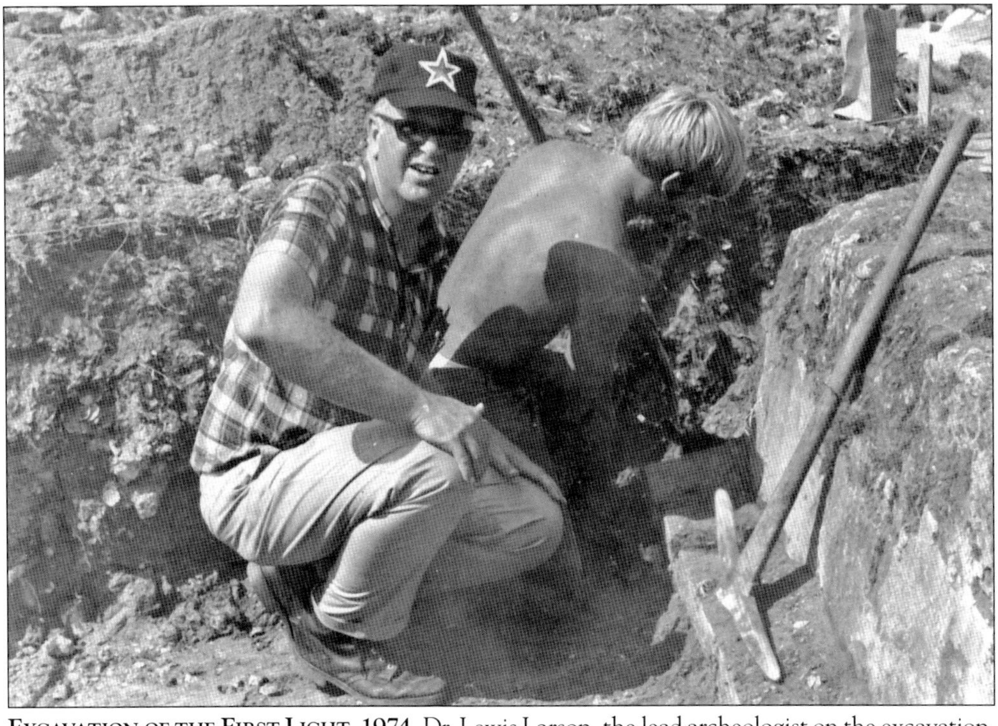

EXCAVATION OF THE FIRST LIGHT, 1974. Dr. Lewis Larson, the lead archeologist on the excavation, is in the cap. (Courtesy of Coastal Georgia Historical Society.)

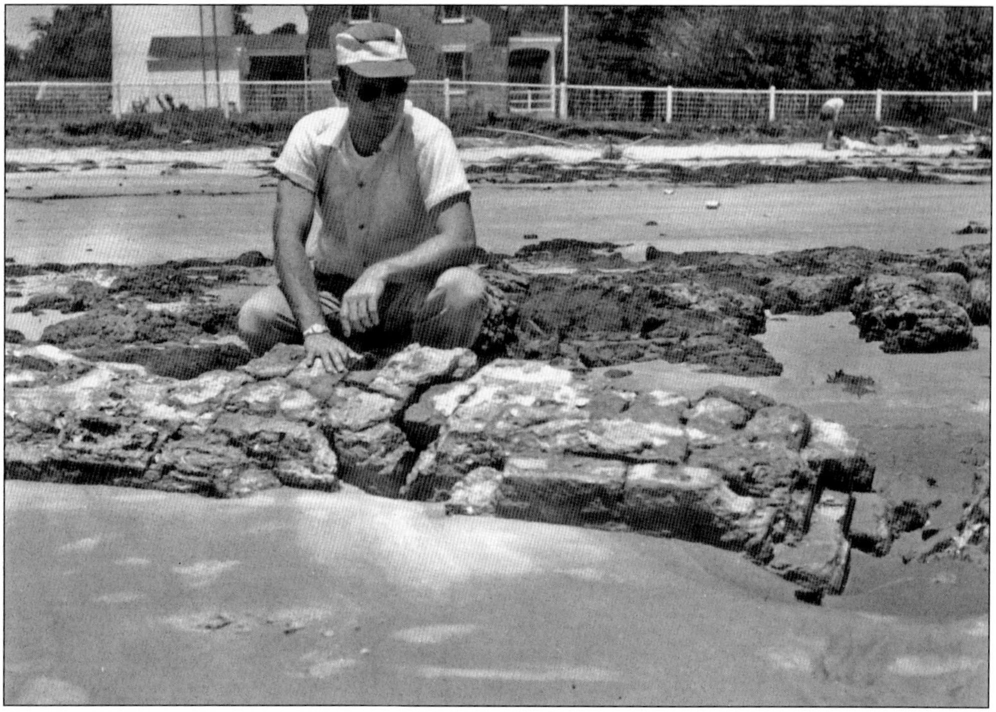

EXCAVATION OF THE WHALE OIL HOUSE, 1974. Excavation of the whale oil building was also completed that summer. (Courtesy of Coastal Georgia Historical Society.)

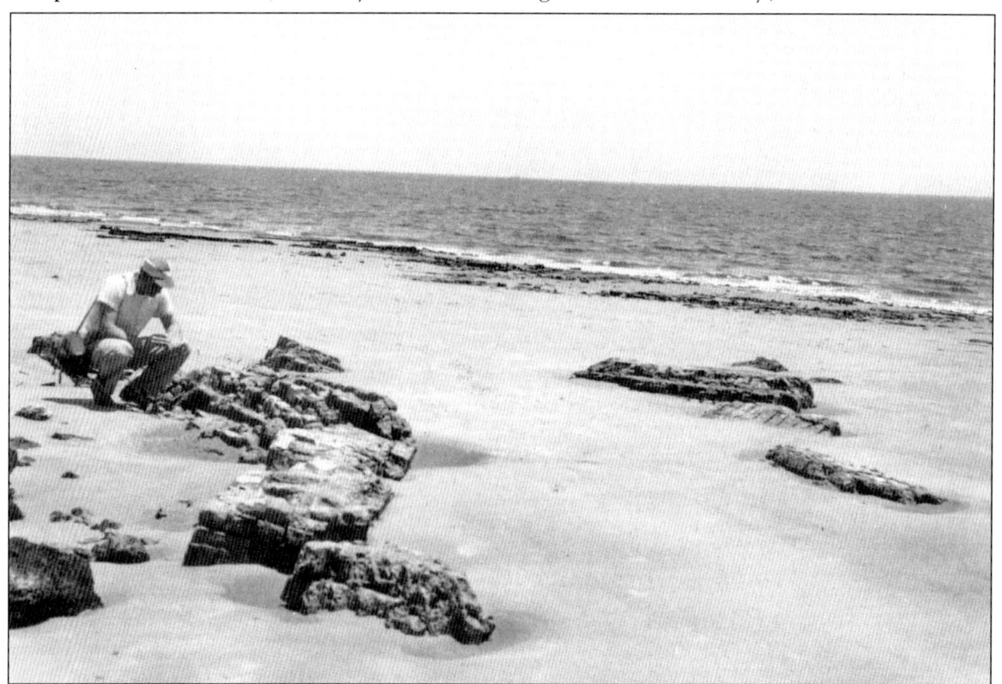

WHALE OIL HOUSE, 1974. Originally the lighthouse was lit with whale oil and later kerosene. The oil house was usually a brick structure used to store the flammable containers away from the lighthouse. (Courtesy of Coastal Georgia Historical Society.)

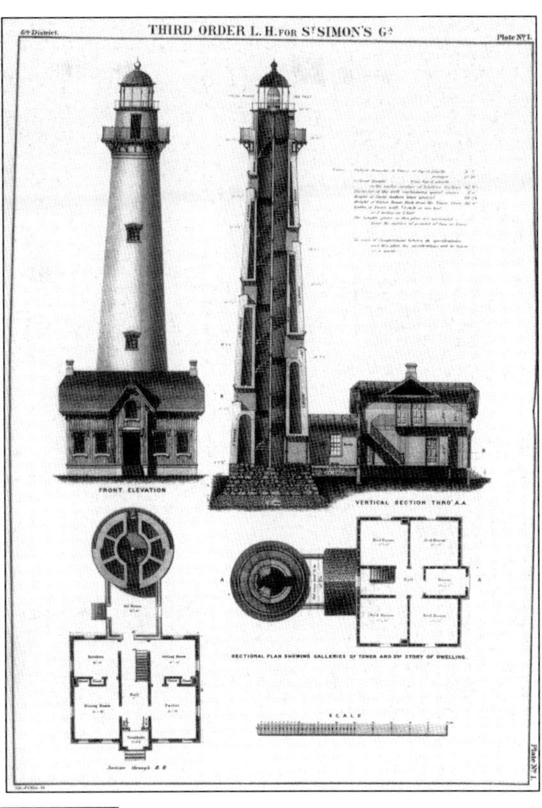

ARCHITECTURAL PLAN, 1872. The building of the second light on St. Simons began in 1867 and was completed in 1872. (Courtesy of Coastal Georgia Historical Society.)

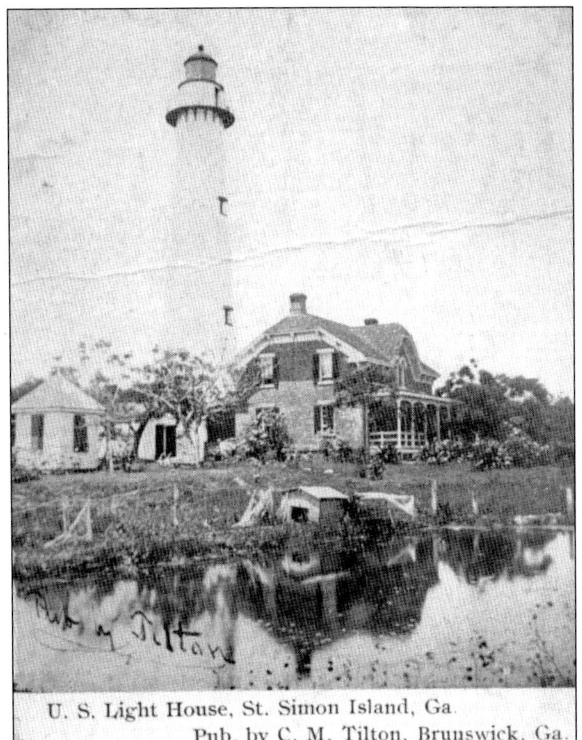

POSTCARD, 1908. It was noted in the official records in 1874 that "this station is very unhealthy, and it is attributed to the stagnant water in several ponds in the vicinity." (Courtesy of Coastal Georgia Historical Society.)

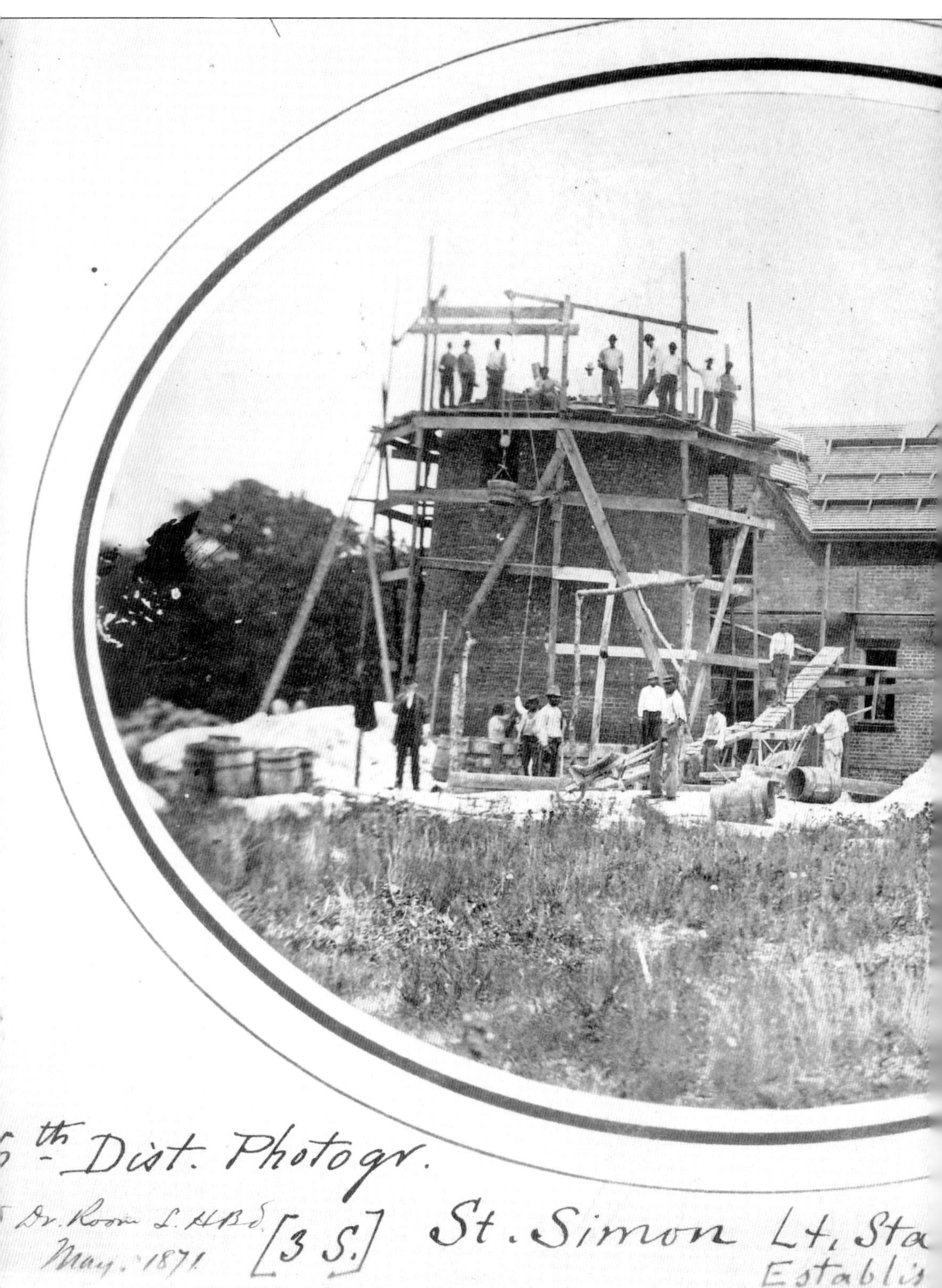
th Dist. Photogr.
Dr. Room L. H. Bd.
May. 1871
[3 S.]
St. Simon Lt. Sta
Establis

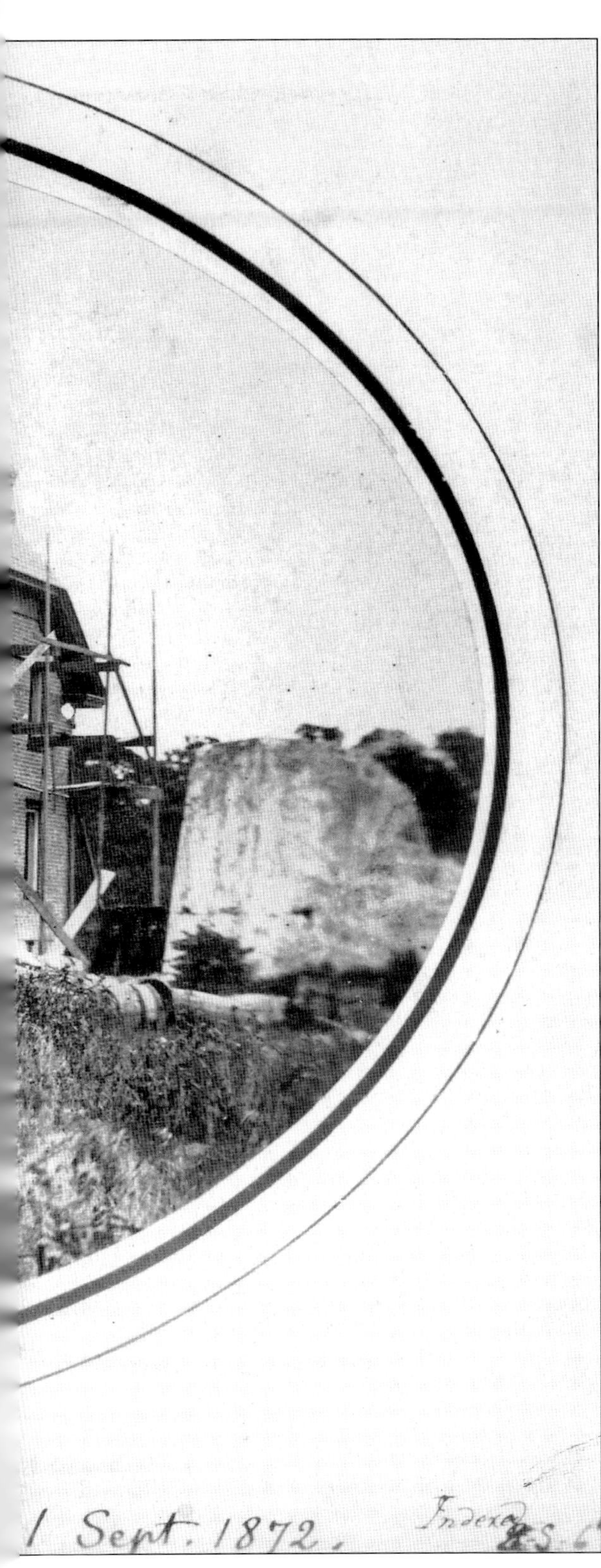

BUILDING OF THE SECOND LIGHT, 1872. Charles Cluskey, a noted Georgia architect, designed and oversaw the project to build the St. Simons lighthouse. Unfortunately, Cluskey died before the construction was completed from malaria contracted while on St. Simons Island. (Courtesy of National Archives.)

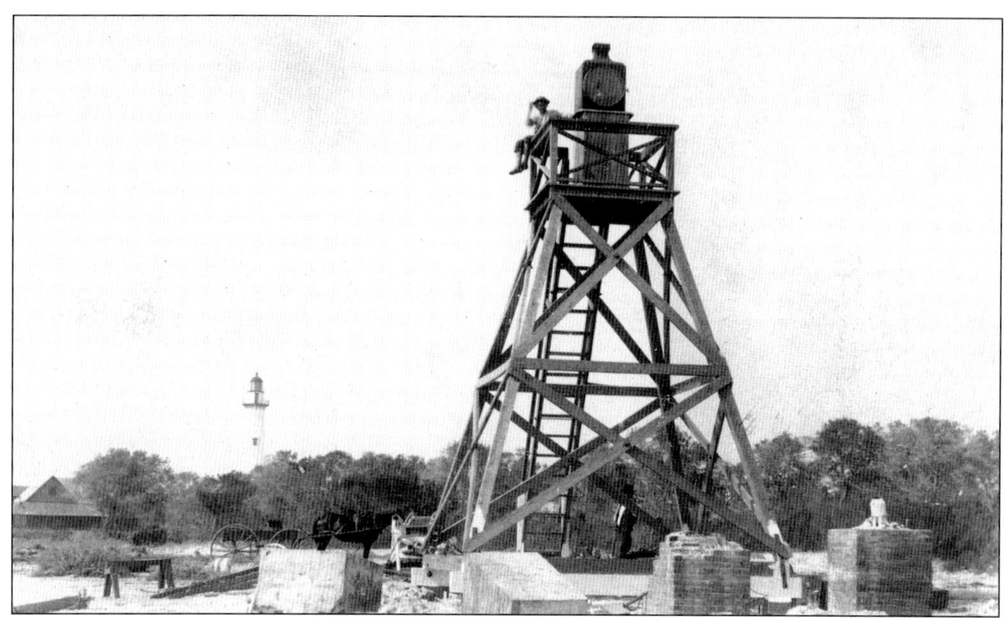

RANGE FRONT BEACON, 1896. Range lights were used to help sailors navigate the port. Range lights are light pairs that indicate a specific line; the higher rear light is placed behind the front light. When the mariner sees the lights vertically in line, the vessel is on the range line and can enter the port safely. (Courtesy of National Archives.)

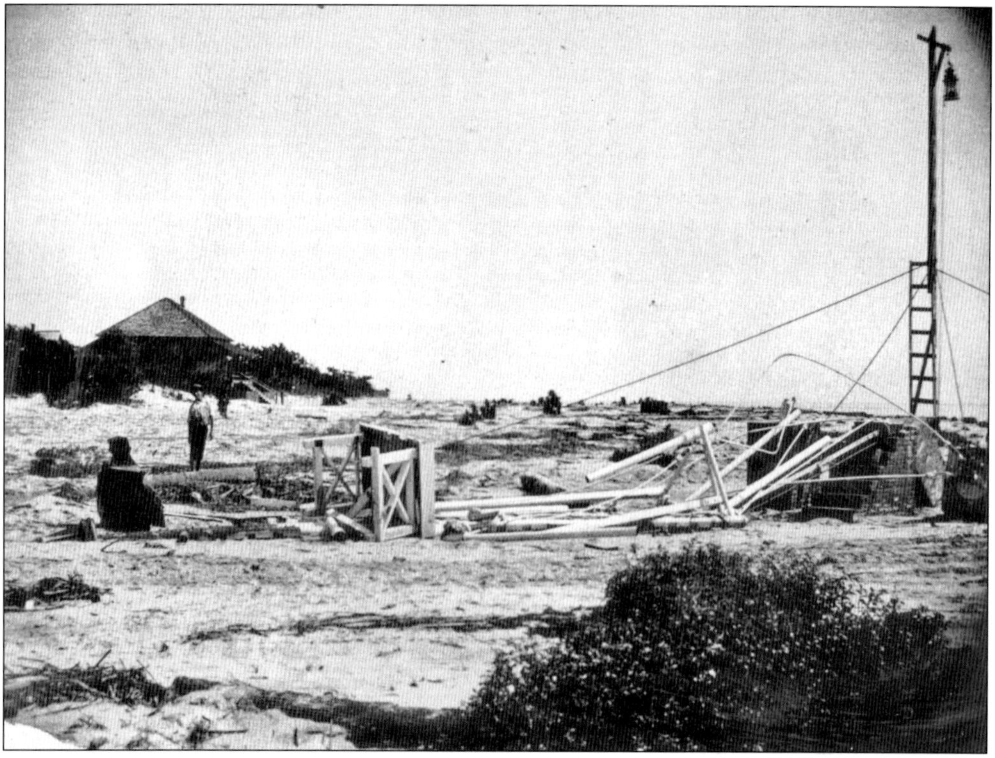

RANGE FRONT BEACON, 1898. The range light was destroyed in an 1898 hurricane. This view is looking north. (Courtesy of National Archives.)

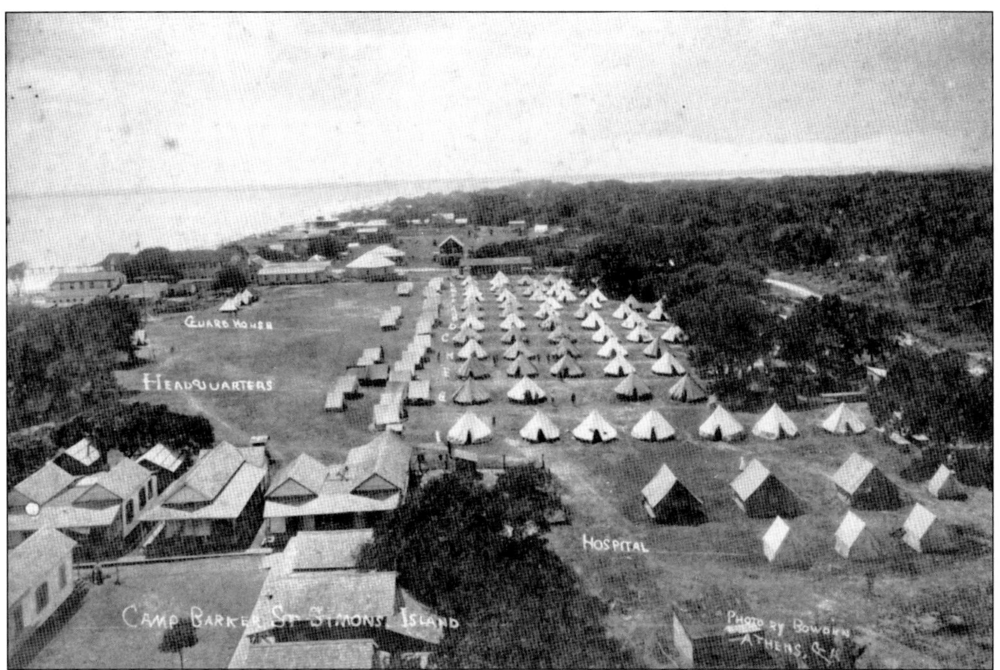

Camp Gorden, 1898. Established by a company of the 3rd Texas Volunteers Infantry Regiment in 1898, Camp Gordon (misidentified as Camp Barker) was named for Confederate major general and Georgia governor John B. Gordon. (Courtesy of Coastal Georgia Historical Society.)

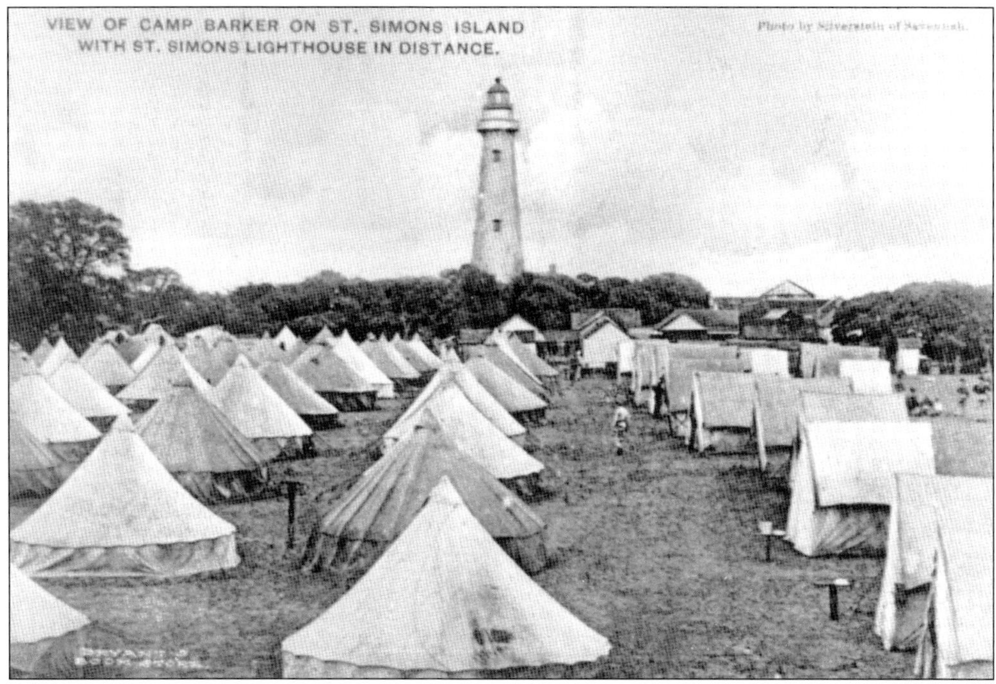

Postcard. Camp Gordon is shown here with St. Simons Lighthouse in the background. The camp was located at the base of the light. (Courtesy of Coastal Georgia Historical Society.)

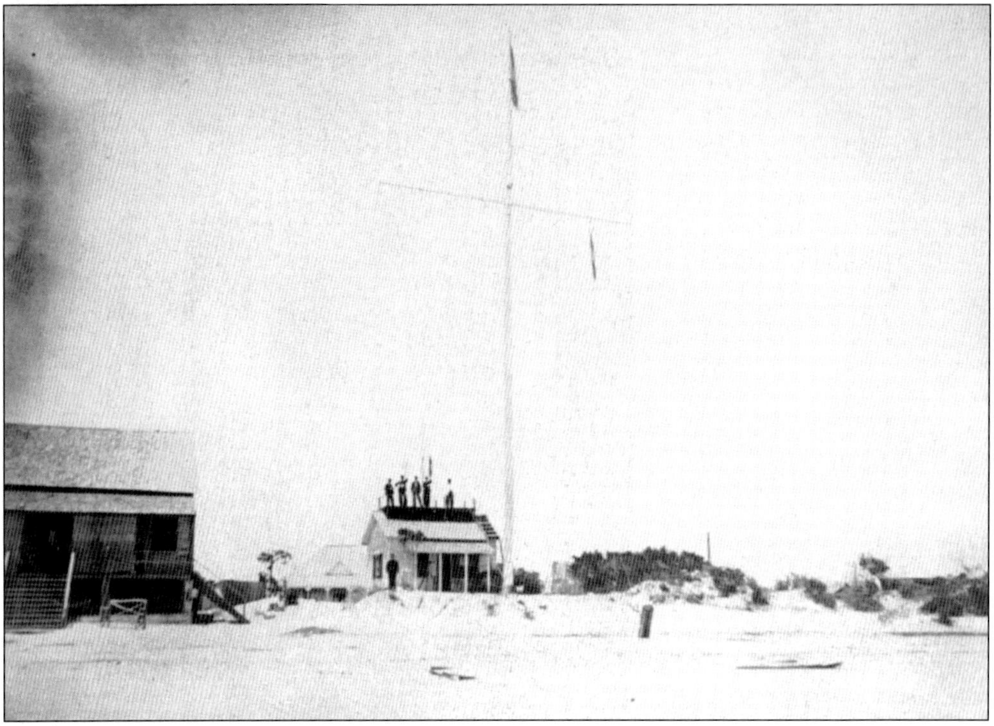

SIGNAL STATION, 1996–1998. This was a signal station by the lighthouse during the Spanish-American War. (Courtesy of National Archives.)

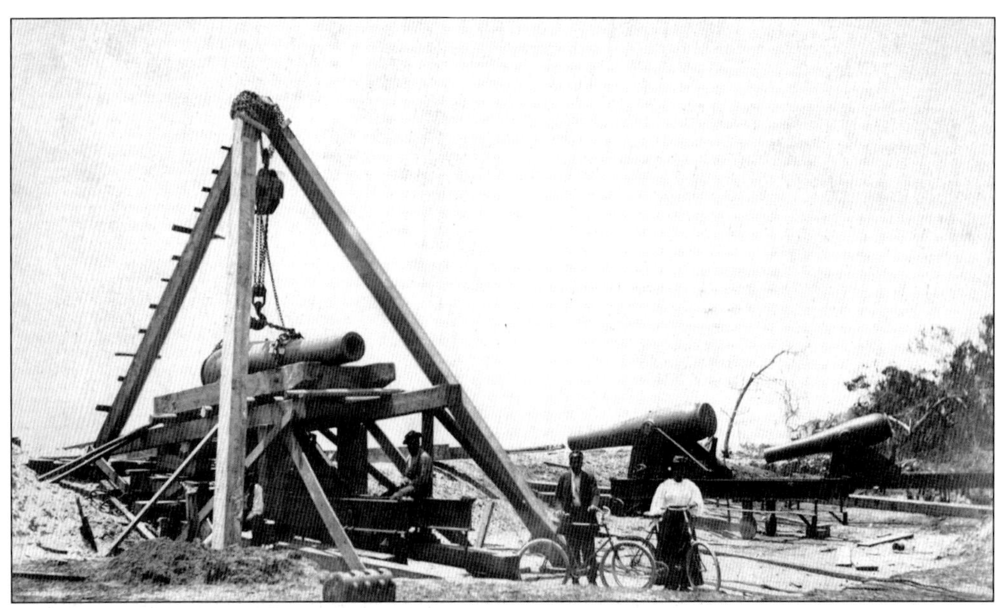

CANNONS IN FRONT OF STRACHAN COTTAGE, C. 1898. Strachan Cottage was located near the lighthouse. In 1898, the Spanish-American War caused concern along the coast. This conflict between the United States and Spain ended Spanish colonial rule in the Americas. (Courtesy of Coastal Georgia Historical Society.)

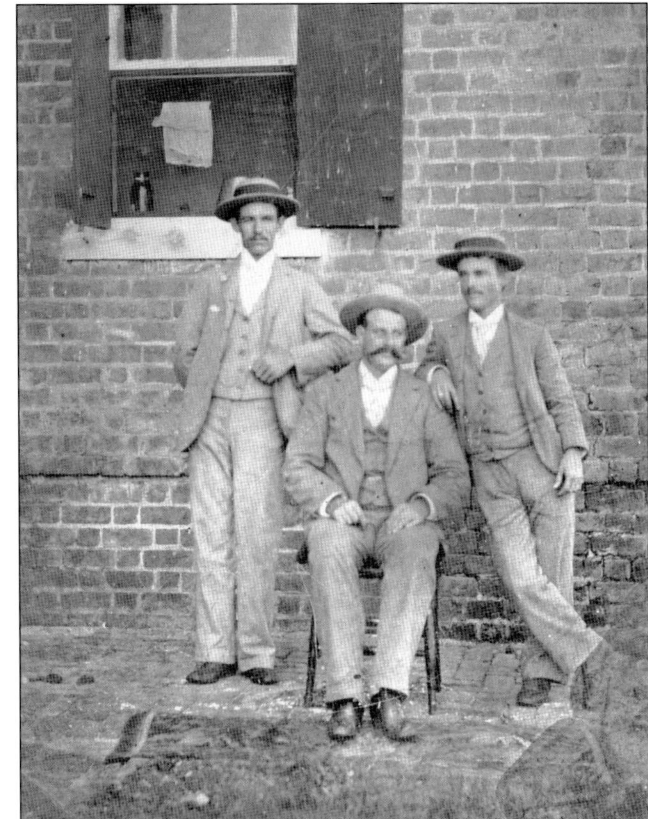

UNIDENTIFIED GENTLEMEN, EARLY 1900S. This daguerreotype of visitors to the light at the beginning of the 20th century is typical of the type of visitor that would stop at the lighthouse while on the island. (Courtesy of Coastal Georgia Historical Society.)

LIGHTHOUSE, C. 1900. Much of the land on the south side of the building has been lost to erosion due to storms. (Courtesy of Coastal Georgia Historical Society.)

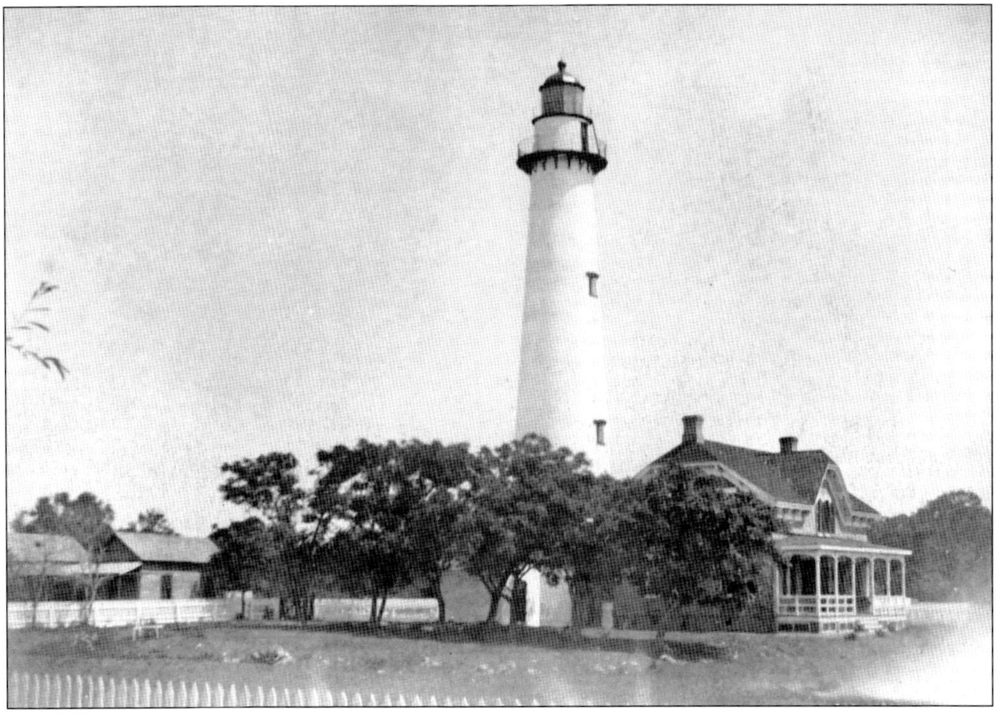

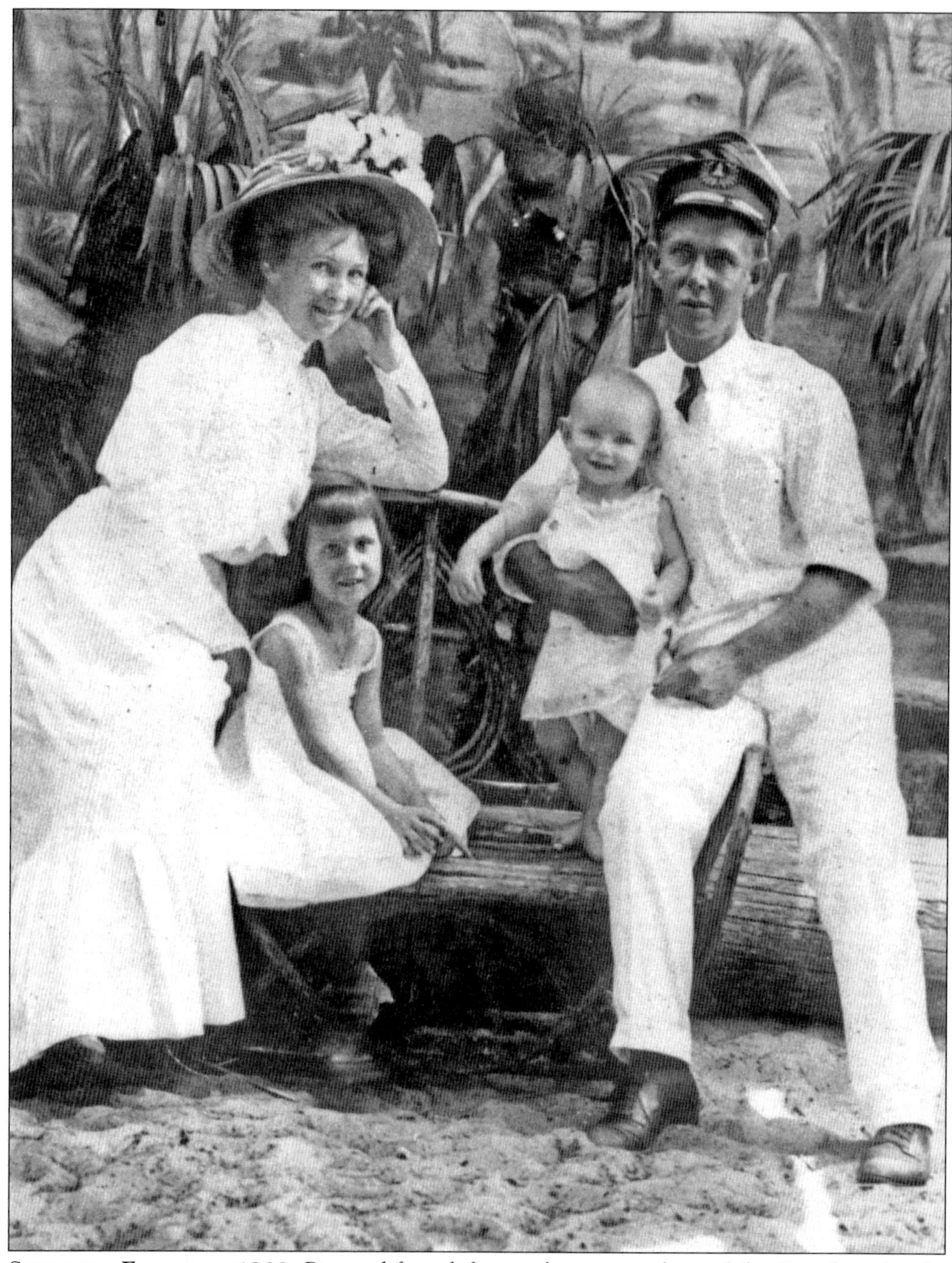

SVENDSEN FAMILY, C. 1908. Pictured from left to right are members of the Svendsen family, Anna, Happy, Carl Jr., and Carl Sr. This formal portrait was taken shortly after the Svendsens arrived on St. Simons Island. (Courtesy of Coastal Georgia Historical Society.)

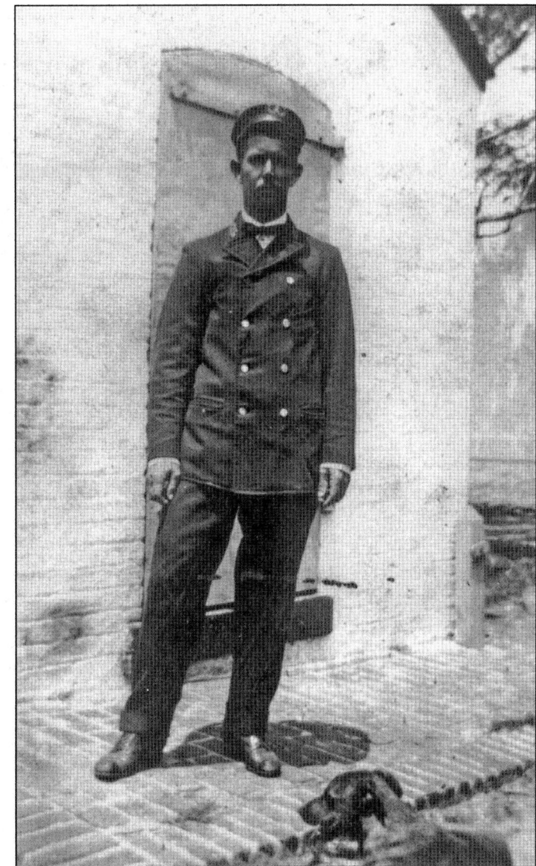

LIGHTHOUSE KEEPER, 1907–1936. Carl Olaf Svendsen was keeper from 1907 until 1936 when the U.S. Coast Guard took over jurisdiction. (Courtesy of Coastal Georgia Historical Society.)

KEEPER'S QUARTERS, C. 1920. When Carl O. Svendsen arrived in 1907, the keeper and his assistant shared the dwelling, with the head keeper's family living downstairs and the assistant's living upstairs. A central stairway connected the two households. (Courtesy of Coastal Georgia Historical Society.)

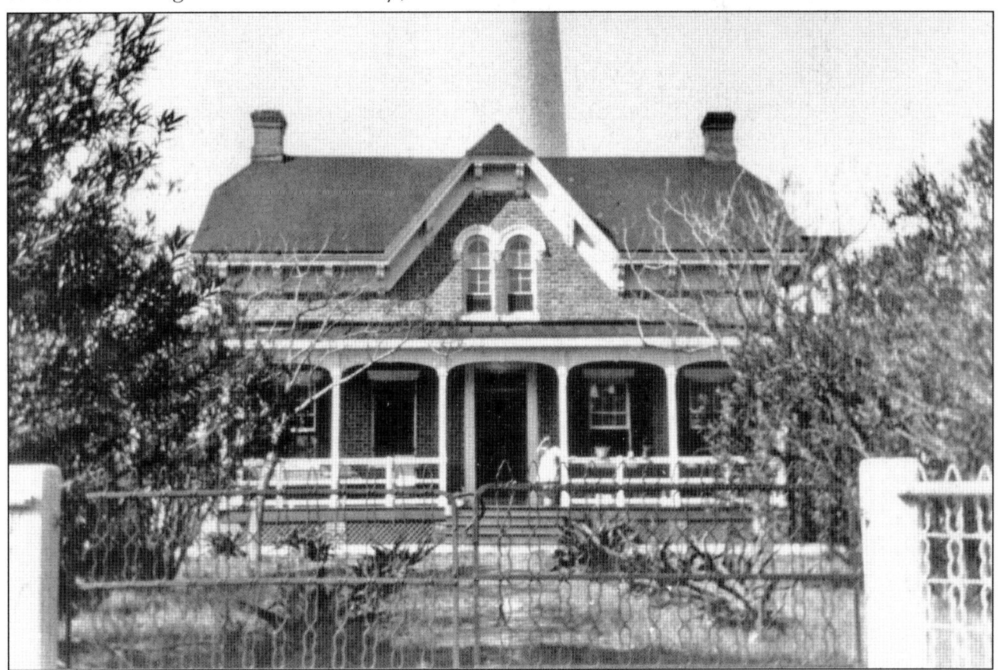

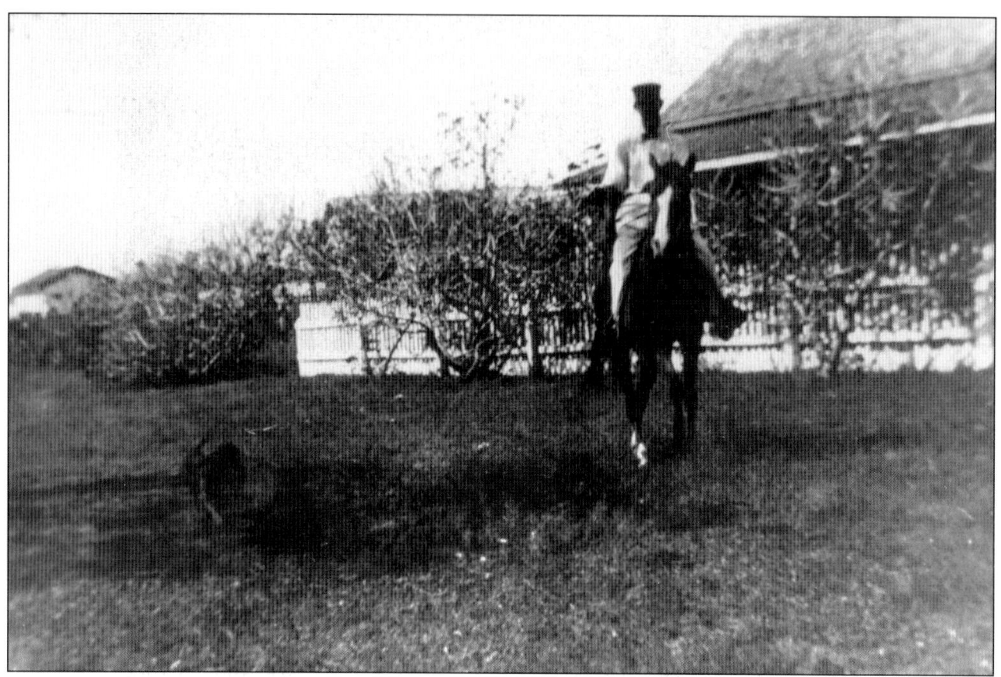

Carl O. Svendsen Near the Boathouse, c. 1920. Horses were the only way to get around the island for many years. The Svendsen's horse, J. L., was considered part of the family. (Courtesy of Coastal Georgia Historical Society.)

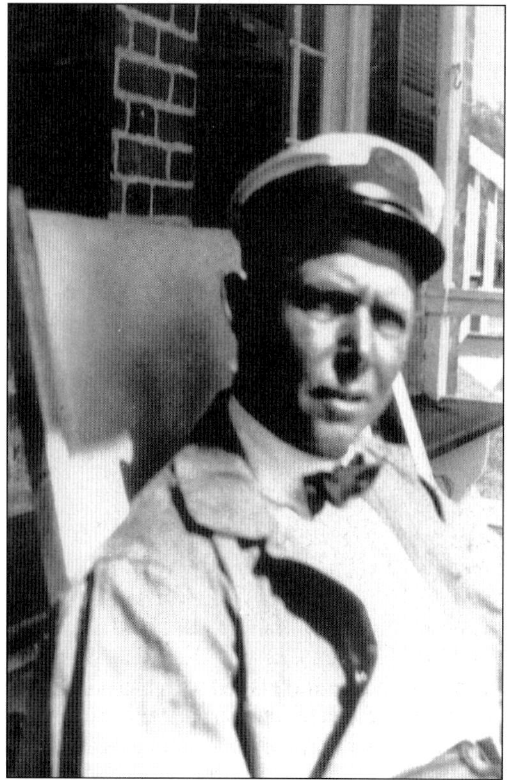

Svendsen on the Porch, 1922. Carl O. Svendsen served as the lighthouse keeper for 29 years. He retired in 1936. (Courtesy of Coastal Georgia Historical Society.)

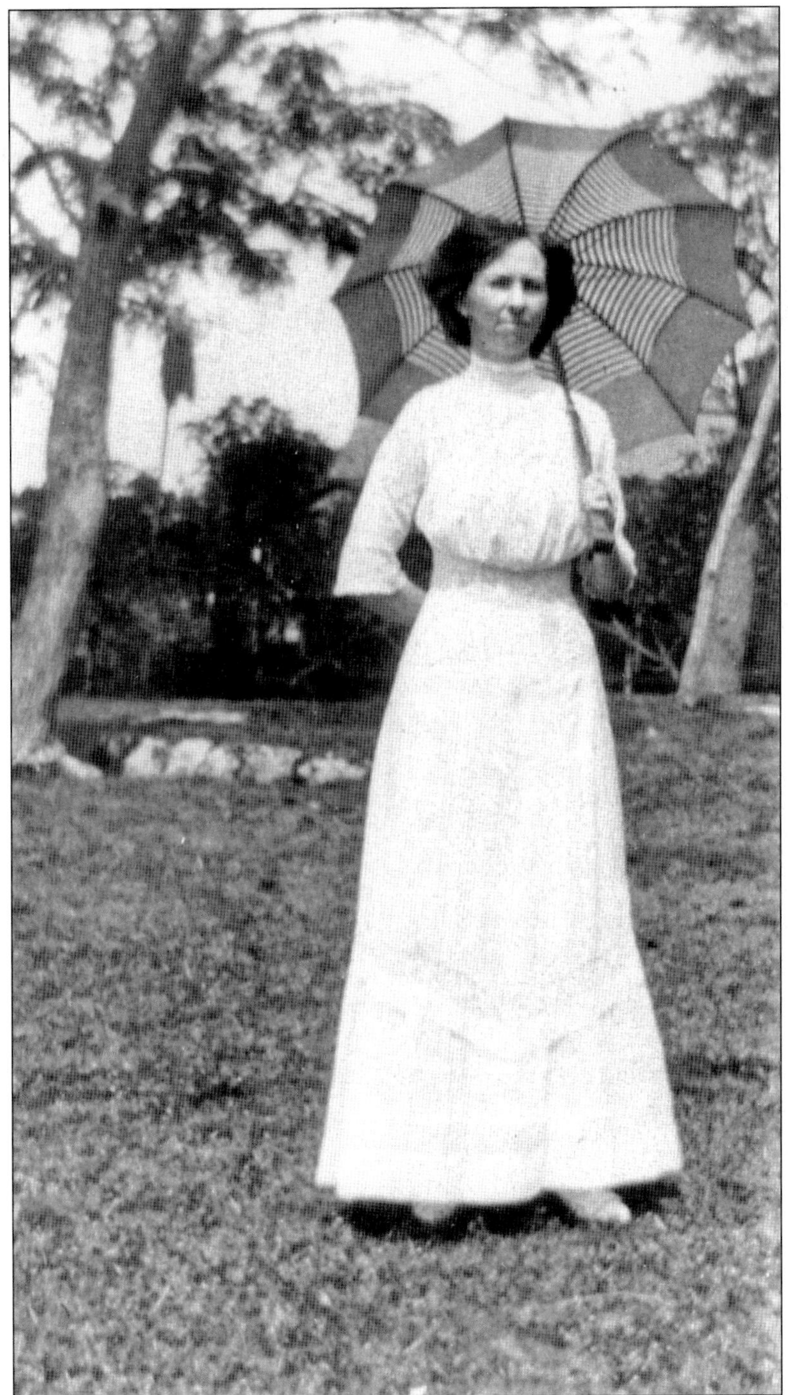

ANNA SVENDSEN, C. 1912. Anna met and married Carl O. Svendsen in 1902 and assisted him with keeping the station's records. As ships passed the lighthouse and saluted with blasts from the ship's whistle, Anna would raise the flag in return if it was daylight and wave a lantern if it was night. Anna rigged the flag so she could raise it from the porch. (Courtesy of Coastal Georgia Historical Society.)

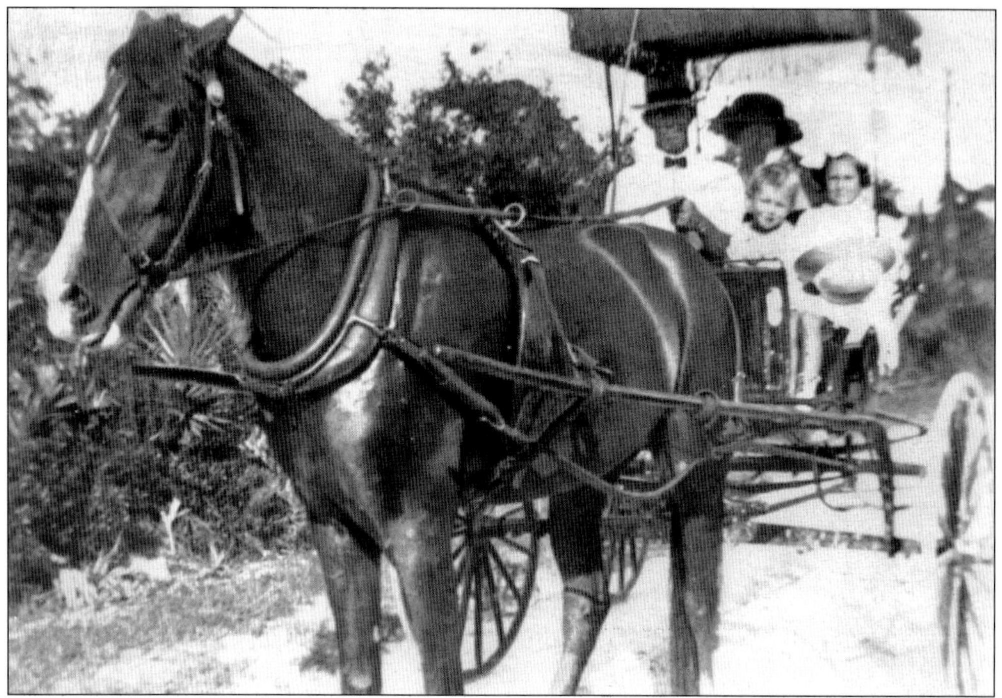

SVENDSEN FAMILY GOES TO CHURCH. The Svendsen family took their horse-and-buggy to Christ Church, located close to Fort Frederica. Christ Church was founded in the 1740s by Charles Wesley for the spiritual guidance of the Frederica settlers on St. Simons Island. The current building was erected in 1889. (Courtesy of Coastal Georgia Historical Society.)

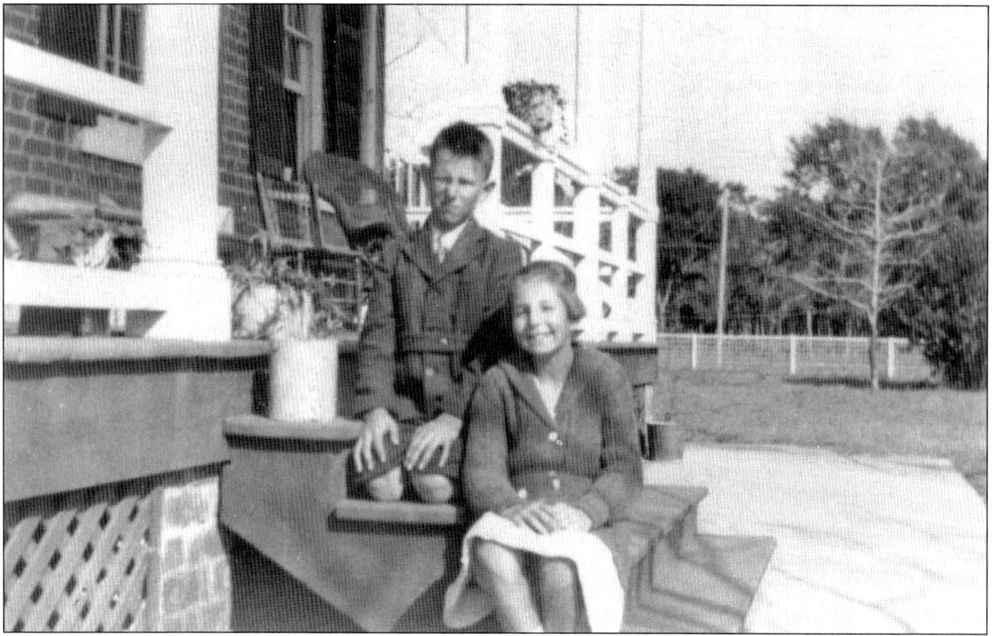

CHILDREN ON THE FRONT PORCH, 1922. Carl Svendsen Jr. and his sister Happy grew up at the St. Simons Light. Carl Jr. later became the assistant keeper. (Courtesy of Coastal Georgia Historical Society.)

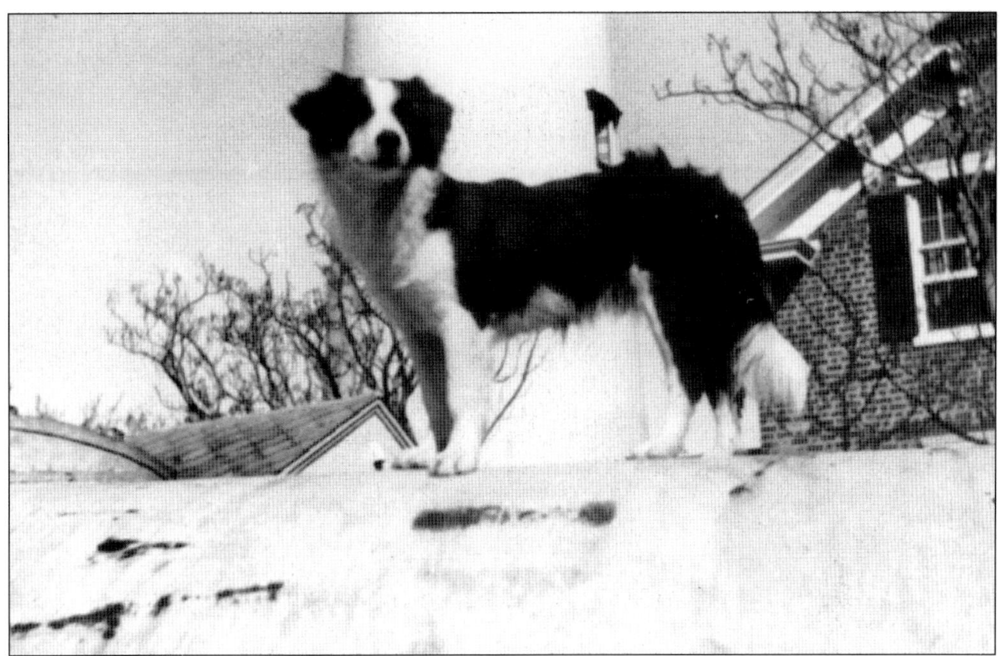

JINX, THE SVENDSEN'S DOG. Jinx was often credited with hearing the footsteps of an earlier keeper, Frederick Osborne, the lighthouse keeper from 1874 until 1880. He was killed by John Stevens, an assistant keeper, during a fight. (Courtesy of Coastal Georgia Historical Society.)

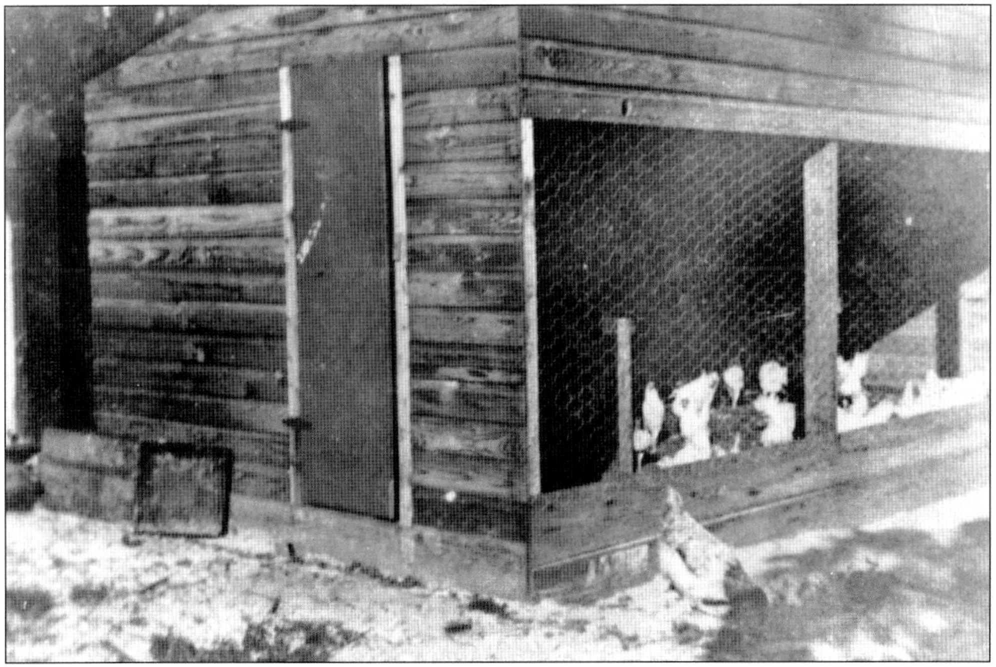

CHICKEN COOP. Lighthouse keepers often cultivated gardens and raised chickens to help feed their families. Many keepers took second jobs to make ends meet. (Courtesy of Coastal Georgia Historical Society.)

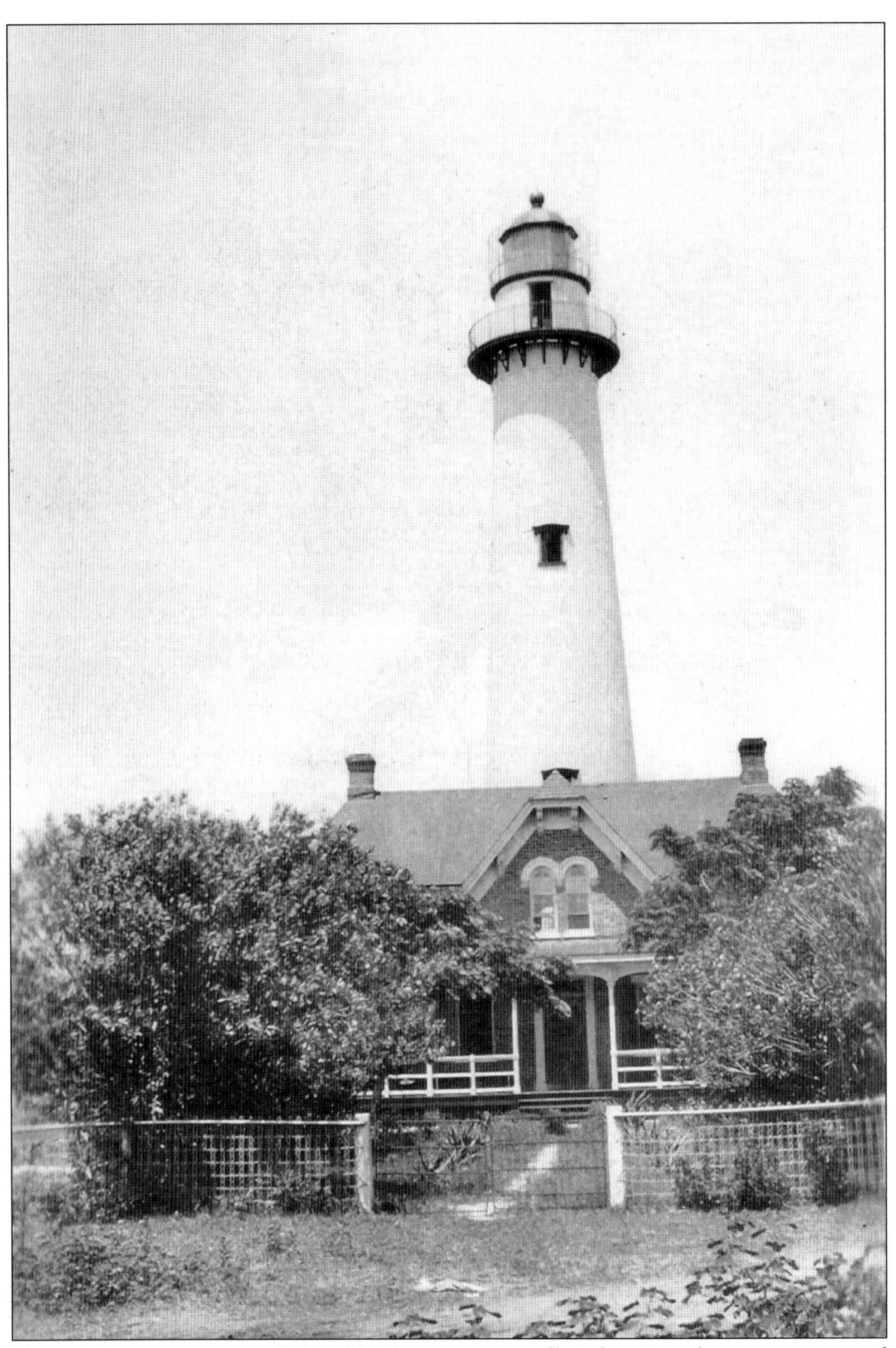

KEEPER'S QUARTERS, EARLY 1920S. Lighthouses were usually in locations that were remote, and conditions were often difficult. (Courtesy of Coastal Georgia Historical Society.)

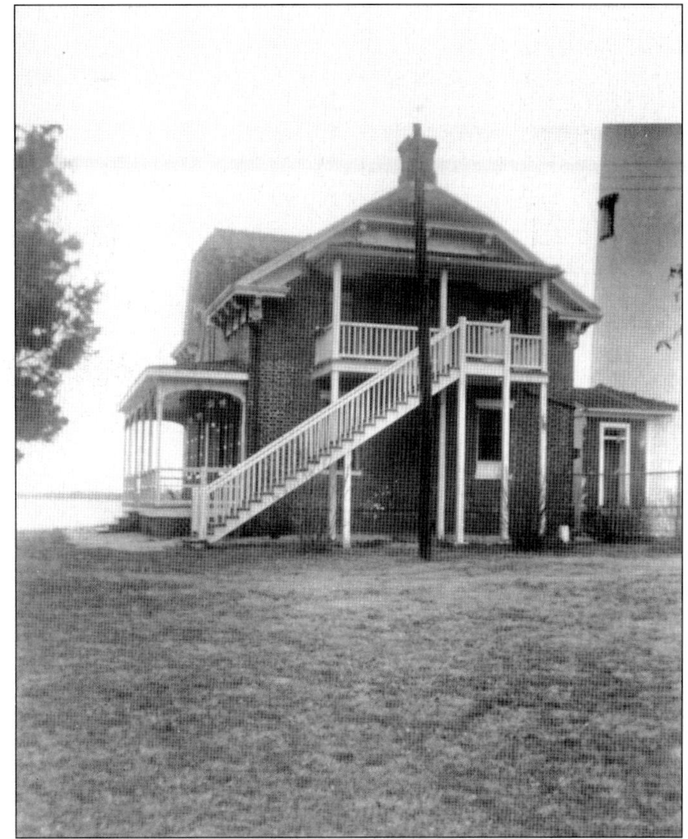

NORTH VIEW OF THE KEEPER'S QUARTERS. Around 1910, the dwelling was altered into two apartments by removing the central staircase and adding an exterior staircase, stoop, and door on the north side. (Courtesy of Coastal Georgia Historical Society.)

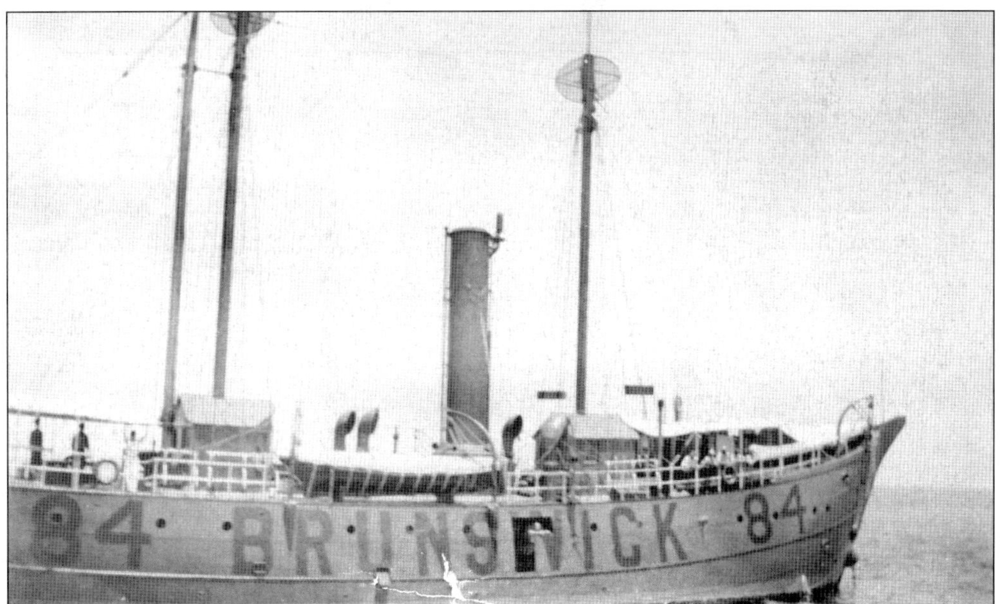

BRUNSWICK LIGHT SHIP, C. 1913. The Brunswick Light Ship was stationed 25 miles out to sea and had a crew of 25 men. It was in use from 1907 to 1929. The ship was replaced by the Brunswick lighted whistle buoy. (Courtesy of Coastal Georgia Historical Society.)

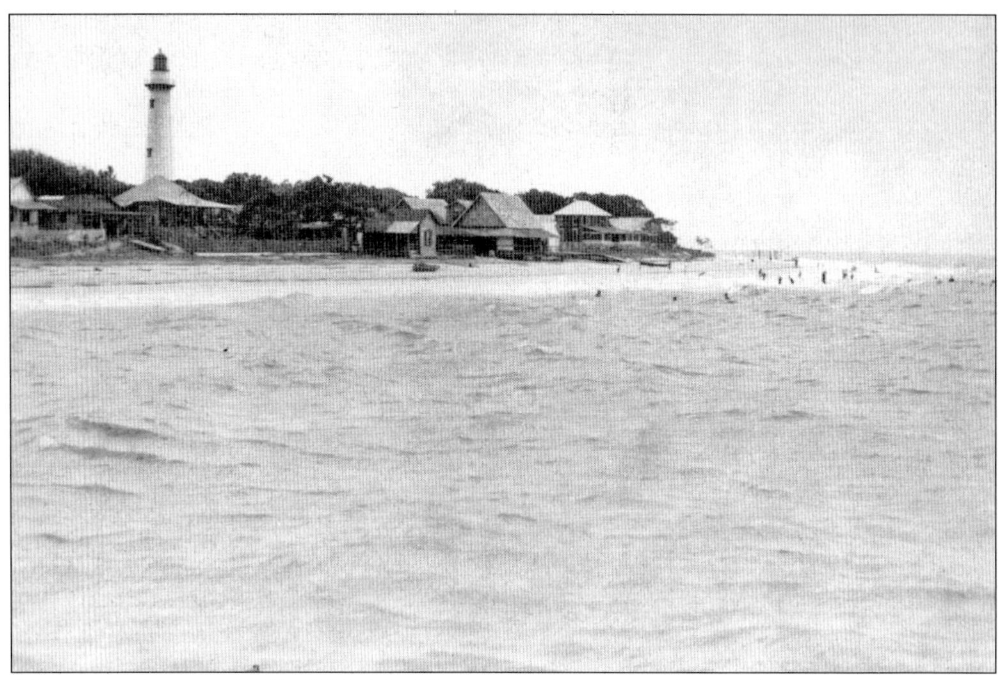

WAYCROSS COLONY, 1890–1900. The Waycross Colony was a cluster of rough cottages built at the base of the light. (Courtesy of Coastal Georgia Historical Society.)

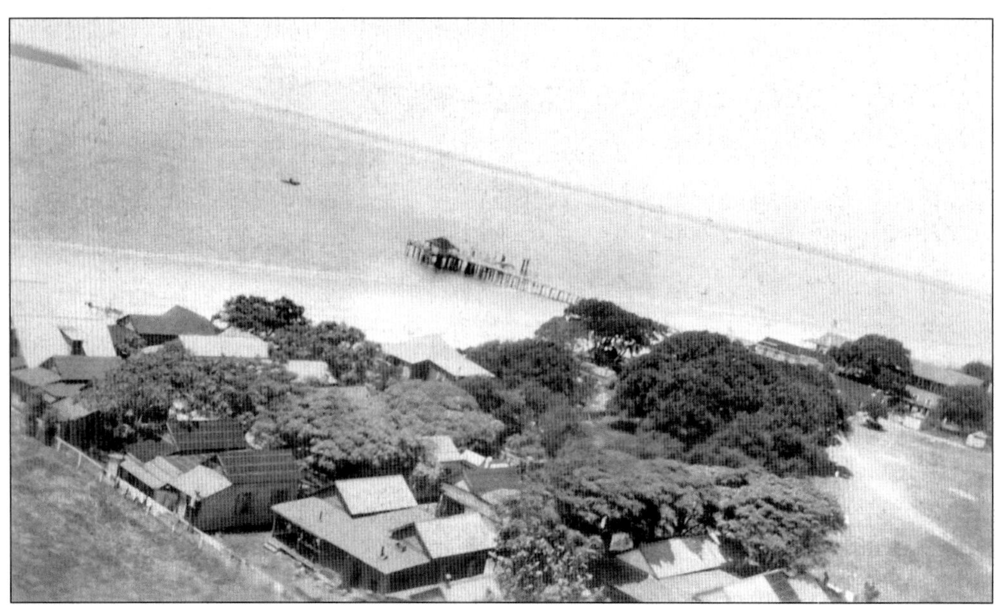

WAYCROSS COLONY. The colony burned in 1934. Here is a view from the top of the lighthouse. (Courtesy of Coastal Georgia Historical Society.)

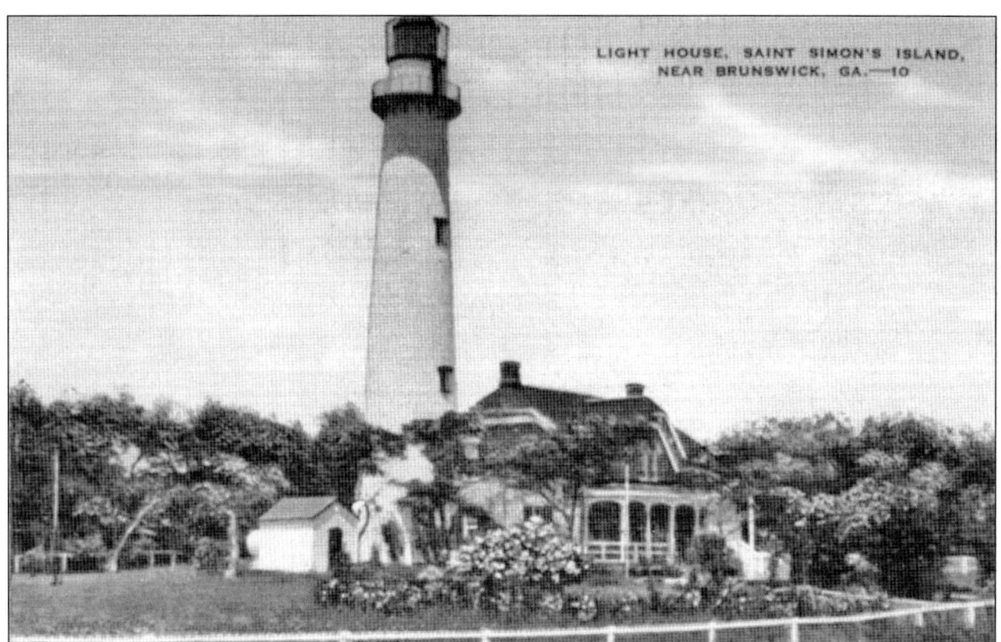

POSTCARD, C. 1940. In this postcard sent to Mrs. E. C. Bruce, the writer asks if anything can be done about cars speeding on East Beach. (Courtesy of Coastal Georgia Historical Society.)

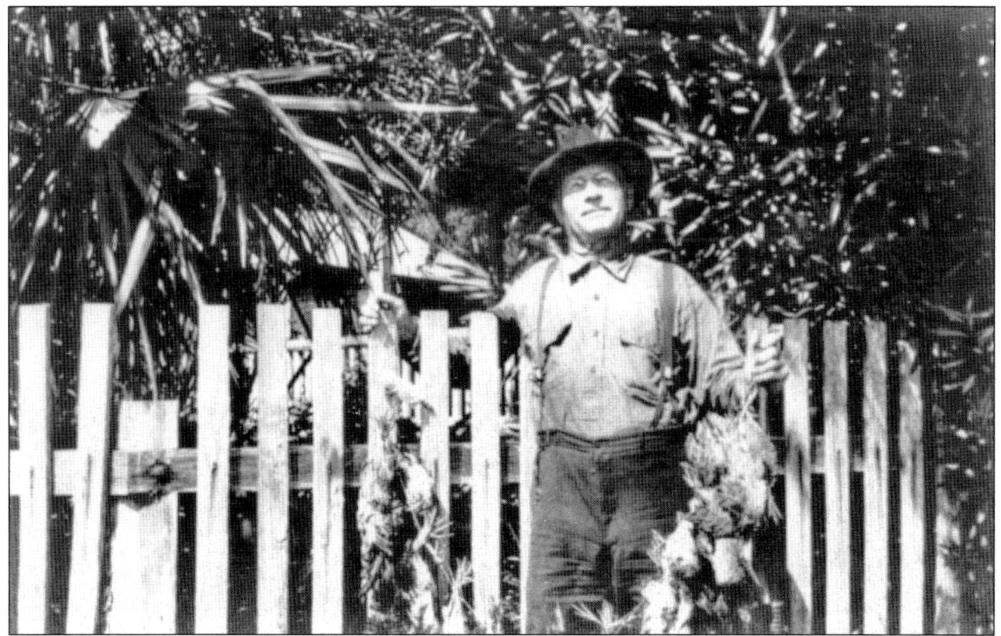

UNIDENTIFIED ASSISTANT, 1930S. This assistant keeper standing in the yard has shot himself quite a collection of birds. There were many stories of the good fishing and hunting available on St. Simons Island. (Courtesy of Coastal Georgia Historical Society.)

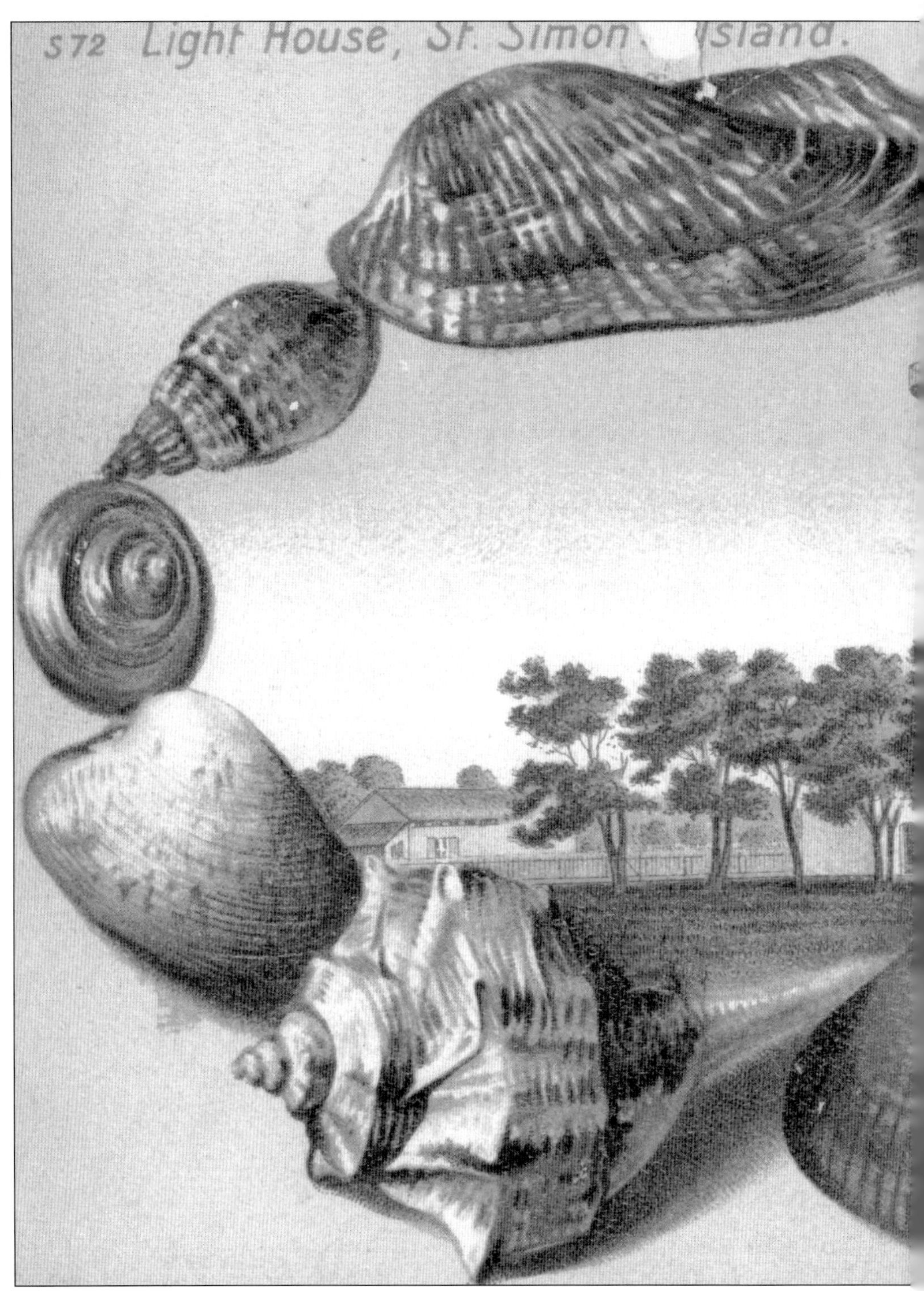

Postcard, 1940. A view of the lighthouse was often a favorite postcard to send home. On this card sent to Atlanta in 1940, the writer is also concerned about the automobiles speeding on the

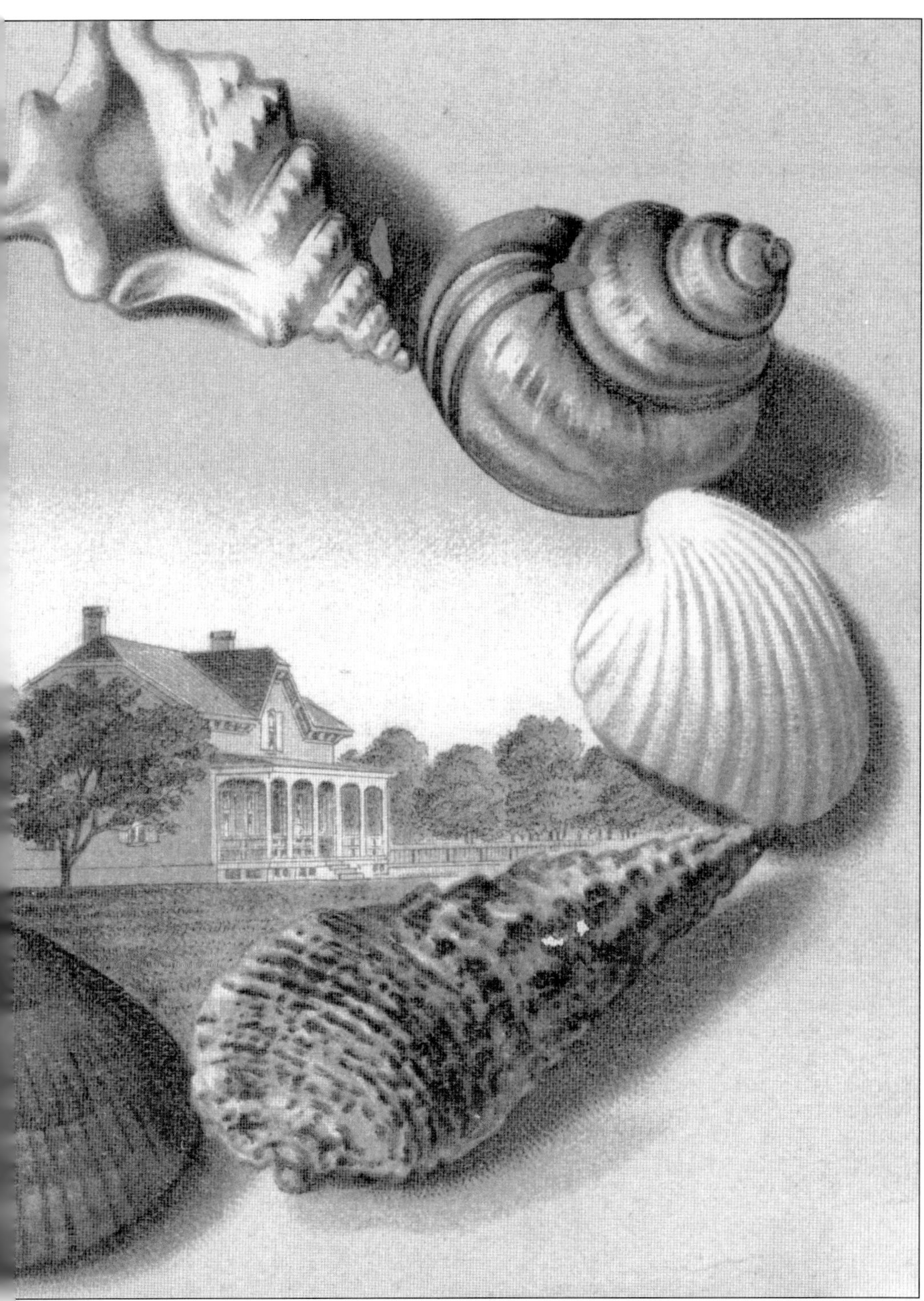

beach. (Courtesy of Coastal Georgia Historical Society.)

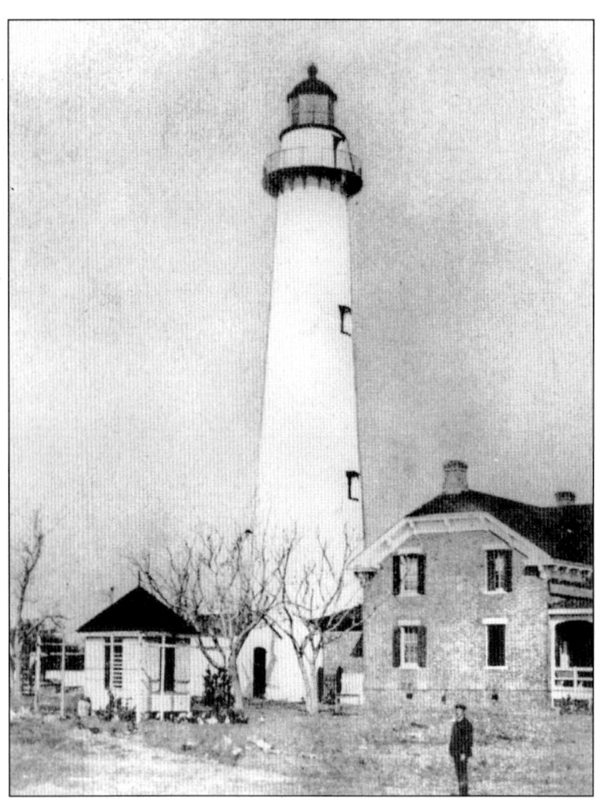

KEEPER IN YARD, 1936. Lighthouse keeper Arthur F. Hodge arrived on the island after the U.S. Coast Guard took over the administration of the lighthouse. (Courtesy of Coastal Georgia Historical Society.)

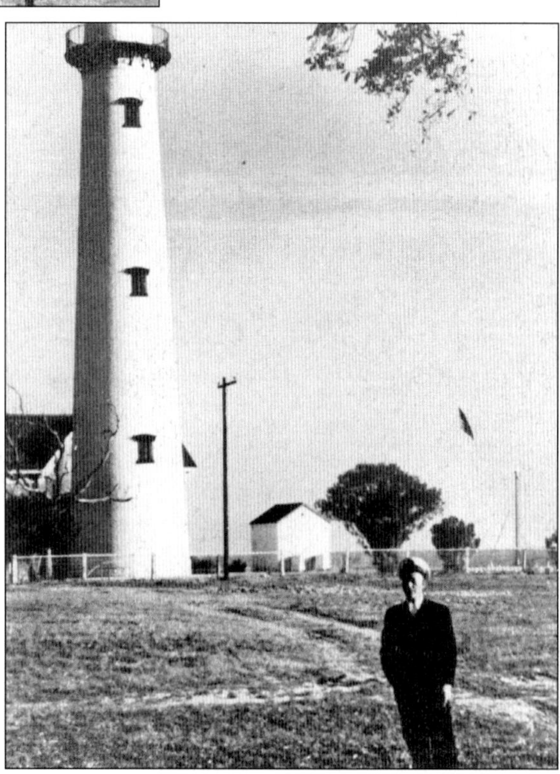

ARTHUR HODGE, C. 1936. Previously, lighthouses were administered by U.S. Lighthouse Establishment. (Courtesy of Coastal Georgia Historical Society.)

CHILDREN ON PORCH, LATE 1930S. Visitors were always welcome at the lighthouse. Neighborhood children often visited head keeper Arthur Hodge. (Courtesy of Coastal Georgia Historical Society.)

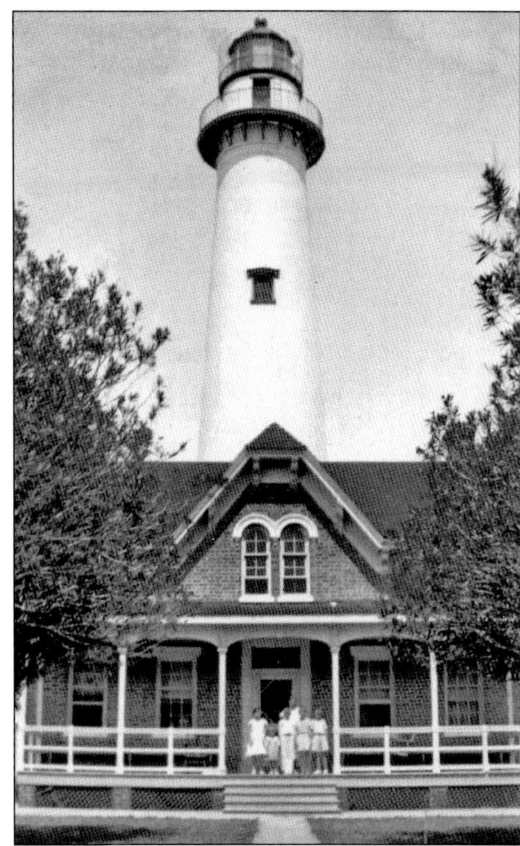

RELIEF KEEPER RAYMOND PINSON, 1944–1945. A relief keeper was someone who would fill in for a keeper who might be on vacation or ill. (Courtesy of Coastal Georgia Historical Society.)

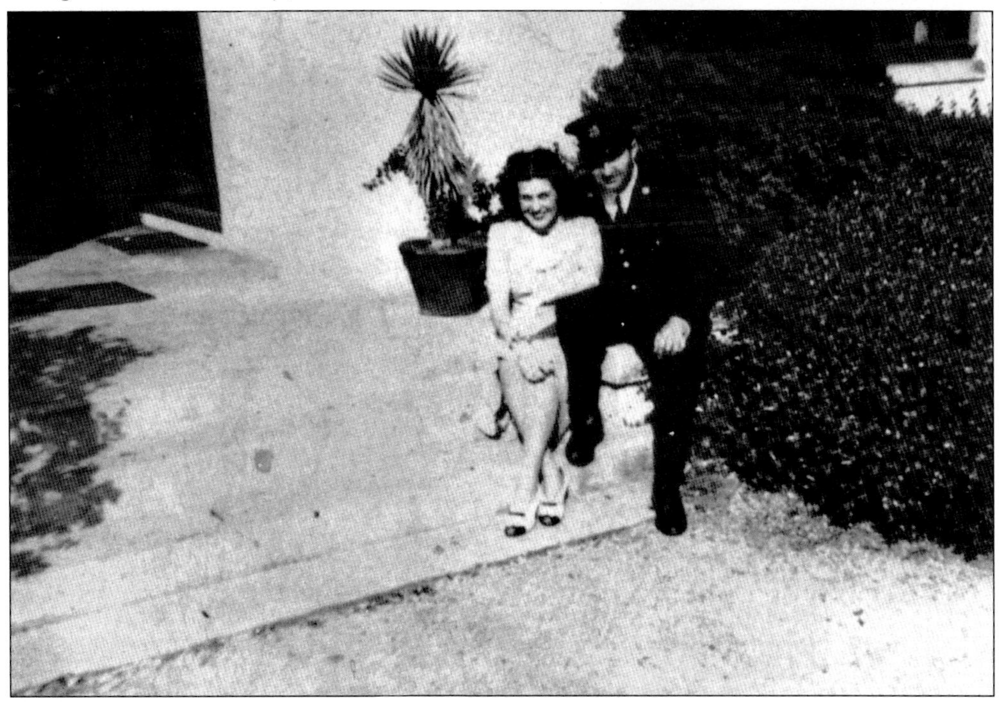

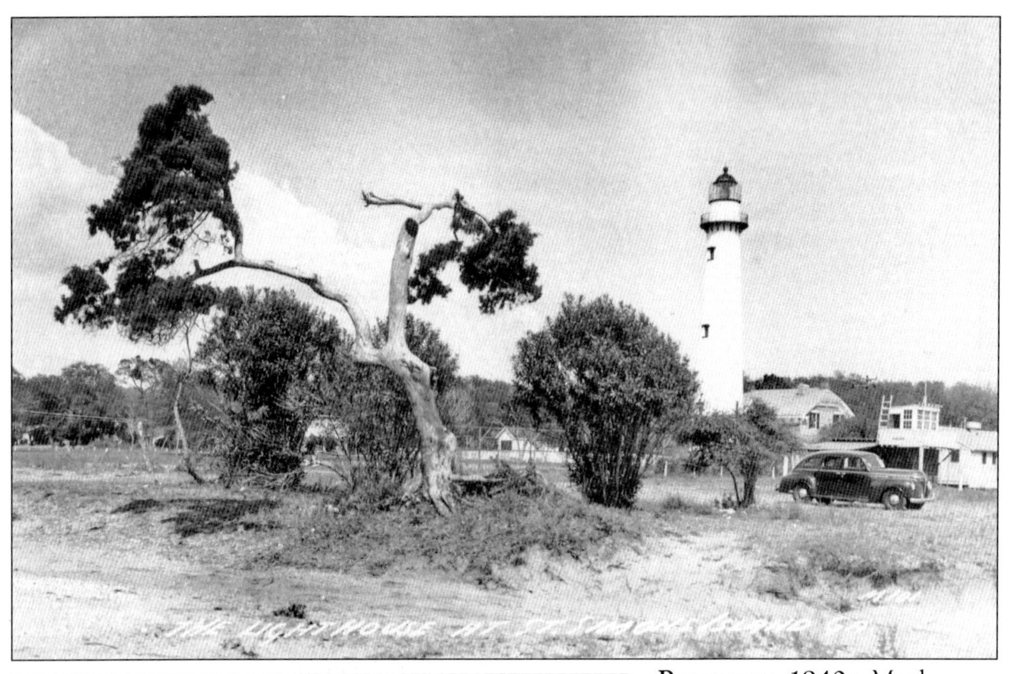

POSTCARD, 1940S. Much of the land seen in this photograph is no longer there. (Courtesy of Coastal Georgia Historical Society.)

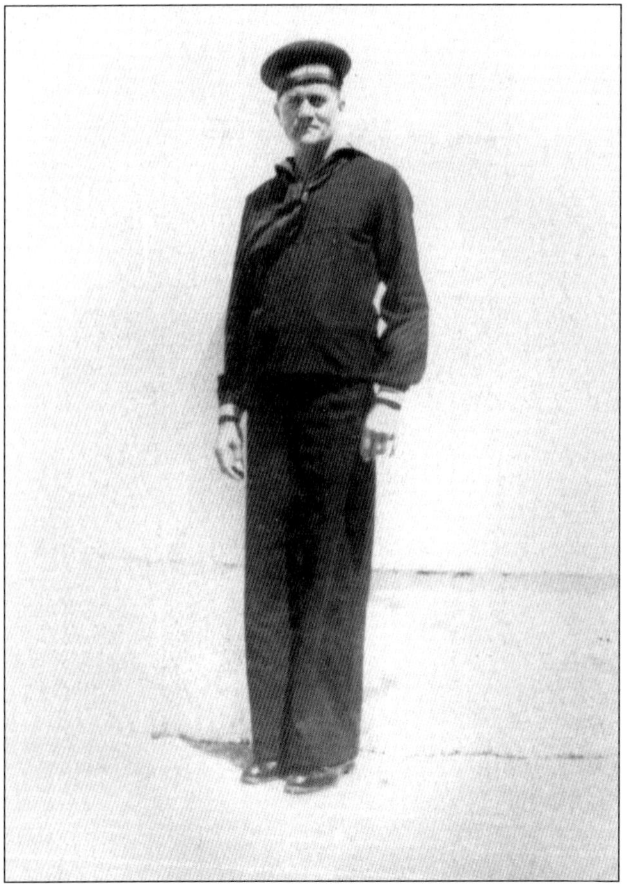

LAST KEEPER, C. 1942. The last lighthouse keeper was David O'Hagan, seen here. In 1953, the light was automated, and Chief O'Hagan retired. At that time, the tower room was removed. (Courtesy of Coastal Georgia Historical Society.)

David O'Hagan and Unidentified Mate. Light keepers were also responsible for search-and-rescue operations and were required to have skills in boating. (Courtesy of Coastal Georgia Historical Society.)

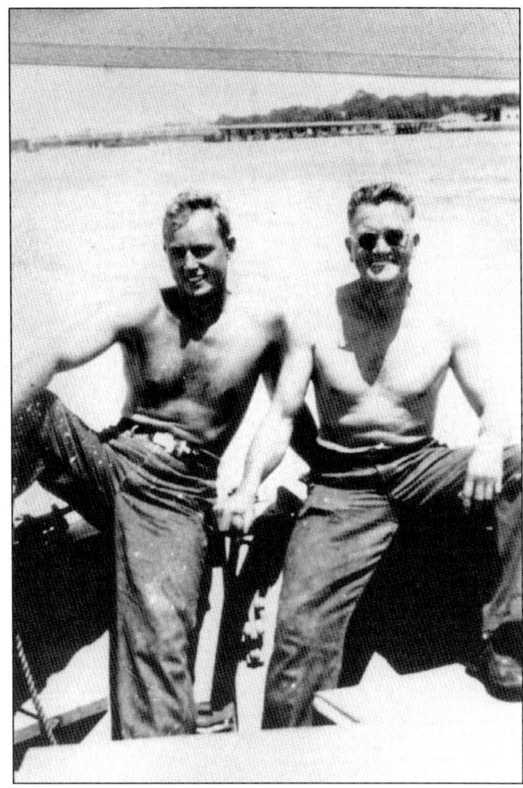

Lighthouse Maintenance, c. 1947. Work on the lighthouse never seemed to end. Here painting the lighthouse are, from left to right, Mr. Gregg, Chief O' Hagan, and Raymond Hale. (Courtesy of Coastal Georgia Historical Society.)

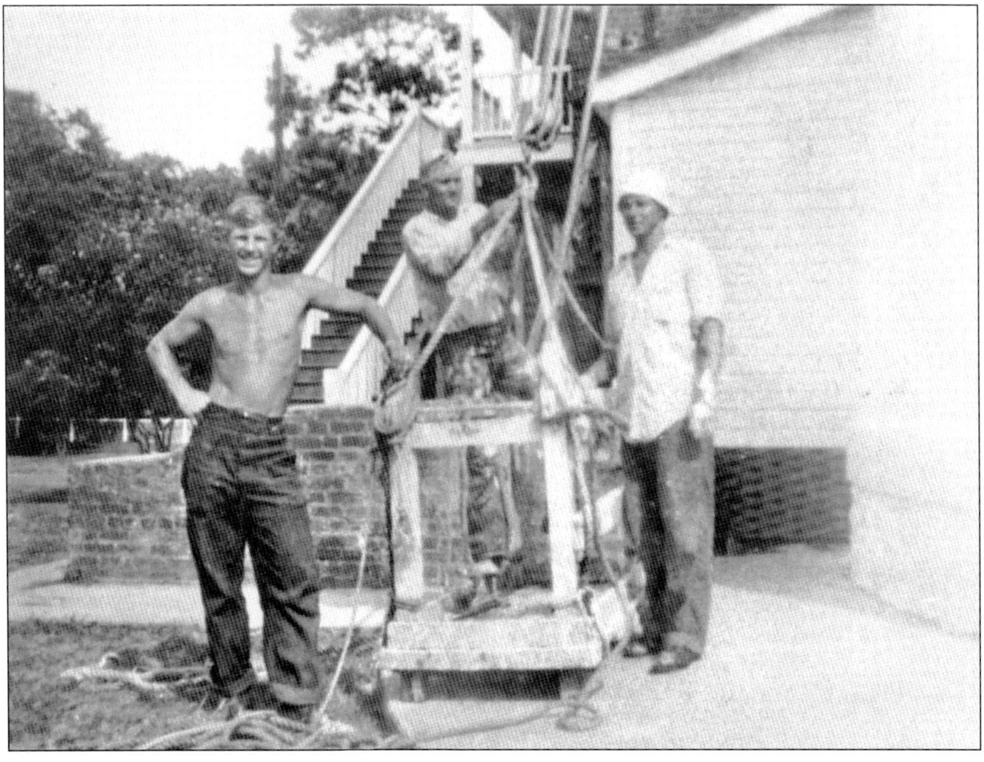

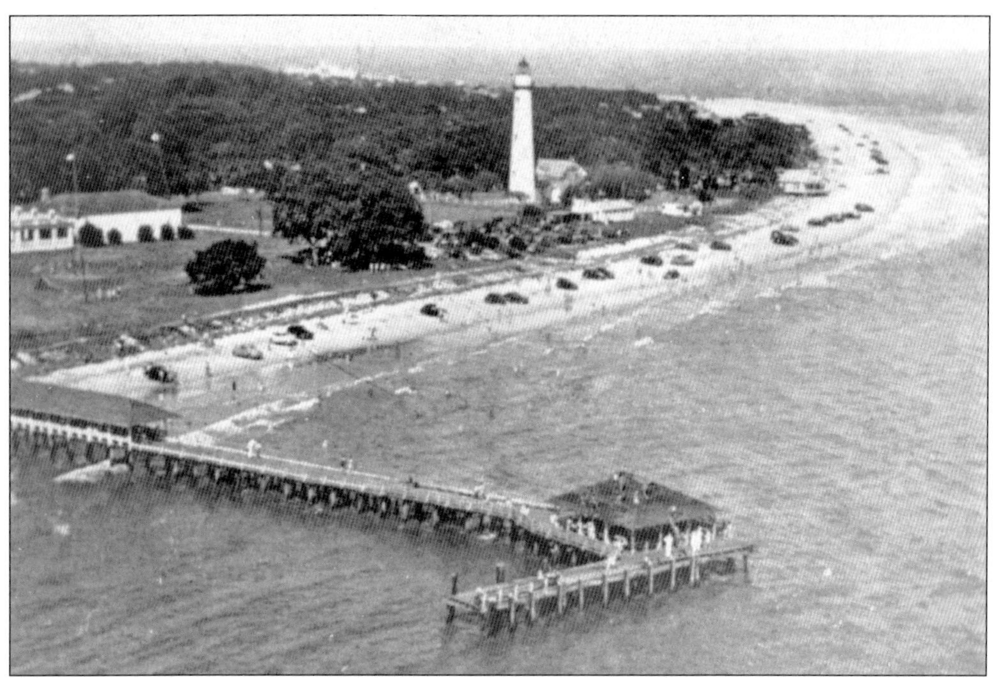

AERIAL OF BEACH. In the 1940s and 1950s, driving on the beach was popular along the eastern coastline. Today most beaches ban cars. (Courtesy of Coastal Georgia Historical Society.)

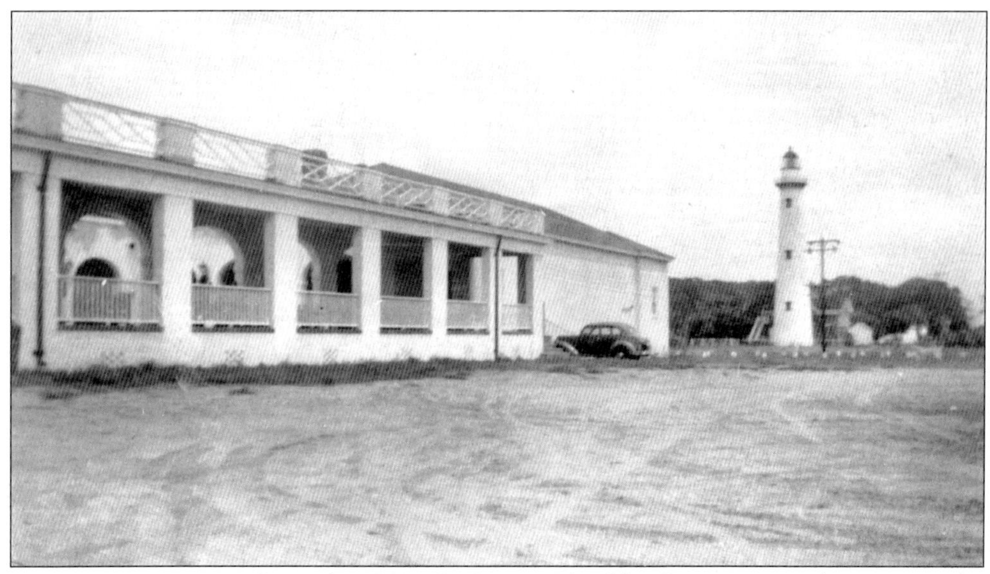

CASINO, EARLY 1940S. Since the 1880s, St. Simons Island has been a tourist destination. The old casino building, constructed between 1939 and 1940, was a place of recreation, like dances and socials, but never gambling. It still remains today, housing the library, a theater, and a visitor's center. (Courtesy of Coastal Georgia Historical Society.)

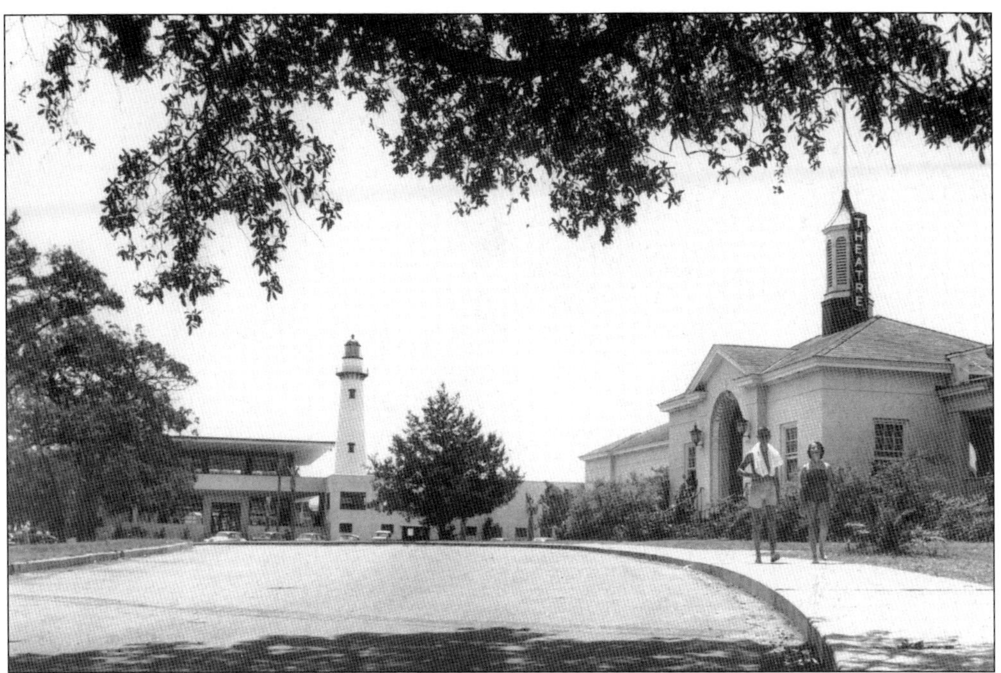

New Casino, c. 1970. In the early 1950s, a new casino was built next to the lighthouse. It is no longer standing. (Courtesy of Coastal Georgia Historical Society.)

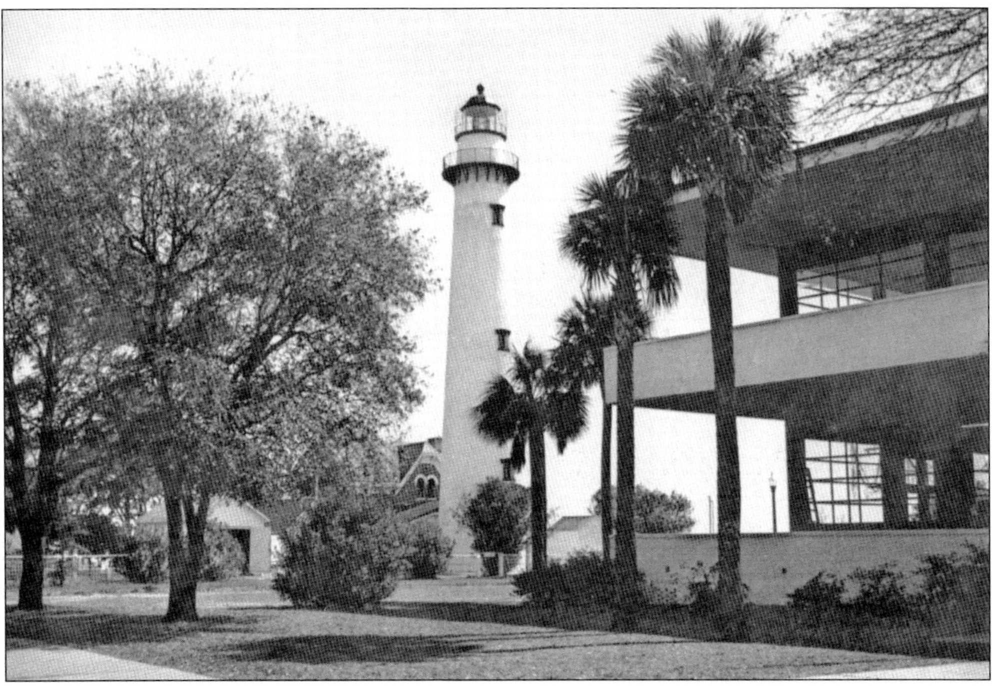

New Casino, c. 1990. This public building featured a community pool, two large rooms that could be opened for maximum airflow, and a bowling alley. The pool remains today. (Courtesy of Coastal Georgia Historical Society.)

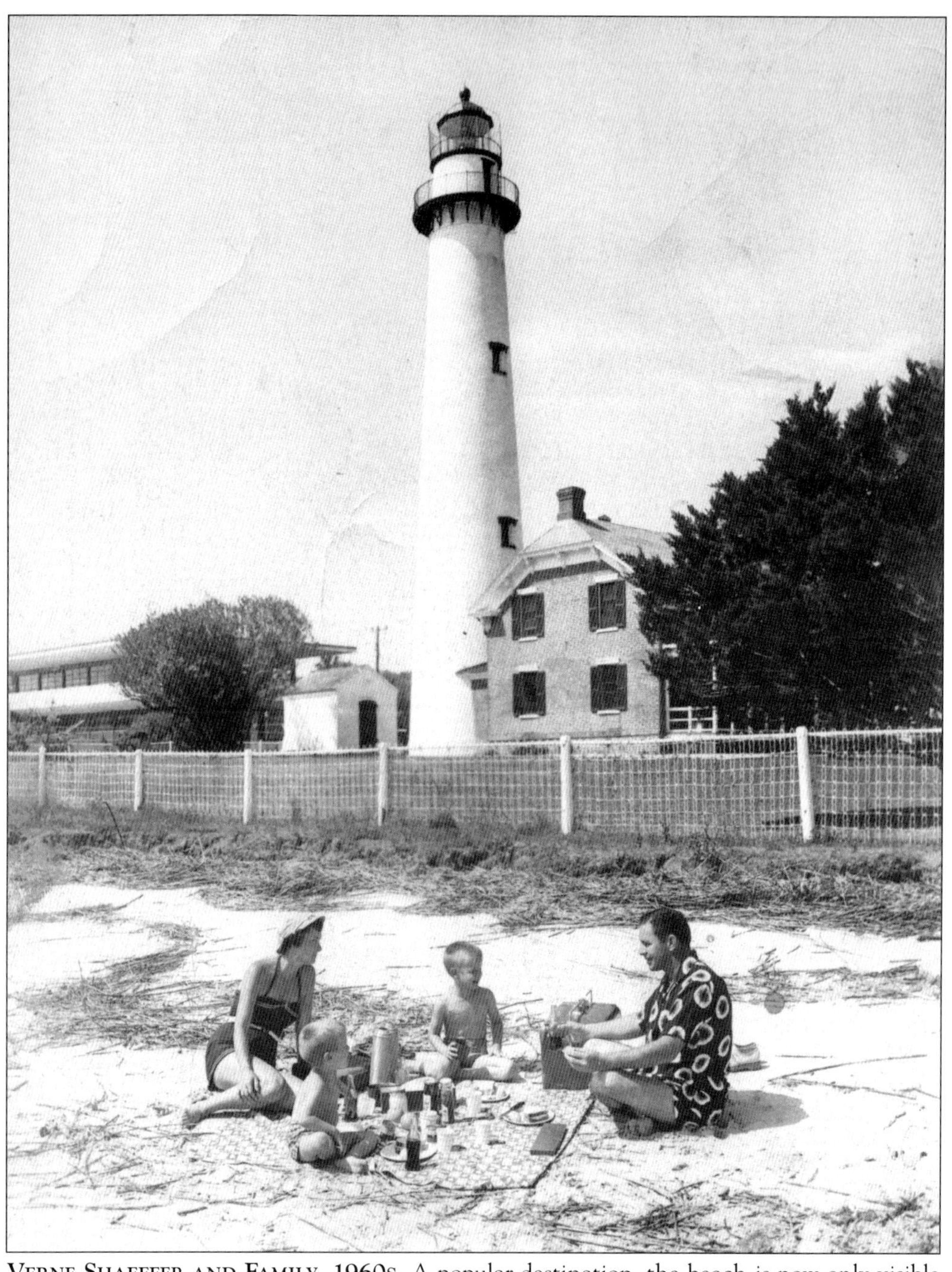

VERNE SHAEFFER AND FAMILY, 1960S. A popular destination, the beach is now only visible during low tides. (Courtesy of Coastal Georgia Historical Society.)

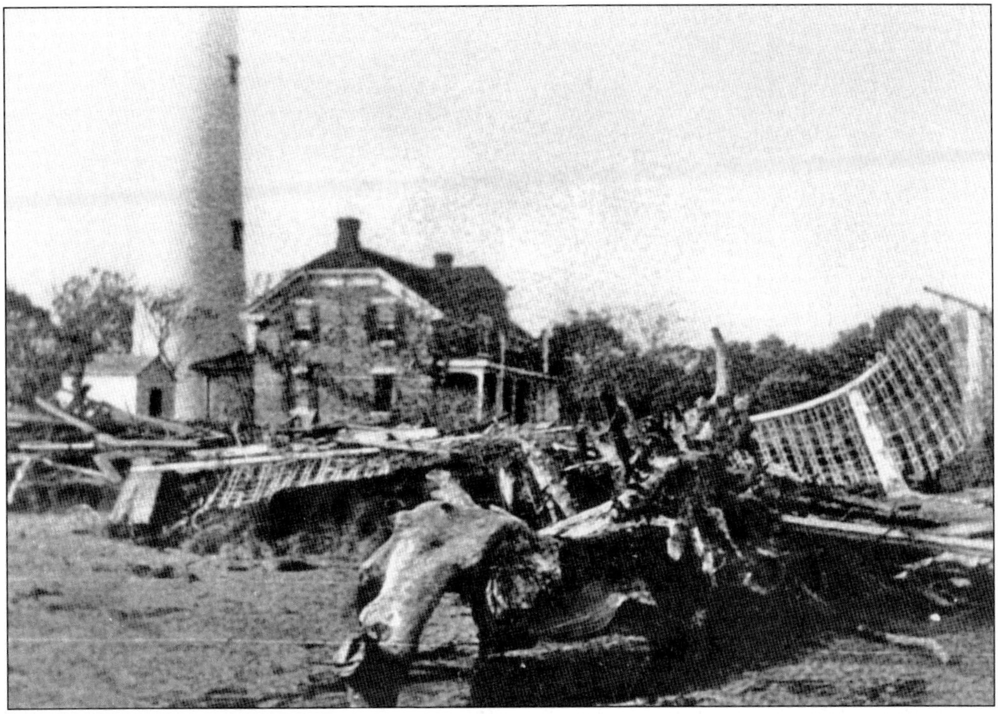

STORM, 1926. Storms have altered the coast of Georgia for many generations. After a 1926 storm, debris is scattered along the beach. (Courtesy of Coastal Georgia Historical Society.)

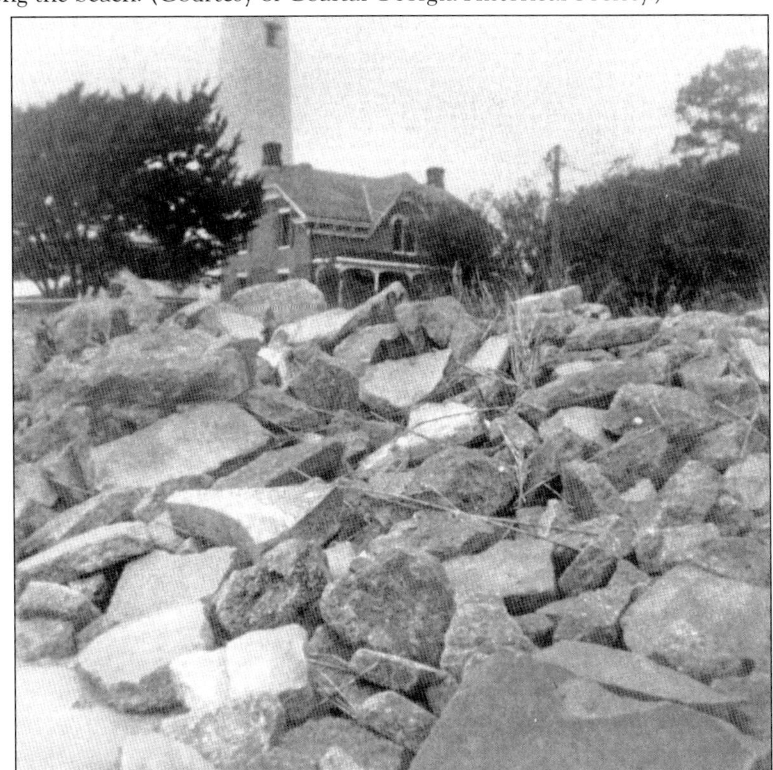

JOHNSON ROCKS, 1995. After Hurricane Dora in 1964, rocks were put in place along the beach by the lighthouse to help slow erosion. Today they are known as the Johnson Rocks, named for Pres. Lyndon B. Johnson. (Courtesy of Coastal Georgia Historical Society.)

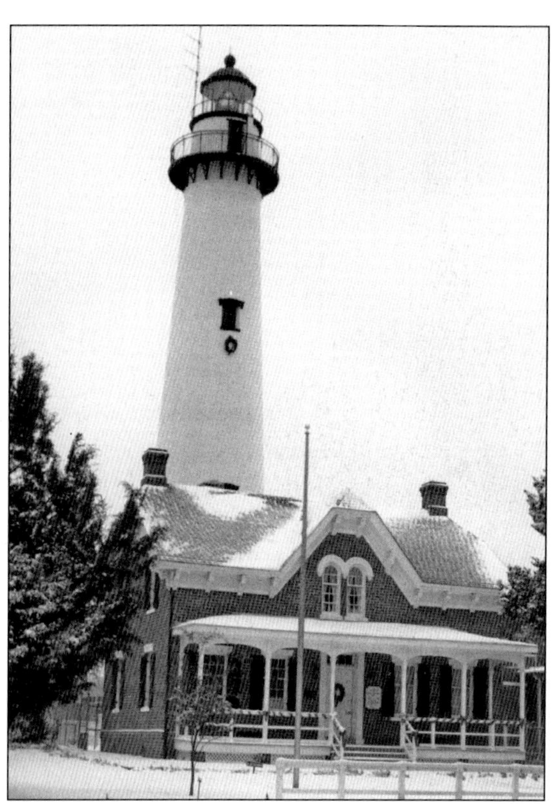

UNUSUAL WEATHER, 1989. A freak snowstorm along the Georgia coast dusted the light. (Courtesy of Coastal Georgia Historical Society.)

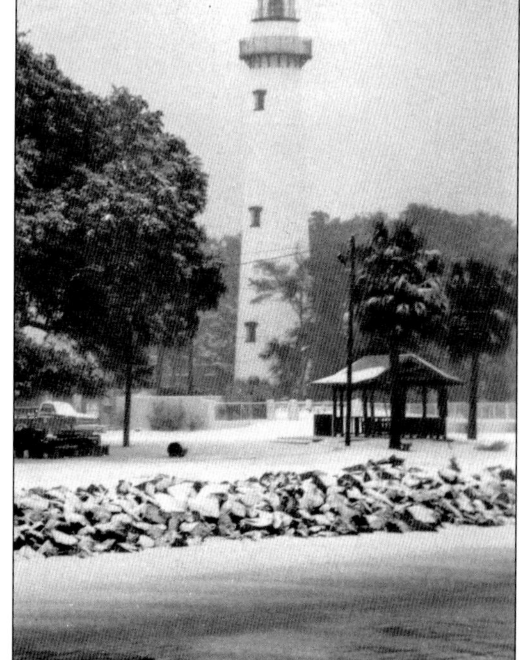

SNOWSTORM, 1989. While it is common for many lighthouses around the world to be covered in snow part of the year, this region of Georgia had not seen snow since the early 1970s. (Courtesy of Coastal Georgia Historical Society.)

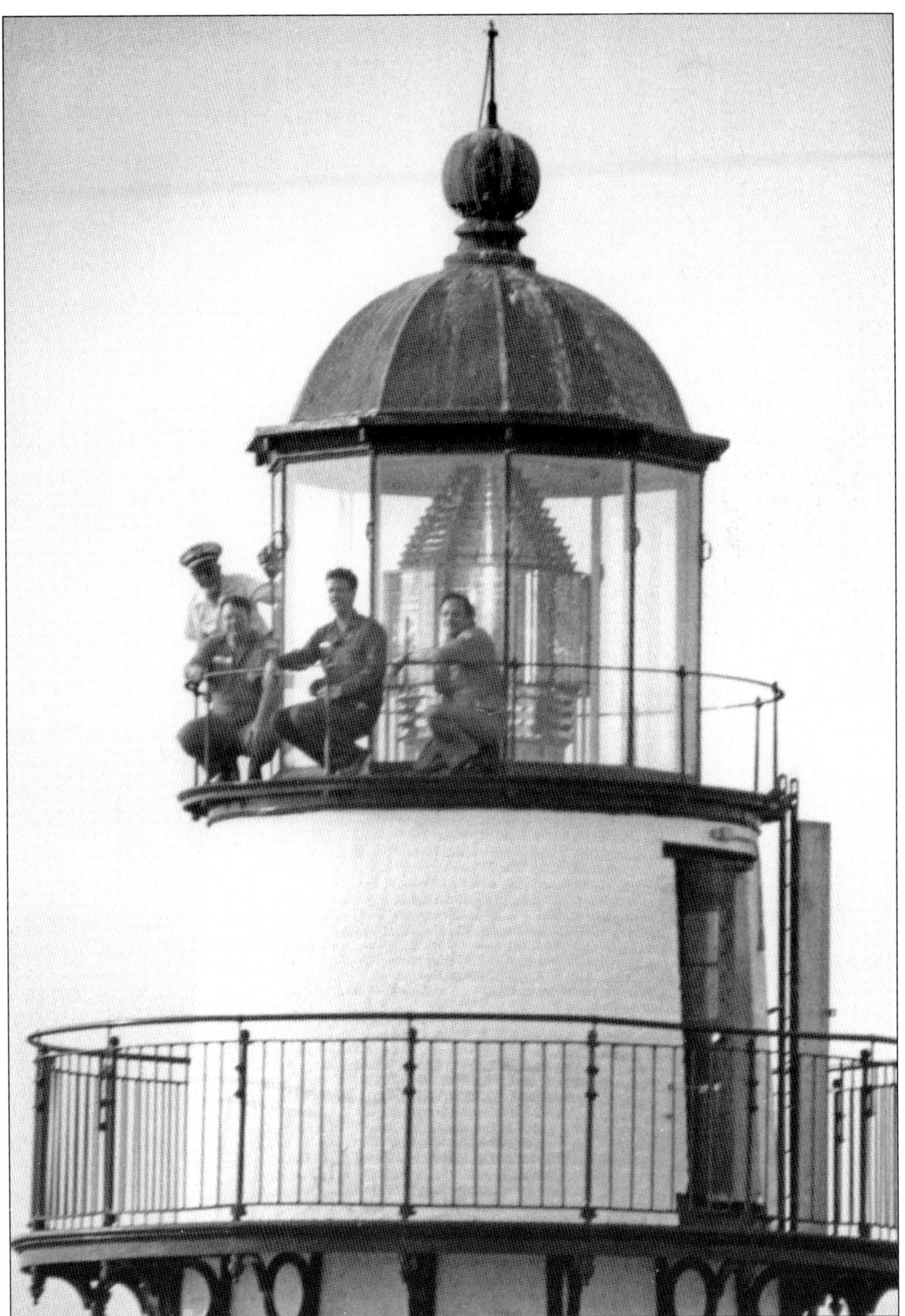

COAST GUARD AUXILIARY, 1997. The light remains active and is maintained by the U.S. Coast Guard Auxiliary. Pictured from left to right are Burney Long, Bob West, Jeff Cole, and David Melvin. (Courtesy of Coastal Georgia Historical Society.)

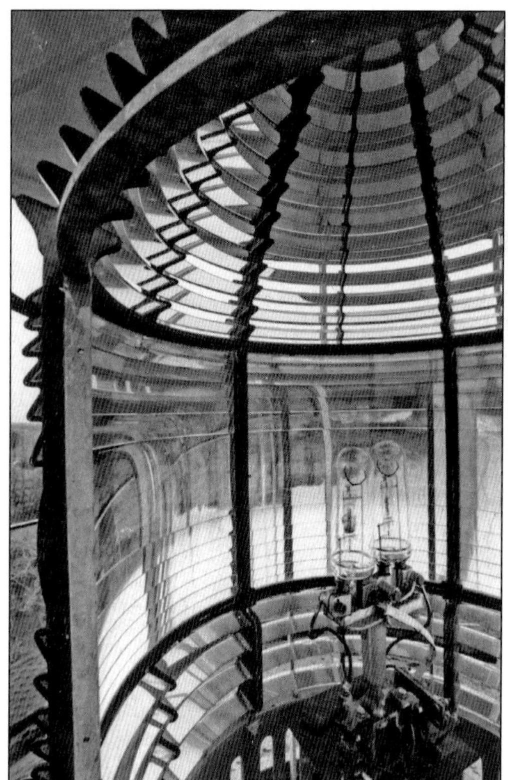

LIGHTHOUSE LENS, 1996. The original, third-order Fresnel lens from the 1872 lighthouse remains today. (Courtesy of Coastal Georgia Historical Society.)

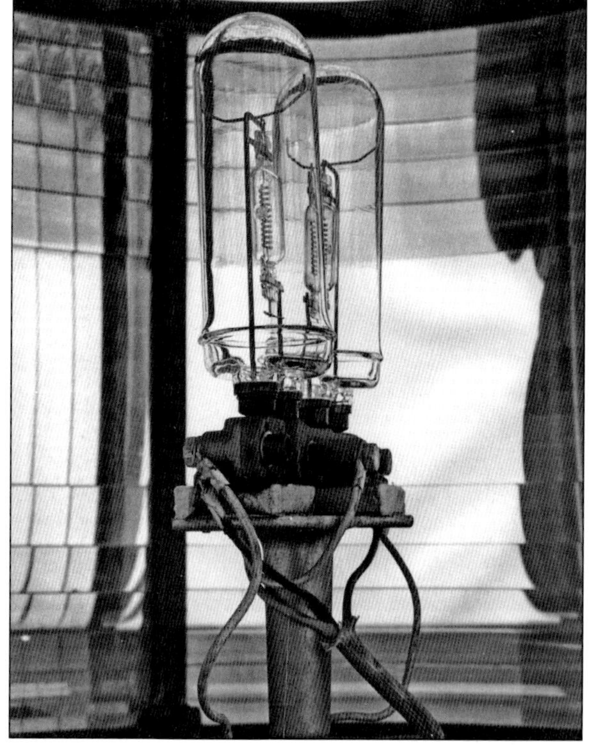

BULB CHANGER, C. 1978. The light is equipped with a bulb changer. When one bulb burns out, the other automatically switches on. The light has a rotation pattern of one flash per minute and can be seen 23 miles out to sea. (Courtesy of Coastal Georgia Historical Society.)

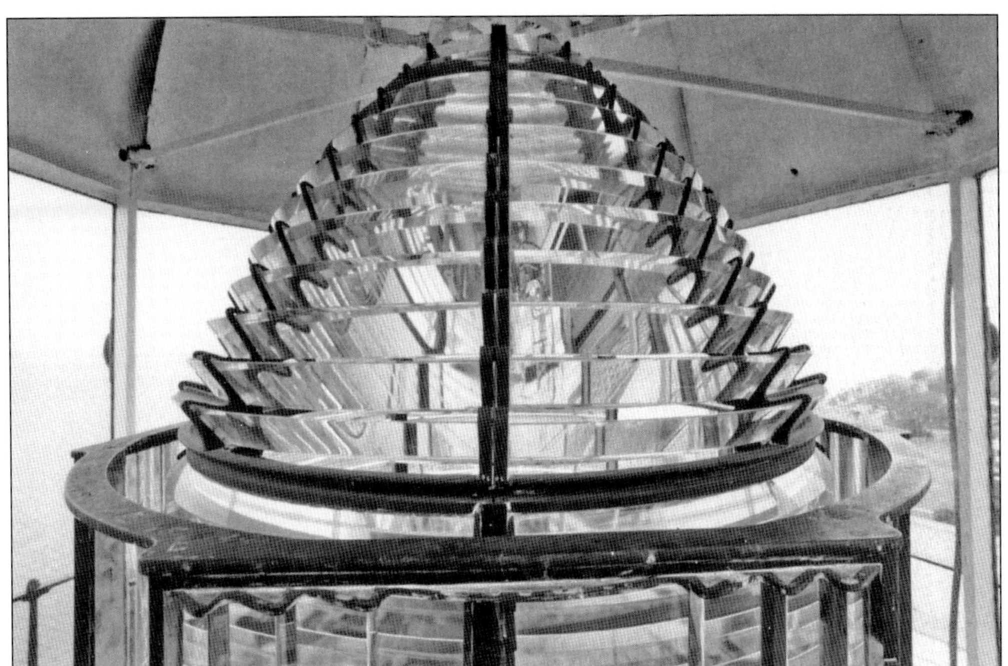

Fresnel Lens, 1996. This type of lens was developed in France by Augustin-Jean Fresnel, a physicist. His design enabled the construction of lenses with a large aperture and a short focal length without the weight and volume of a large amount of material. Compared to earlier lenses, the Fresnel lens is much thinner, thus passing more light and allowing lighthouses to be visible over much longer distances. (Courtesy of Coastal Georgia Historical Society.)

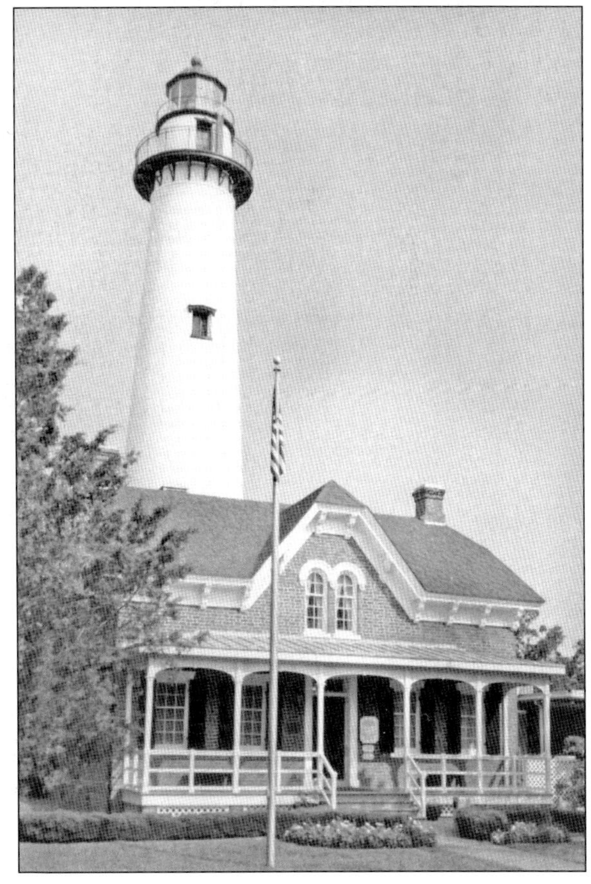

St. Simons Light and Keeper's Dwelling, 1995. In 1975, the Coastal Georgia Historical Society leased the building, completed its restoration, and opened the dwelling as a museum. In 1984, the society leased the lighthouse, allowing people to again climb to the top. (Courtesy of Coastal Georgia Historical Society.)

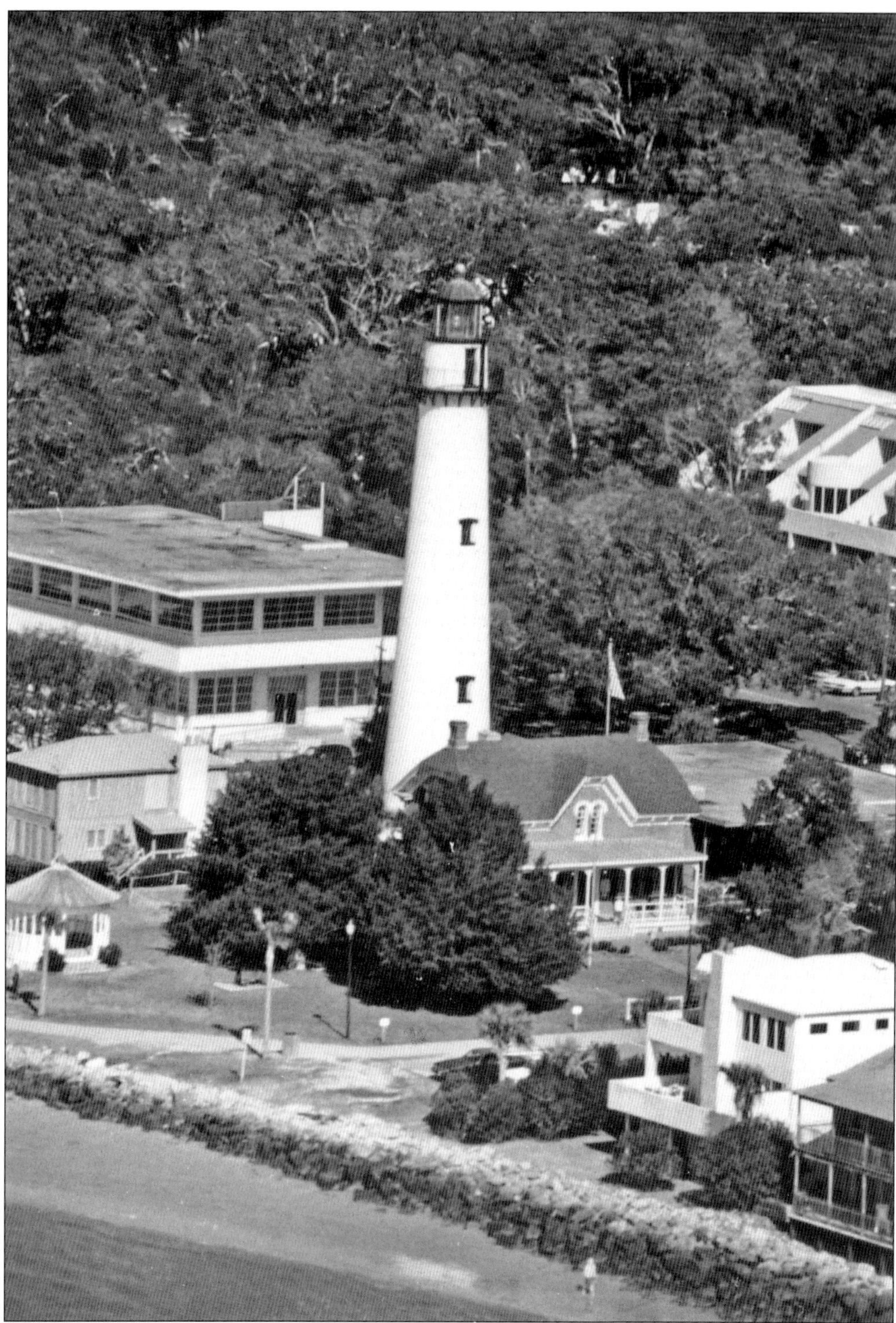

AERIAL VIEW, 1996. Today the light remains active and is owned by the Coastal Georgia Historical Society. It was turned over to the society in 2004 through the National Lighthouse Preservation Act. (Courtesy of Coastal Georgia Historical Society.)

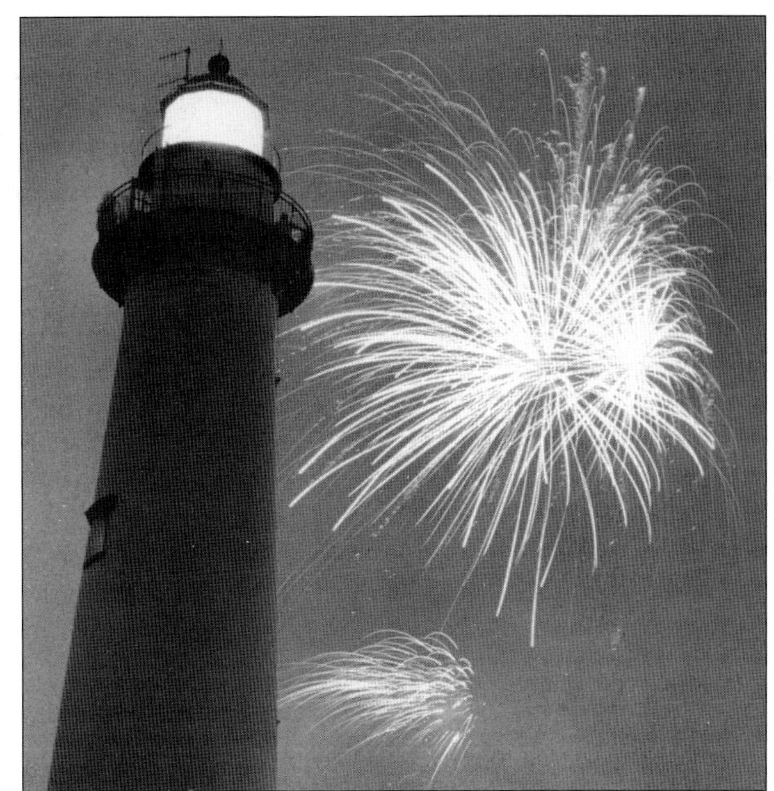

FOURTH OF JULY FIREWORKS, 1990S. Today the St. Simons Island Lighthouse continues to greet ships coming into the port of Brunswick. (Courtesy of Amelia Island Images.)

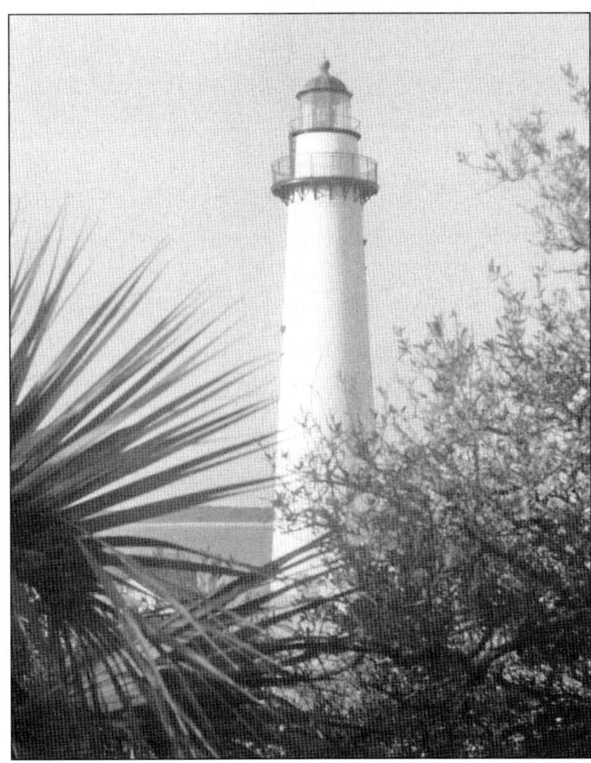

LIGHT THROUGH THREE PALMS, C. 1993. The St. Simons Island Light remains an icon for many in the Golden Isles. (Courtesy of Coastal Georgia Historical Society.)

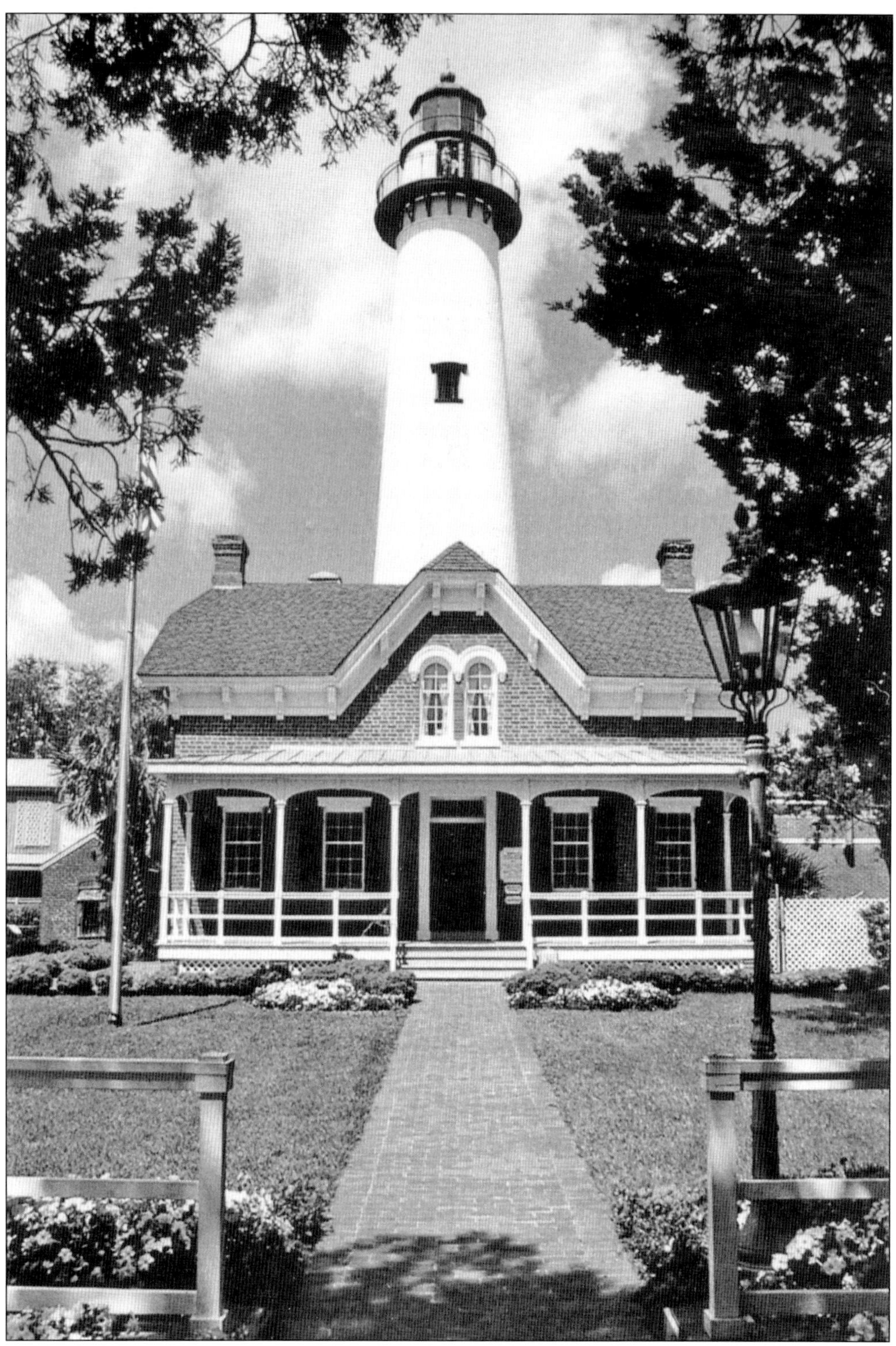

ST. SIMONS ISLAND LIGHT, C. 2000. Known today as the gem of the coast, the St. Simons Island Lighthouse stands as a remembrance to past generations. (Courtesy of Amelia Island Images.)

Four

GEORGIA'S OTHER LIGHTS

Many lighthouses had other lights close to their locations that complemented them. Directly across Doboy Sound from the Sapelo Island Lighthouse was the Wolf Island Light. Lit in 1822, this small lighthouse was built out of Georgia pine. The purpose of this light was to act as a range beacon.

The Savannah River lights also helped guide ships into port. This river navigation system included such lights as the New Channel Range and the Fort Jackson lights: the Fort Jackson Range (front) and the Barnwell Place Range.

About 12 miles east of the Savannah port, the Cockspur Lighthouse marks the south channel of the Savannah River and is still standing today. This light sits on a small islet, which is covered during high tide and just off the southeastern tip of Cockspur Island. The first constructed, brick tower was built on Cockspur Island between March 1837 and November 1839. This tower was used as a day mark. In 1848, a New York architect named John Norris was contracted to supervise construction of an illuminated station. Norris's duties were to repair, alter, and put up lanterns and lights on Cockspur Island and to erect a suitable keeper's house.

However, in 1854, the structure was destroyed by a hurricane. The tower was rebuilt and enlarged on the same foundation the next year. With the beginning of the Civil War, and the Cockspur light was temporarily extinguished, but the lighthouse suffered only minor damage during the war. On April 25, 1866, the lighthouse was relit and painted white for use as a day mark.

Hurricanes plague all lighthouses, and the Cockspur light was no exception. Massive storms struck Cockspur Island in 1881 and 1893. In 1881, the water rose to 23 feet above sea level and destroyed the keeper's residence. The residence was again destroyed in 1893, after which a two-story house was built atop Fort Pulaski for the light keeper. The light was finally extinguished in 1909. After many years of neglect, the Cockspur Lighthouse, now under the care of the National Park Service, was relit in a 2007 ceremony.

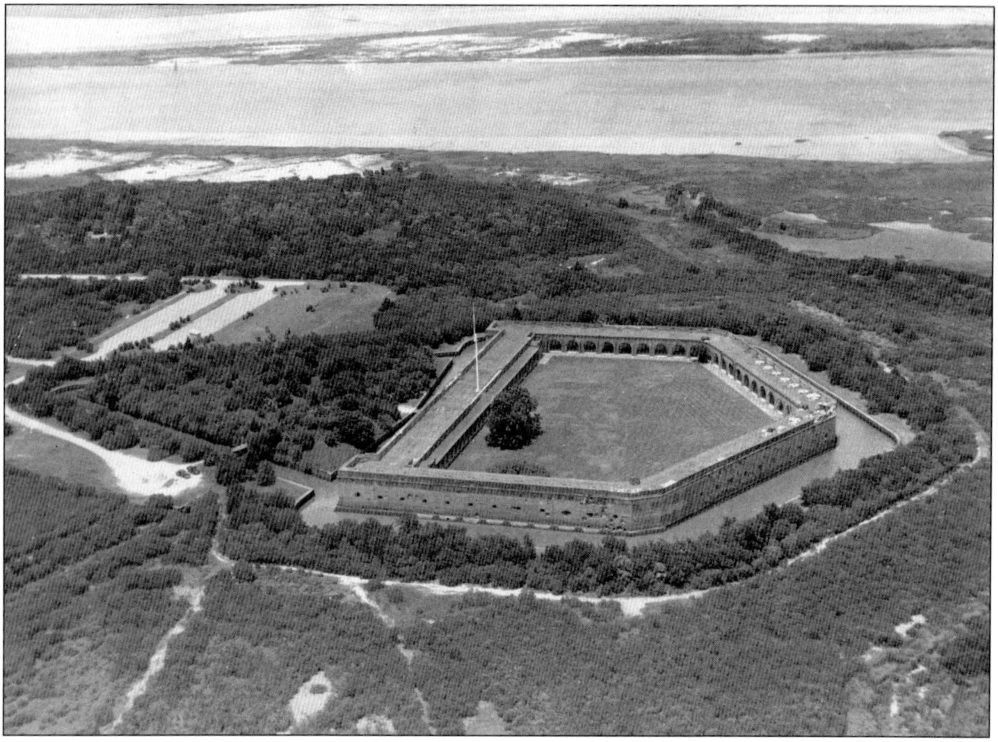

FORTIFICATIONS. After the War of 1812, Pres. James Madison ordered a new system of coastal fortifications to protect the United States against foreign invasion. Construction of a fort to protect the port of Savannah began in 1829. The new fort was to be located on Cockspur Island at the mouth of the Savannah River. (Courtesy of Fort Pulaski National Monument.)

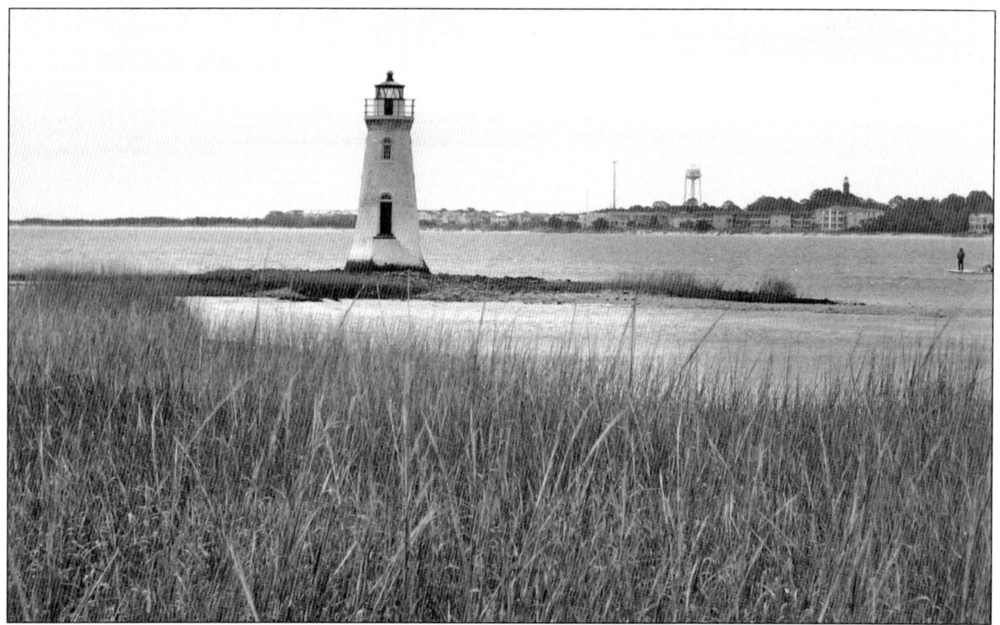

VIEW FROM FORT. The Cockspur Island light was first built as a day mark between 1837 and 1839. (Courtesy of Fort Pulaski National Monument.)

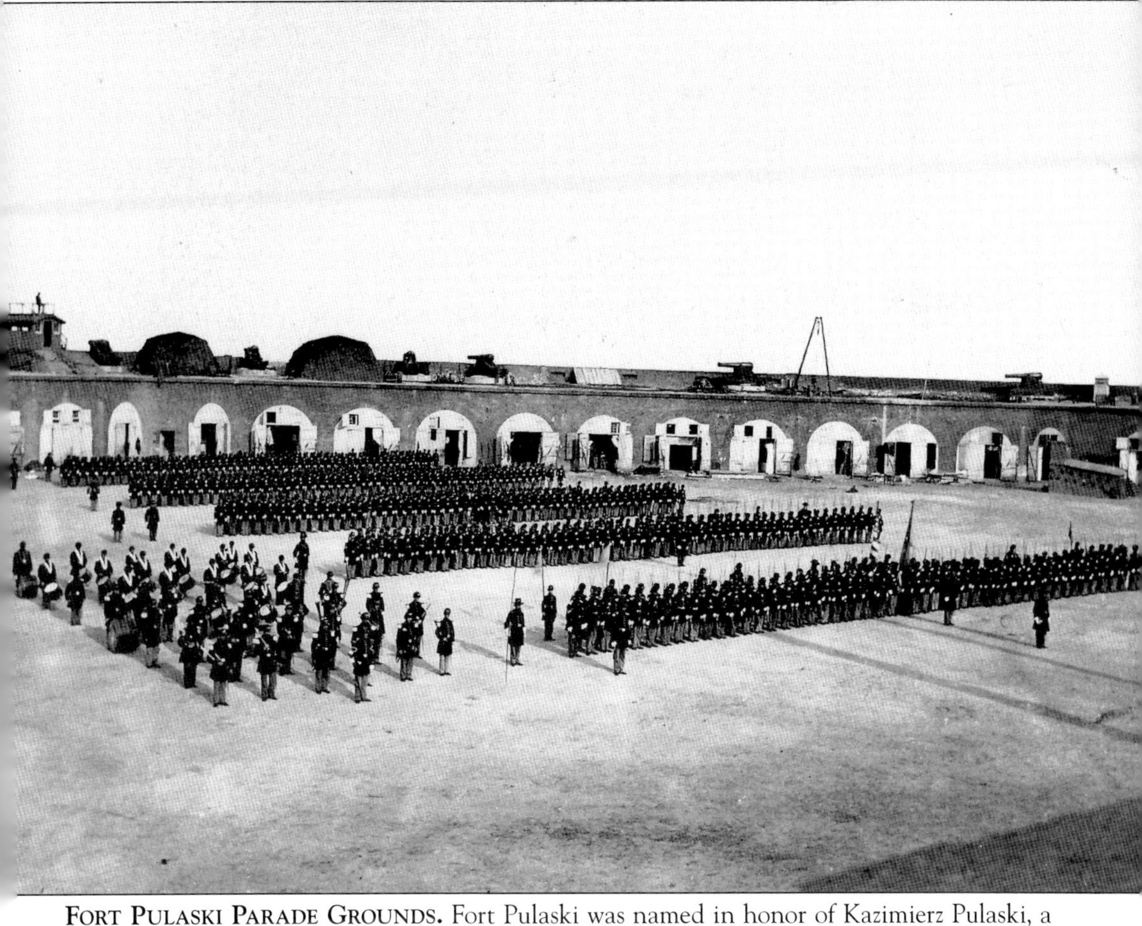

FORT PULASKI PARADE GROUNDS. Fort Pulaski was named in honor of Kazimierz Pulaski, a Polish soldier and military commander who fought and died during the Battle of Savannah during the American Revolution. The Cockspur Light can be seen in the distance. (Courtesy of Fort Pulaski National Monument.)

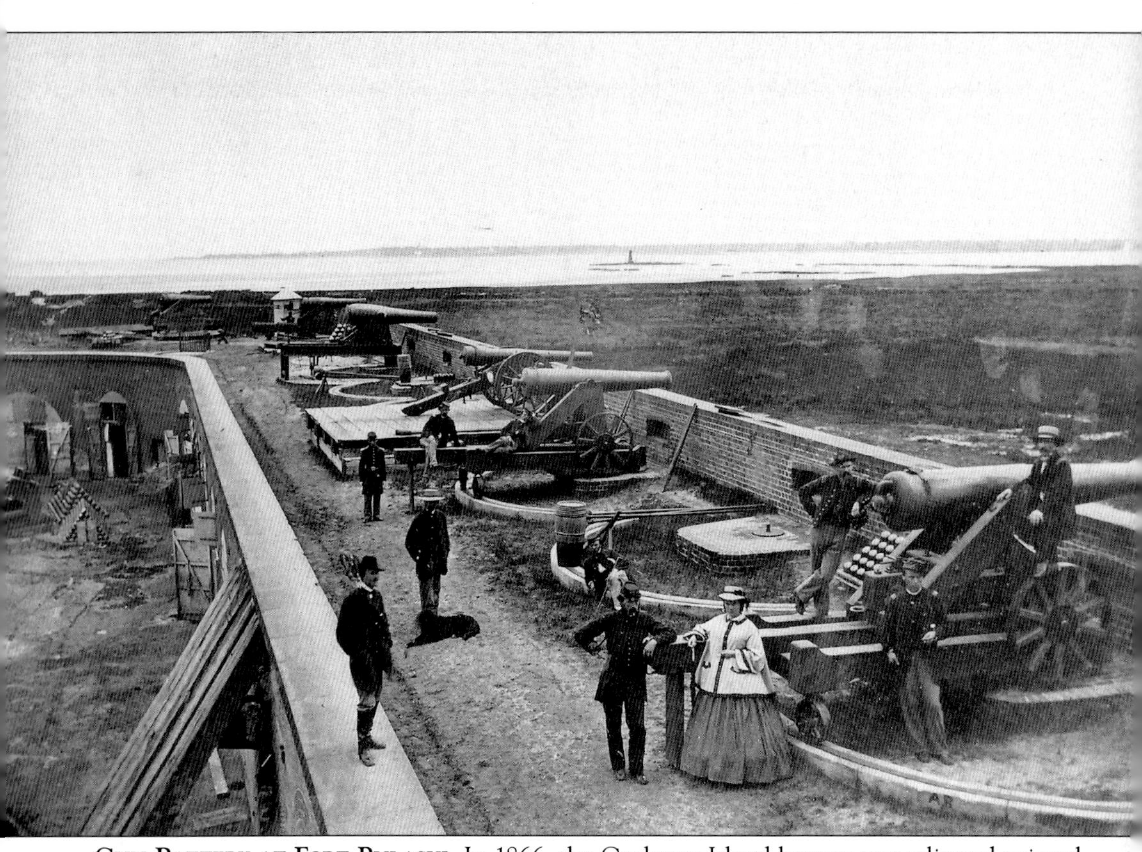

GUN BATTERY AT FORT PULASKI. In 1866, the Cockspur Island beacon was relit and painted white for use as a day mark. (Courtesy of Fort Pulaski National Monument.)

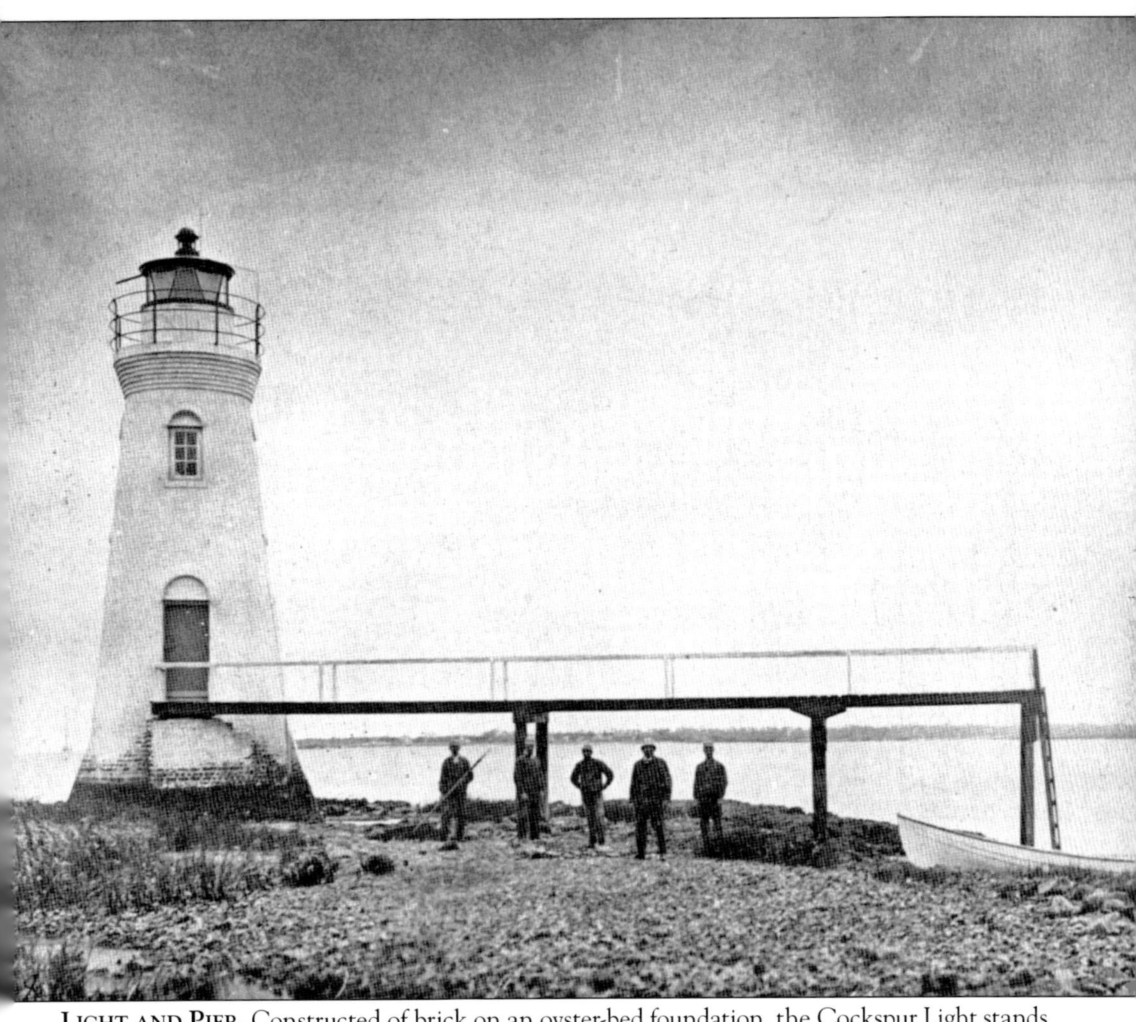

LIGHT AND PIER. Constructed of brick on an oyster-bed foundation, the Cockspur Light stands only 46 feet tall. (Courtesy of Fort Pulaski National Monument.)

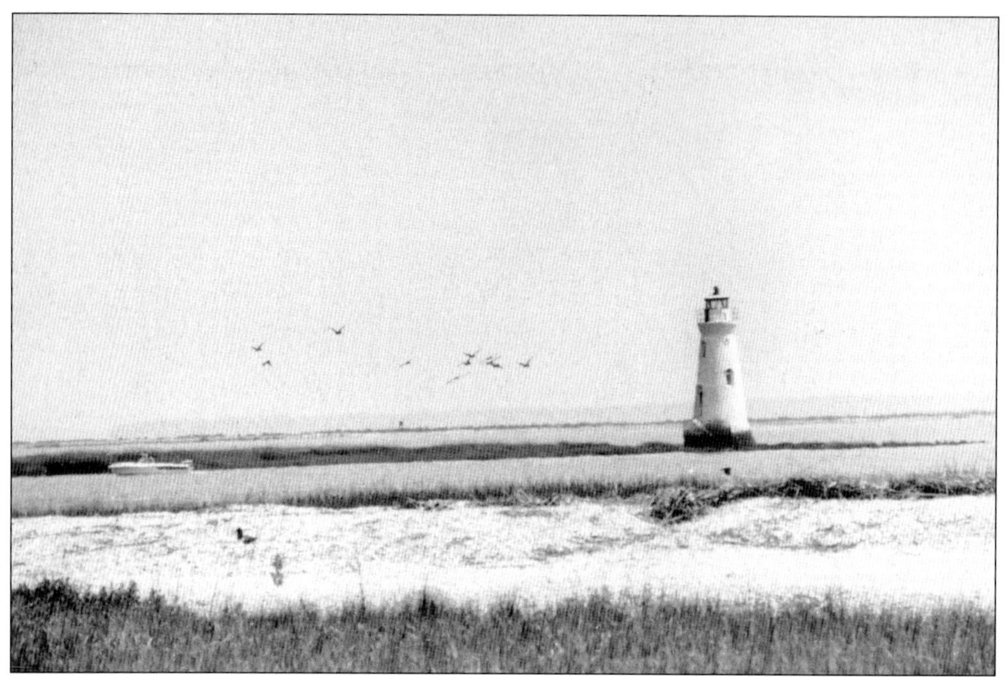

Cockspur Light. Located on an islet off the southeastern tip of Cockspur Island, the small lighthouse marks the south channel of the Savannah River. (Courtesy of Fort Pulaski National Monument.)

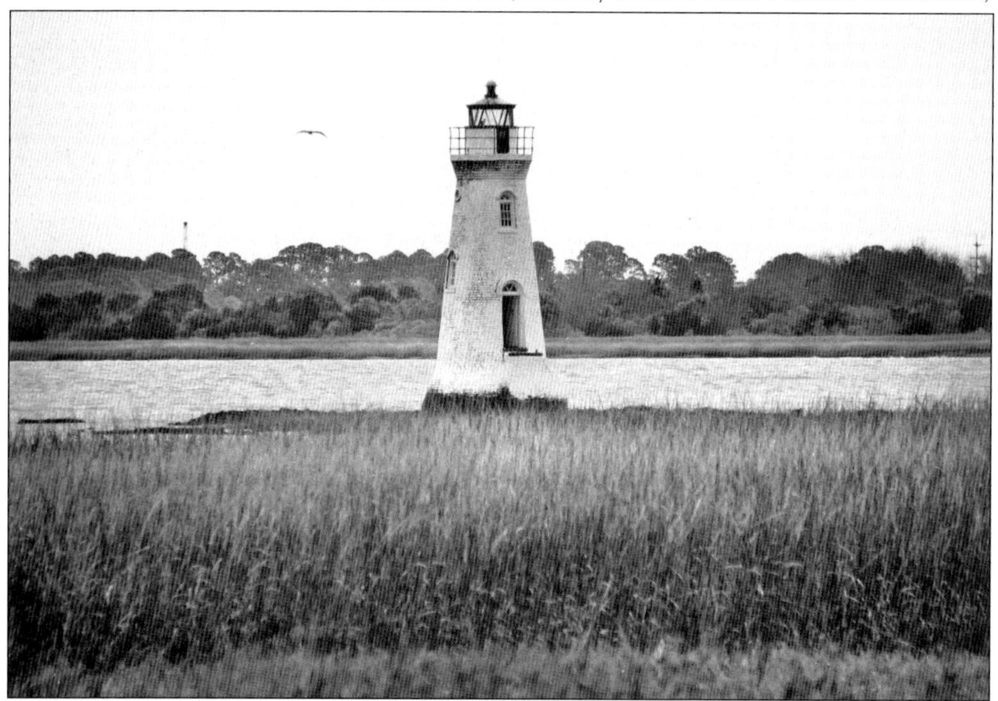

View from Marsh. Cockspur Island is approximately 12 miles east of the port of Savannah. The islet is often covered by high tide and is comprised of oyster shells and marsh grass. An islet is a small land feature, isolated by water and lying off the shore of a larger island. (Courtesy of Fort Pulaski National Monument.)

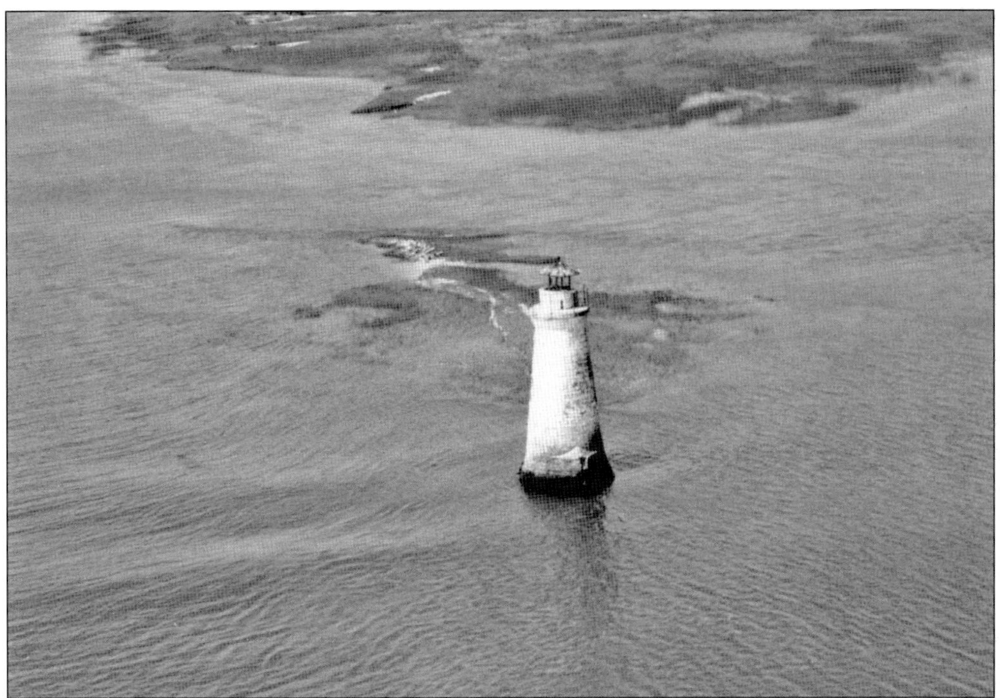

COCKSPUR LIGHT AT HIGH TIDE. The Cockspur Light was also known as the North Light. It is often underwater at high tide. (Courtesy of Fort Pulaski National Monument.)

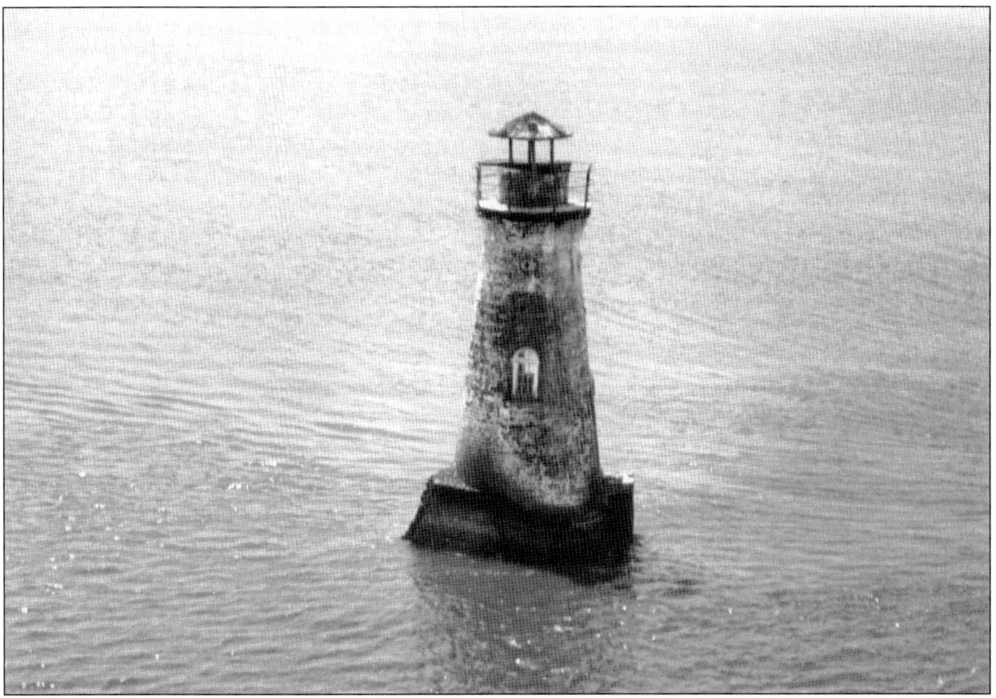

COCKSPUR LIGHT AT HIGH TIDE, 1996. The lighthouse was deactivated in 1909. Use of the shallower southern channel by larger commercial vessels had decreased over time. (Courtesy of Fort Pulaski National Monument.)

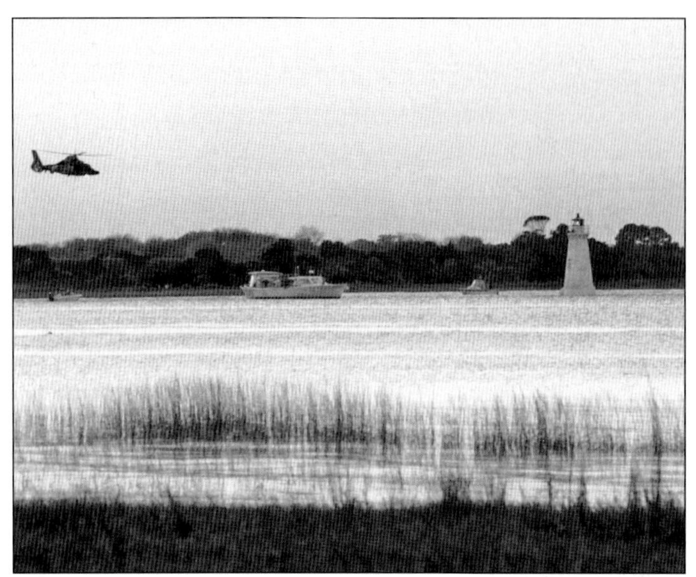

COCKSPUR RELIT, 2007. On March 18, 2007, the Cockspur light was shining once again. The U.S. Coast Guard participated in the celebration. (Courtesy of Fort Pulaski National Monument.)

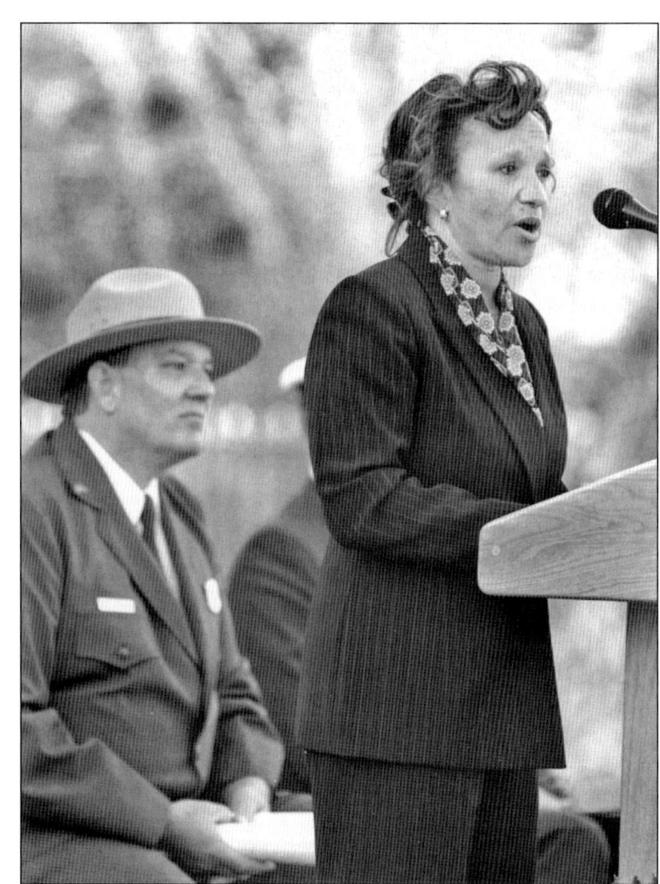

RELIGHTING CEREMONY, 2007. Rededicating the lighthouse are superintendent Charlie Fenwick (seated left) and Pat Hooks, southeast region director of the National Park Service. (Courtesy of Fort Pulaski National Monument.)

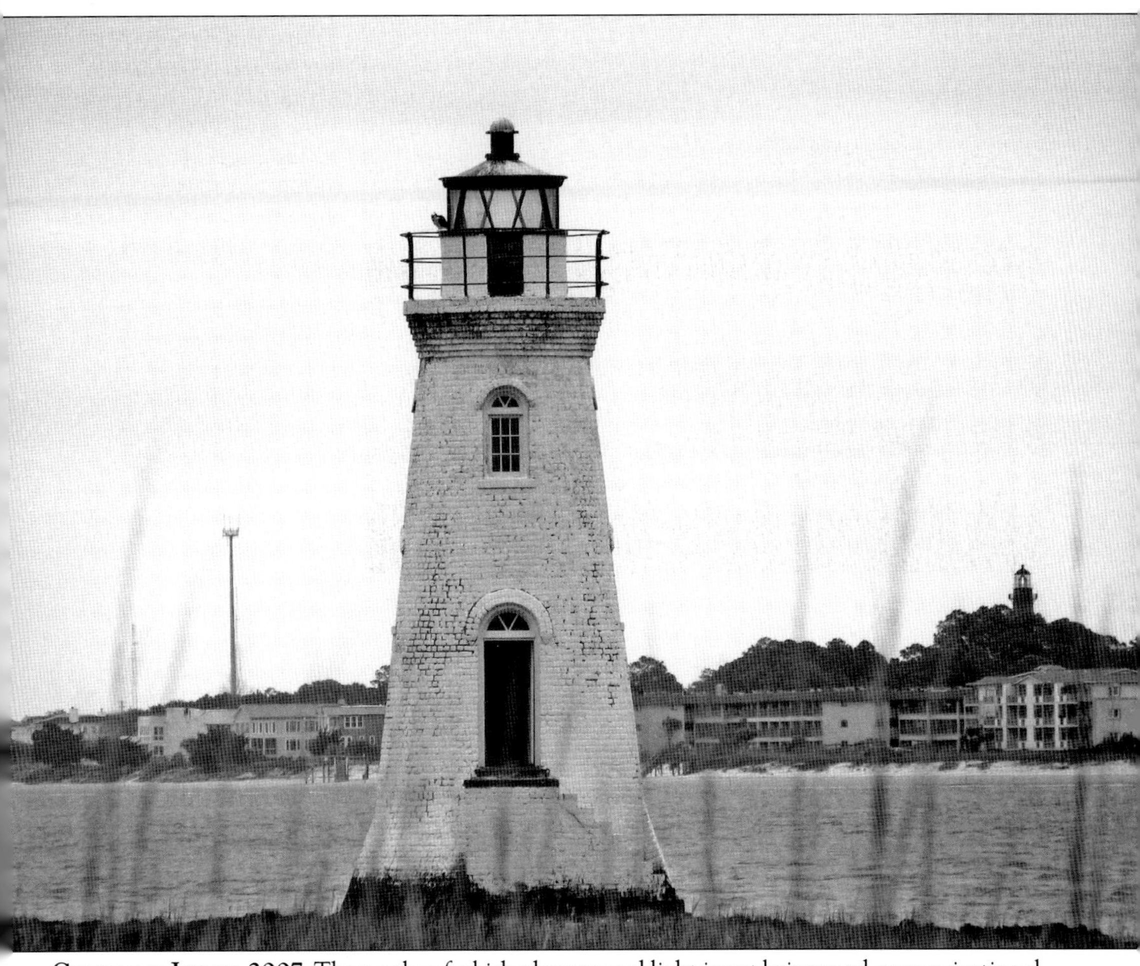

COCKSPUR LIGHT, 2007. The newly refurbished tower and light is not being used as a navigational aid. (Courtesy of Fort Pulaski National Monument.)

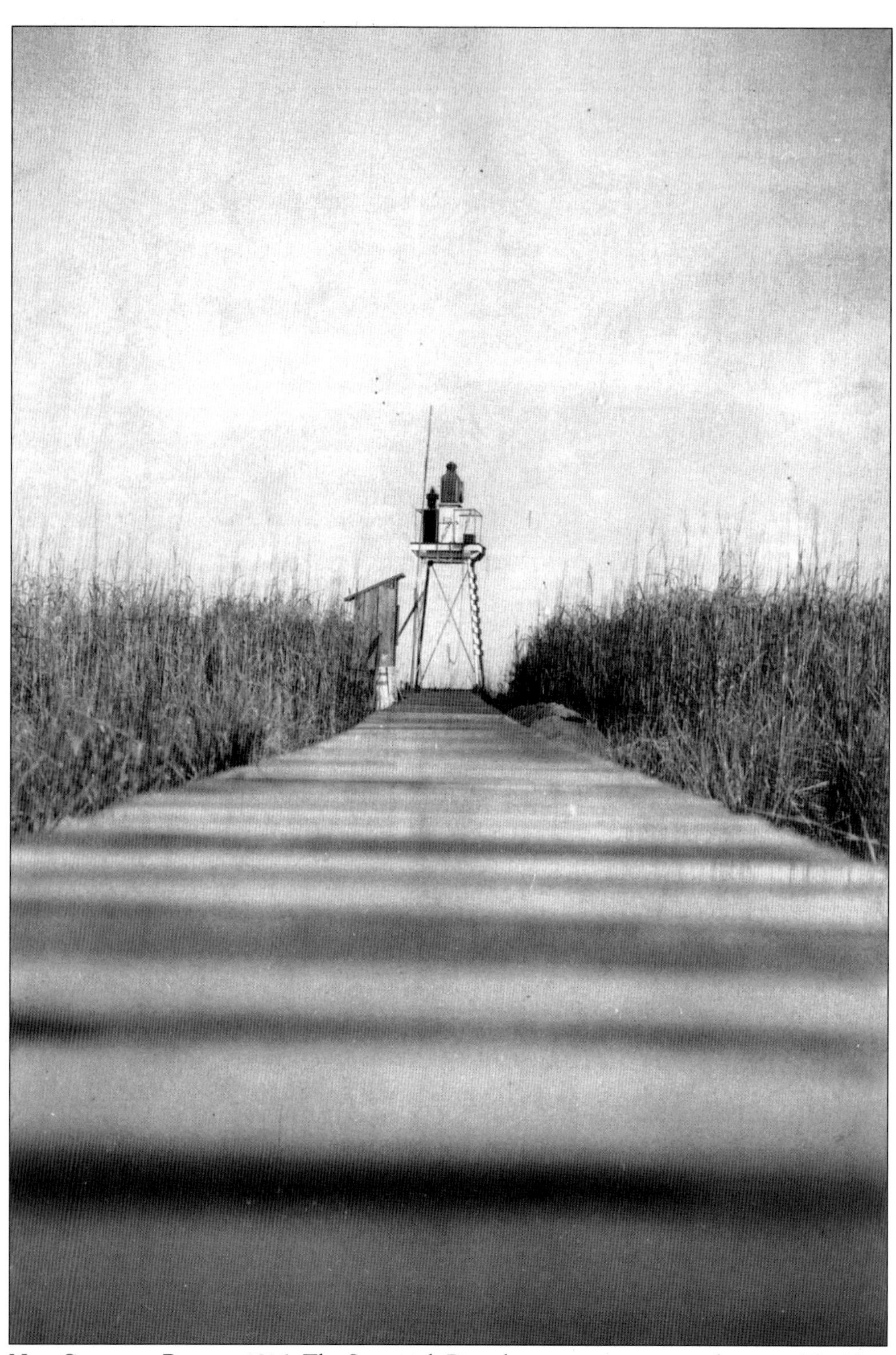

NEW CHANNEL RANGE, 1916. The Savannah River has a river navigational system. The New Channel Range was part of that system. (Courtesy of National Archives.)

FORT JACKSON RANGE, 1915. Though called range lights, the Fort Jackson lights were part of the Savannah River navigational system and not connected to any specific lighthouse. This is the Fort Jackson Range (front). (Courtesy of National Archives.)

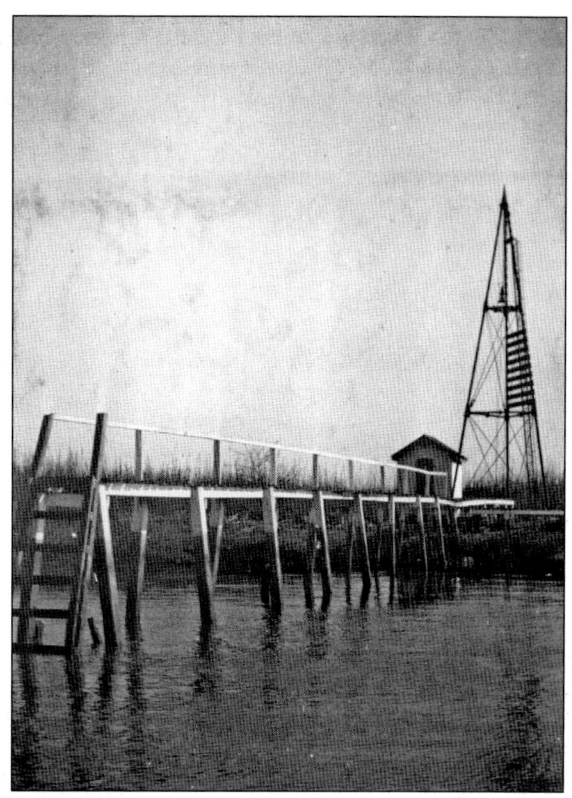

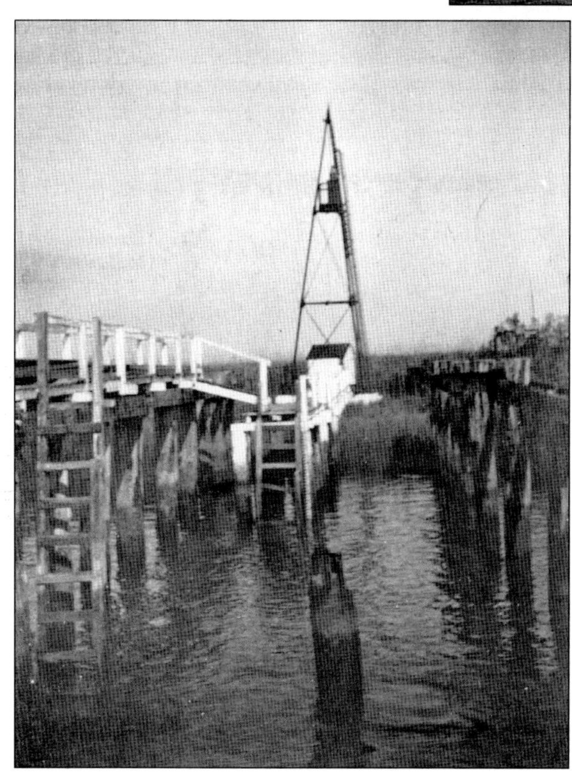

BARNWELL PLACE, 1915. Also located at Fort Jackson was the Barnwell Place Range. (Courtesy of National Archives.)

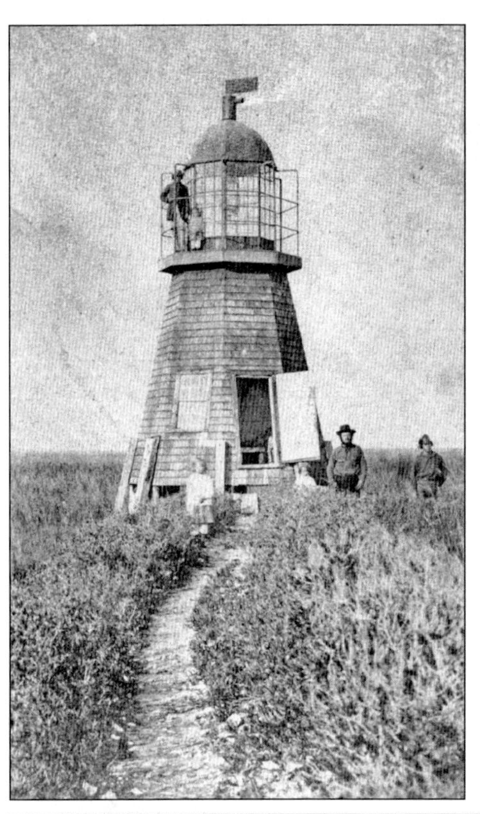

WOLF ISLAND LIGHT, C. 1860. Located on the south end of Doboy Sound near Darien, the Wolf Island Lighthouse was completed in 1822. Apparently, this beacon was to complement the recently completed lighthouse on Sapelo Island. The first appointed keeper was William Donnelly. (Courtesy of National Archives.)

WOLF ISLAND LIGHT. During the 1824 hurricane, the lighthouse and keeper's quarters were swept away. It was repaired and in service until 1899. (Courtesy of National Archives.)

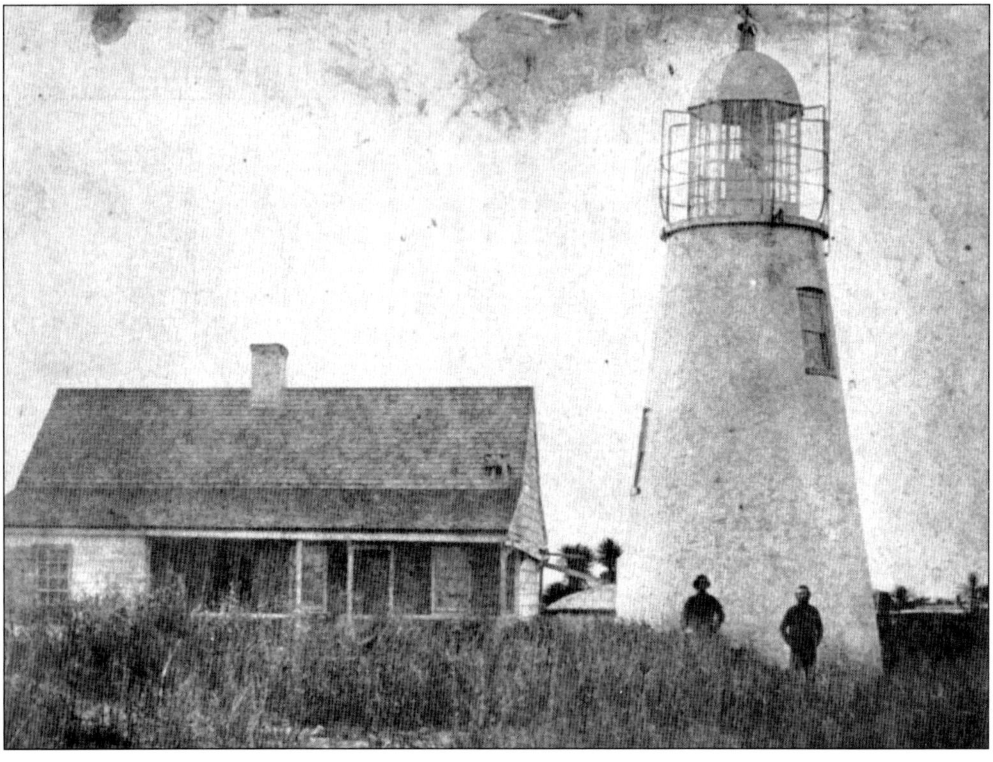

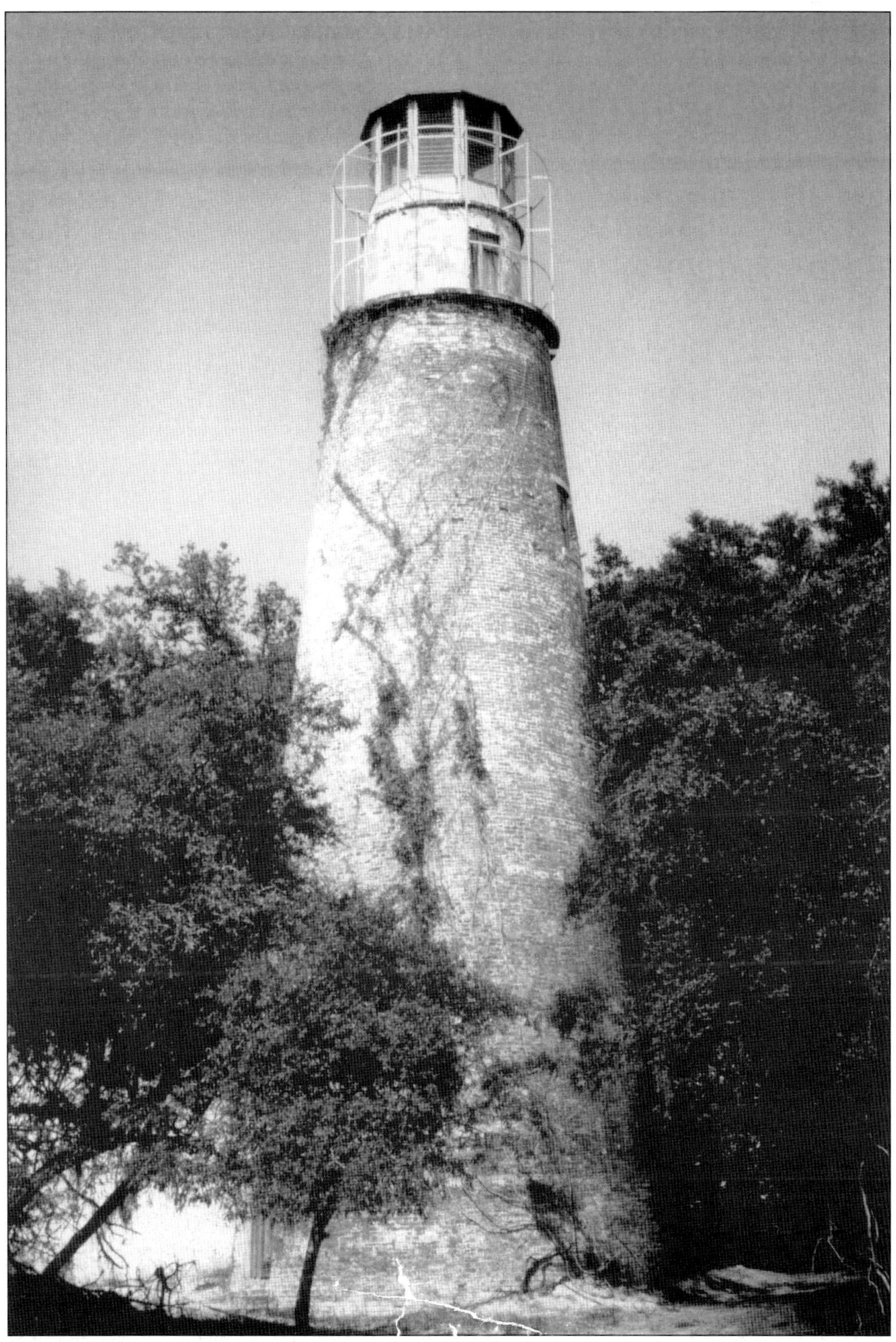

LITTLE CUMBERLAND LIGHT. Established in 1838, the Little Cumberland Light was sometimes referred to as the St. Andrews light. (Courtesy of Cumberland National Seashore.)

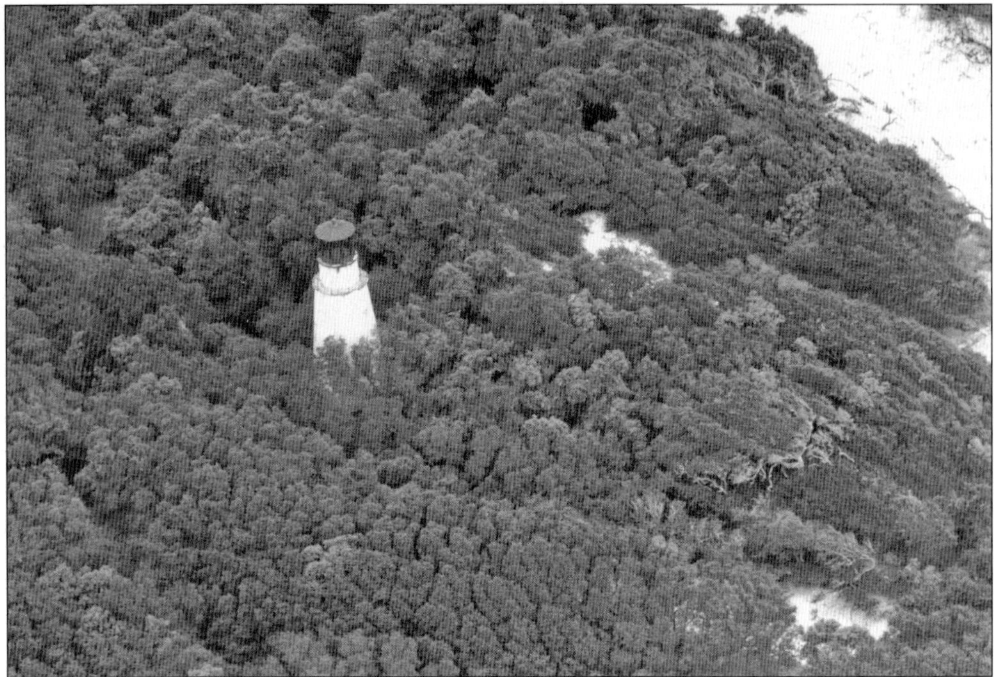

AERIAL VIEW. This Little Cumberland Light is the most southern of the Georgia lighthouses today. The light is located on the north end of Little Cumberland Island on St. Andrews Sound. (Courtesy of Tybee Island Historical Society.)

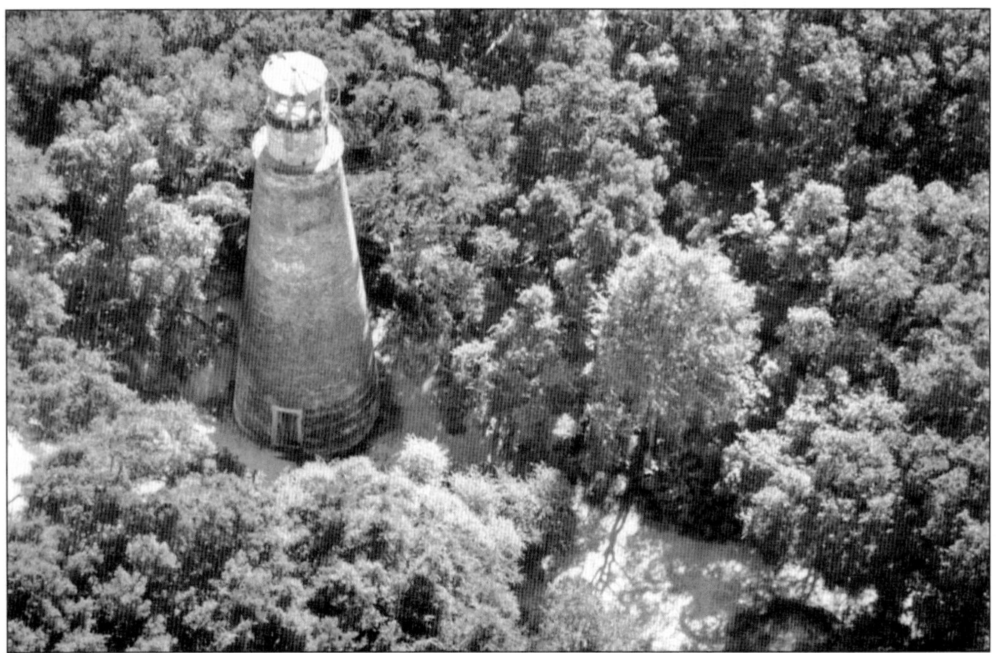

CLOSER VIEW OF THE LITTLE CUMBERLAND LIGHT. Another light was placed on the southern end of Cumberland Island in 1820 and was in service for 18 years. It was dismantled, brick by brick. (Courtesy of Amelia Island Images.)

LENS ROOM, 1999. The Little Cumberland Light had 14 lamps generating a fixed light, which distinguished it from the older tower to the south that had a revolving light. (Courtesy of Coastal Georgia Historical Society.)

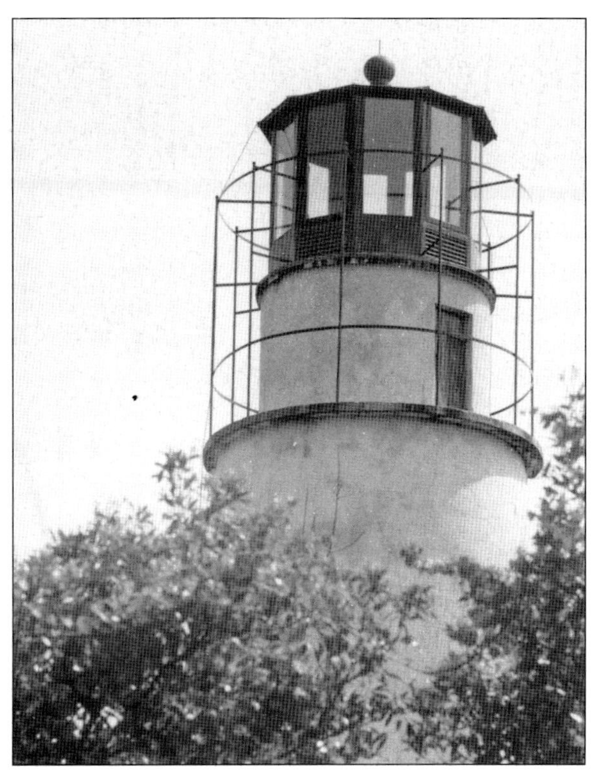

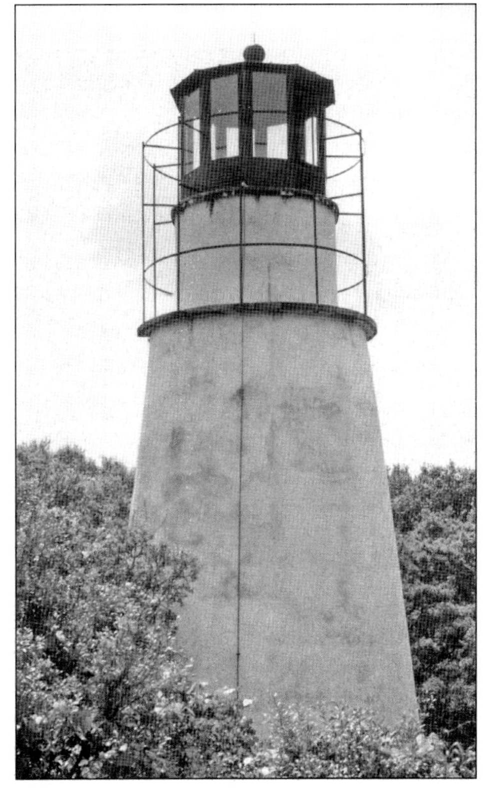

LENS ROOM RESTORATION, 1999. This photograph was taken during a restoration of the lens room. The light remains dark today. (Courtesy of Coastal Georgia Historical Society.)

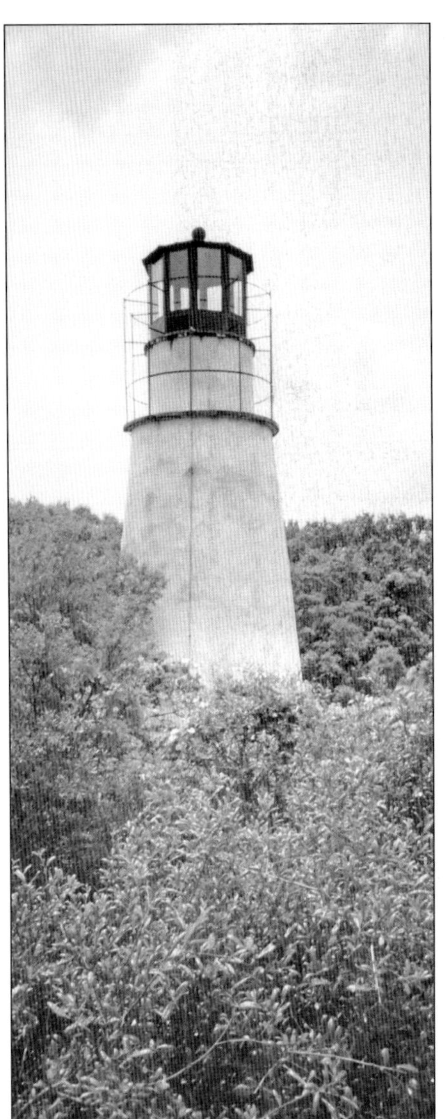

TOP OF THE LIGHT, 1999. Today the Little Cumberland Light is surrounded by dunes and a heavy stand of trees. (Courtesy of Coastal Georgia Historical Society.)

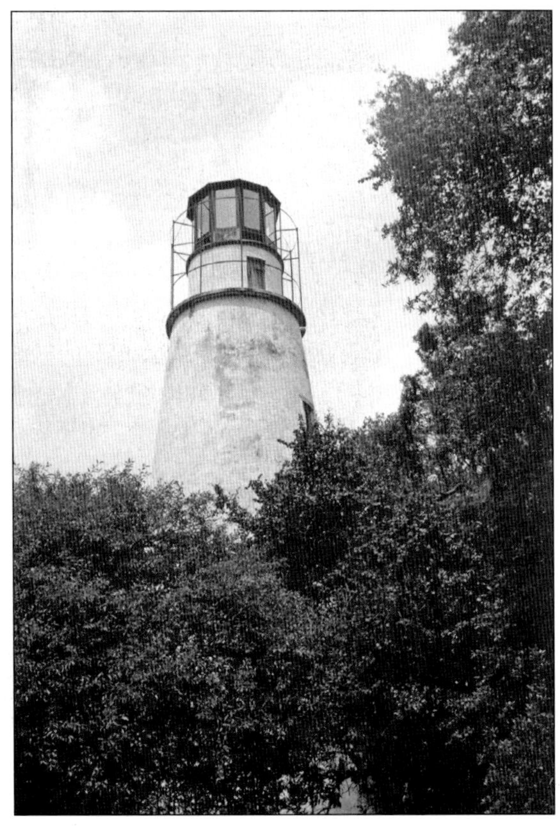

LITTLE CUMBERLAND LIGHT, 1999. Seen here, the light is barely visible from the water. (Courtesy of Coastal Georgia Historical Society.)

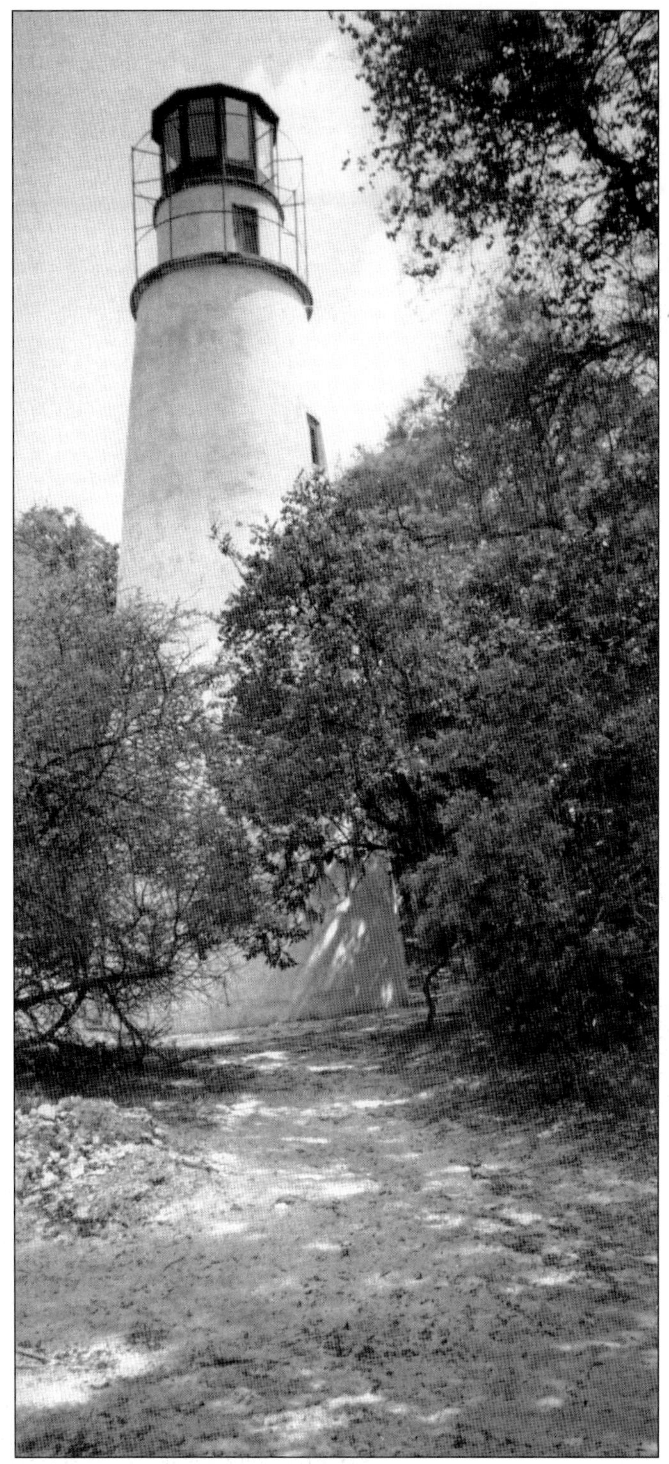

LITTLE CUMBERLAND LIGHT PRESERVED, 1999. Renovated in 1998 by the Little Cumberland Association, the lighthouse is privately owned and not open to the public. (Courtesy of Coastal Georgia Historical Society.)